ACPL ITEM

Advance praise f

DISCARDE

D0196889

"You must read this book to conquer communication concerns once and for all. Nannette Carroll's *The Communication Problem Solver* is content-rich with how-tos and step-by-step processes that you can apply immediately. It is bursting with stories of real managers wrestling with actual situations."

—Dr. Tony Alessandra, author, *Communicating at Work* and
The NEW Art of Managing People

"Examine any career setback and it's likely to stem from problems in interpersonal communication. It may be unclear expectations, a lack of listening, not empathizing, or any number of other preventable problems. This book will show you, easily and practically, just how to change problems into successes and how to avoid future communication problems. Nannette Carroll has done a fine job of building your tool kit. Keep it handy every day."

—Jim Cathcart, founder, www.Motivation.tv, and author,
Relationship Intelligence®

"An employee misses a deadline—again. Two coworkers aren't getting along. A meeting deteriorates into blaming and shaming. Would you like to know how to handle these all-too-common workplace challenges? Buy this book. It's packed with specific suggestions on how to turn conflict into cooperation and reasons into results. Read it and reap."

—Sam Horn, author, *POP!*, *Tongue Fu!*, and *What's Holding You Back?*

THE COMMUNICATION PROBLEM SOLVER

Simple Tools and Techniques for Busy Managers

Nannette Rundle Carroll

American Management Association

New York • Atlanta • Brussels • Chicago • Mexico City • San Francisco
Shanghai • Tokyo • Toronto • Washington, D.C.

This publication is designed to provide accurate and authoritative information in regard to the subject matter covered. It is sold with the understanding that the publisher is not engaged in rendering legal, accounting, or other professional service. If legal advice or other expert assistance is required, the services of a competent professional person should be sought.

Library of Congress Cataloging-in-Publication Data

Carroll, Nannette Rundle.
    The communication problem solver : simple tools and techniques for busy managers / Nannette Rundle Carroll.
        p.   cm.
    Includes index.
    ISBN-13: 978-0-8144-1308-1 (pbk.)
    ISBN-10: 0-8144-1308-0 (pbk.)
    1. Communication in management.   2. Problem solving.
3. Interpersonal communication.   I. Title.

    HD30.3.C3564   2010
    658.4' 5—dc22

                                                    2009031662

Printing number

10   9   8   7   6   5   4   3   2   1

To Chuck and Danielle,
communicators extraordinaire,
who are my muses and loving support

and

In loving memory of Coach Bob Rankin,
who energized athletes, business colleagues,
family, and friends with his message,
"Stay Positive!"

Contents

Foreword

As a professional speaker, author, professor, and motion picture actor I like to think of myself as a good communicator. Yet, there are always times when I just don't know how to express what I want or what I say is not perceived the way I had intended.

Communication seems so simple—so why is it so hard? It is the most important skill for success in business as well as in life. Studies show that people in organizations typically spend over 75 percent of their time in interpersonal situations.

That is why Nannette Rundle Carroll's book, *The Communication Problem Solver: Simple Tools and Techniques for Busy Managers*, is so valuable. It is a practical, hands-on, no-nonsense approach to how to get your message across clearly and concisely. What I believe separates this book from others on the topic are the practical tools like the step-by-step how-to's and the real-world management examples. They cut through the theories to enable you to analyze your communication skills and challenges.

Most important, *The Communication Problem Solver* shows how to develop clarity that builds trust, relationships, and communication with others. I wish I could have had this resource on my bookshelf when I was the dean of a university business school. Dealing with students, faculty, staff, and administration challenged all of my communication skills and then some. This book would have made my life so much easier. I trust it will help you in all of your communications, regardless of the situation.

Each chapter in *The Communication Problem Solver* examines a vital component of communication. You will learn how to improve your leadership communication skills, including handling difficult situations, questioning abilities, feedback techniques, and more. I think busy managers will find Chapter 6, "How to Break the Judging Habit," particularly unique and valuable.

In my current work as a diversity consultant, communication is crucial because language and culture add to the challenges of building trusting and lasting relationships. An added bonus of this book is that the knowledge you acquire will benefit you well beyond the business world. If you can communicate expectations, ask appropriate questions, and avoid judgment, your business, as well as personal, relationships are likely to improve.

I know you will find *The Communication Problem Solver* well worth your time.

———————

May you always communicate with clarity,

Michael Soon Lee, MBA
Diversity Consultant
Author: *Black Belt Negotiating* and
Cross-Cultural Selling for Dummies

Preface

If you were to think about your work communication issues, what would they be? Are you paying attention to the "uh-oh" feeling in your gut when tension arises among people at work? Or do you ignore your intuition about these communication challenges and hope they will go away on their own?

As a professional speaker, management trainer, consultant, and former manager, I have worked with leaders from all over the world. They have ranged from potential managers to the most senior executives and officers. All had professional competence and were committed to their organizations' success.

These managers work hard to continually expand their knowledge and skills. Yet, no matter what management topic we address, communication is usually the *underlying* problem. When a manager has difficulty giving feedback, coaching, or delegating, it most often is due to "people problems"—challenges the manager would rather avoid or does not know how to handle.

Regardless of where they work or how long they have managed, many managers struggle to develop work relationships and communicate more effectively. Managers know the "what" and the "how" of the job. Problems erupt when communicating tasks and discussing progress. People get upset and communication breaks down. "Work would be great if it weren't for the people," many managers joke. But people problems are the predicaments that keep them awake at night.

So why not solve the people problems first? Perhaps it is because these challenges are both the most uncomfortable and the ones without deadlines. Or maybe it is because busy managers simply do not know how.

If you are reading this book, you are probably interested in improving communication at your workplace. This book will make your life easier by:

➤ Expanding your confidence to handle the "tough stuff"
➤ Showing how to energize your work environment
➤ Boosting your ability to delegate, give feedback, and coach
➤ Slashing wasted time due to misunderstandings about assignments
➤ Increasing productivity in your team by enhancing relationships
➤ Diminishing friction
➤ Perking up your communication proficiency

The Communication Problem Solver: Simple Tools and Techniques for Busy Managers offers a dramatically different approach to management communication. This book guides you through communication minefields and helps you prevent them in the future. Once you have read it, you will want this problem-solving book on your desk for continual reference.

Real-world stories and practical examples will capture your interest and illustrate proven action steps. You will be able to lift the solutions off the page or adapt the ideas to your own solutions.

In any economy, managers need topflight communication skills to keep staff productive and collaborative. This book will help you set clear expectations, develop collaborative relationships, and avoid imprecise judgments. It will sharpen your listening skills to grasp information better in every conversation.

Many communication issues seem overwhelming because they are vague and trigger emotional responses. *The Communication Problem*

Solver is your key to redefining communication problems in factual terms, then solving them once and for all.

The examples in this book are true, but the names have been changed to provide privacy. The exception is when someone has given authorization to be quoted: Their full names are shown.

Acknowledgments

A special thanks to Ellen R. Kadin, executive editor, and Barry H. Richardson, senior development editor, at AMACOM Books, who made this book a reality. Thanks also to the thousands of thoughtful managers and seminar participants who worked with me over the years. I am deeply grateful to the many people who participated so generously with quotes and stories, which enriched the book. Warm thanks also to the many people who supported this project:

- Paula Rankin, whose strong belief that I would succeed energized me.
- In memory of Loretto and Joseph Rundle, my loving parents, who gave me faith and education, and always told me I could achieve anything I set my mind to.
- Hugh Rundle, Jane Rundle, Mary and David Baker, Virginia and Ken Paulin, and their families.
- Elizabeth Koehler-Pentacoff, who helped me launch this project and advised me throughout.
- Michael Soon Lee, who mentored me through the process.
- Dr. Edward P. Miranda, plastic and reconstructive surgeon of San Francisco, for his successful surgeries on my hand during the writing of this book.
- Sharon Lawrence for the meditation classes and great energy work.
- Ian Griffin, president, National Speakers Association Northern California, for interviewing me about my book for his first podcast.
- Camille Minichino (aka Margaret Grace) for advice and help.

➤ Critique group friends: Susan Berman, David George, Cheryl Spanos, Jack Russ, Fran Cain, Margaret Ramirez, Elisabeth Tuck, and Jill Hedgecock.

➤ And all the relatives, friends, and colleagues not mentioned by name but always remembered.

THE COMMUNICATION
PROBLEM SOLVER

THE SECRETS TO CREATING AND SUSTAINING ENERGIZED RELATIONSHIPS

Topflight managers develop exceptional skills in forging relationships throughout the organization, and in particular with their own manager and direct reports. Built on trust, respect, and goodwill, a good relationship eases the exchange of information on expectations, and therefore enables successful cooperation. People more freely express their ideas when a trusting connection exists. Clarity contributes to sustaining good relationships because people learn to trust each other when they have the same understanding of roles, responsibilities, and levels of authority.

Trust, in the management context, means that you and your employees have confidence that the other person's work behavior is consistent. Employees can rely on you for honest, direct communication of expectations. You can depend on them to get the work done as agreed because you share an understanding of what is expected. When you habitually state clear expectations, employees can tackle the assignment with conviction that they are on the right path. Knowing clearly what to do builds commitment to the work. It drives the creation and maintenance of positive working relationships.

Relationships power collegial communication of expectations and earn employee buy-in. Well-developed associations with staff are the most important key to preventing and solving communication problems. Relationships and consistently clear expectations deliver results.

CHAPTER

1

The Power of Relationship

This chapter gives tips on how to reinforce relationships and thus prevent performance disappointments—even when dealing with people you don't like. Good working relationships are pivotal to getting positive results and developing team harmony. When interpersonal communication at work is pleasant, people can focus on the projects and tasks instead of being sidetracked by poor relationships.

The manager's intention and decision to form good working relationships is crucial. Leaving it to chance means ignoring a great opportunity to create an environment conducive to people producing their best work.

Your staff know what your intentions are. They know whether or not you value them as persons or just as tools to get what you need done. They know if you like them or not. Managers need to communicate that they value relationships with their direct reports.

What Is a Work Relationship?

Simply stated, a working relationship is a connection between people who deal with each other in some work way. The association can be required by business interactions or can be desired based on enjoyment of productively working together and trusting the other person will contribute and meet deadlines.

Relationships can be kept at the acquaintance level or can involve a continued connection that develops rapport and mutual trust. Some people may go beyond the minimum work requirements and enjoy coffee or lunch together to learn more about each other's backgrounds and interests. Others may choose friendship based on compatibility and common pursuits. I have enjoyed friendships with both my managers and my direct reports. Some of these friendships took place only at work. For others, we chose to socialize outside of work and were close friends. Sometimes people keep up the relationship after they cease working together and sometimes they do not. So there is a wide range of acceptable work-related relationships.

The word "relationship" intimidates some managers because they think it implies friendship or getting close to someone. They don't want to invest time in a relationship and they don't want to get personal with coworkers. In reality, it can have a minimal meaning of being respectful, friendly, and courteous and getting the work done together. It does not have to be personal.

Some managers do want to be somewhat personal but want to know where to draw the line. How personal can we be in establishing work relationships? One senior executive asked, "Most people do want to talk about their kids, but how friendly and personal can we be without being nosy?" Managers do want to play it safe and not offend direct reports. There is no one way to define work relationships. The work must get accomplished and the manager needs to create a comfortable environment with open communication so coworkers can trust and help each other. The types of relationships developed depend on the people and the situation.

Types of Relationships

Years ago I had a friend named Jerry who liked to shop at the corner grocery store. Every time he shopped there he complained about how high the prices were. "Why don't you go to the big chain grocery store?" I asked. "It's two blocks closer to your home." "No," he would always say. "I go to the mom-and-pop store because they know my name."

Jerry felt good because the corner grocers treated him as an individual person. He could not expect this treatment at the chain grocery store where the checkout people would ring up his groceries but not show any interest in him. He was willing to pay more and walk farther because he enjoyed the relationship at the mom-and-pop store.

On the other hand, a relationship can be based on the quality of the work. I have used the same dry cleaner for years because I like the consistent results. Ownership and employees have changed, but the standard of quality remains. My relationship with the current woman at the dry cleaner is friendly, cordial, and surface. We smile, exchange pleasantries, and nothing personal is discussed. Our brief but regular interactions deal only with the task at hand—the dry cleaning of my clothes—and perhaps comments about the weather and other small talk. If there is a button missing or a shirt that needs to be re-ironed, I bring it up in a friendly, nondemanding, nonaccusatory way that leaves the door open for her to suggest the solution. Our relationship is based entirely on the business transaction. If I didn't like the quality of the work, I wouldn't patronize the shop.

Relationships vary depending upon how much both parties want to know about each other. Many neighbors have relationships. Typically they entail showing respect and meeting mutual community goals—cleanliness, safety, and regulations, if the neighborhood has an association. Maybe neighbors collect each other's mail and papers and care for animals during vacations. One household might have neighbors they only say hello to, ones they see only at neighborhood social functions, and others they are friends with. One size does not fit all, because there are at least two people deciding how much to interact and how much personal information to share.

It's the same thing at work. What brings people together is a task or project. Then colleagues choose how much interest to express in getting to know about where their coworkers are from, where they worked before, other places they've lived, hobbies, families, travel, and so on. And they each choose how much to tell. Despite a manager's best intentions, a particular employee may not want to discuss anything personal. Even some managers have said they don't want to disclose personal information.

Work relationships don't need to be personal, but they do need to be congenial. Some managers have mentioned that they don't want to listen to direct reports' stories. But those few minutes of listening can be the bridge to employee commitment and enthusiasm about the work and the manager. Taking a little time to express interest, to show compassion when employees are sad or bereaved or ill, and to feel happiness for them when they celebrate a work achievement or personal feat can make life at the office more pleasurable and productive for everyone. Smiling, laughing, and using open body language show the manager is congenial. Setting a climate of courtesy and cooperation enables teams of coworkers to exchange their thoughts and ideas on common tasks. The better the relationships, the better the chance of collaborative results.

Relationships can make the difference in whether people want to come to work and in how willing they are to help others. A comfortable workplace invites people to be their authentic selves.

Importance of Relationships

Is there "fire" in the bellies of your coworkers? Is it passion for the work or is it sabotage? There are people who will "walk through fire" with and for us to get projects done if they like us. And, if they don't, they might "throw fire at us" to defeat our objective. Think about someone you would do almost any work for. You want to help that person meet objectives and get them done well. Why? Chances are it's because you value the relationship you share. Perhaps you want to preserve and enhance the association and the shared achievement.

For example, when my friend Marilyn and I were college students, we both worked part-time in Manhattan. We rode the train together into the city for work and also on many weekends just for fun. Rarely did we simultaneously have money for eating out. So, whoever had the money that day paid for the meal. We never tracked who spent what. There was no expectation of "you owe me something." The pleasure of helping the other person and having a good time together was the only thought. The relationship superseded fairness, rules, and bookkeeping. We are still friends today.

You have known people on the job for whom you would "walk through fire" despite your own heavy workload and schedule. Perhaps it was taking on an extra project your boss needed done. Maybe you helped a peer who was wrestling with a tough problem. Or could it have been a direct report who needed an extra pair of hands for a crucial deadline? And you have had direct reports and peers and bosses who would work passionately to help you meet a work objective. Why? Sometimes people do the extraordinary for colleagues because it is the right thing to do or because it gets the job done. More times than not, however, it is because they value the relationship and enjoy the interaction of working together toward a goal.

On the other hand, there are some people in the workplace who are always too busy to help a coworker. They may have personal goals, but those objectives may not be aligned with the organization. These people may not buy in to mutual goals because of their nature, personal issues, organizational obstacles, the manager, or even an experience with a previous manager. Many just do their jobs at the minimum level. Other folks will even do what they can to actively sabotage the manager's objectives. Maybe they wanted the management job. Maybe it is personal, and maybe it is just the way they behave at work. These employees are expressing fire, but not the passion of loving their jobs. The blistering behavior seems unlikely from people who have a good relationship with their boss.

There are many reasons people don't have comfortable relationships with their managers. Sometimes it is that the manager doesn't manage the relationship, and sometimes the employee prefers not to engage. Also, some workers are extremely competent technically but don't have a natural aptitude or desire for interpersonal interactions.

Jack, a West Coast computer programmer, complained for years about management because, he said, "They don't know anything about my work but want to interfere with my decisions every now and then." Forthright, friendly communication was not part of Jack's workplace. Jack worked alone and very successfully managed a major project that didn't require much interaction with others. That's the way he liked it. Dealing with others was difficult for him because, in his words, he felt technically and intellectually superior and because he was introverted. He didn't have a relationship with his boss and he didn't want one. Any involvement of the boss was seen as interference. It was easier for Jack to blame the boss than to develop a relationship. When computer systems changed, and continual communication with coworkers or users became a requirement, he chose the "early retirement package" instead of making the transition.

Jack exemplifies some who do not want relationships and exchanges with people; they just want to do the job and be left alone. Some other people are shy about communicating. Still others are willing to learn how to work with people, but they just don't know how.

For example, a manager from Washington state regaled a class I was leading with the following comments: "I'm a geologist. I'm trained to work with rocks. Rocks don't talk back! People do. I told my bosses if they wanted to make me a manager, they would have to send me to management training classes to teach me how to work with people. I still don't know if I want to be promoted to manager because of the people issues." This man was about to make a career decision, which he saw as binary: rocks or people.

Why do some people find it easier to learn the technical aspects of the job than to learn to develop relationships? Managers sometimes say that the work would be easy if it weren't for the people. In many cases, as long as things go smoothly, working with others is fine. It's when individuals disagree or believe there will be confrontation that many have difficulty.

Certain people embrace conflict as just another bump in the road. Some welcome debate so that ideas can be aired and innovation can flourish. But numerous managers fear disagreement will damage a relationship or the other person will attack them or aggressively ask questions that they are unable to answer. In one class, a seminar participant said that if conflict arose in meetings at her workplace, the CEO would cover his eyes with the palms of his hands and peek out through slits in-between his fingers. That's pretty extreme body language from such a senior person, but there's no right or wrong about the fact that some people flee rather than fight. It is reality. Adept managers frame statements in ways that do not generate conflict with coworkers. They also facilitate discussions with agility when inevitable conflicts arise. Managers need conflict radar to ensure that their employees feel free to express themselves and also feel emotionally safe. Are people really debating ideas or are they attacking each other as persons? It is in the best interest of the organization and the individuals who work there to be able to voice their ideas without being personally challenged. When the team critiques ideas against the goals instead of criticizing the person, new thoughts can flourish.

A solid working relationship can make the difference in whether a person wants to come to work or not. The relationship can color the willingness to help others. It can influence the readiness to work out misunderstandings and take mistakes in stride. Opinions and emotions about managers and coworkers vibrate strongly. Managers can take the initiative to nurture relationships and create a positive climate where employees are free to be themselves and voice their concerns without fear. When managers care about employees as human beings, they increase the possibility that employees will shape their strong emotions about work and the team into supportive excitement instead of actions that undermine the group's success.

Surprises Cause Communication Problems

Some of us like surprise parties and some of us don't. Most of us, however, do not like being surprised about work. Blindsiding direct reports, bosses, peer managers, and people in other departments can cause stress, frustration, and organizational workflow problems. Surprises can negatively affect relationships when employees' schedules and work suddenly shift them into high-adrenaline mode. Employees want to know what management's expectations are—both planned and as unexpected things happen. Minimizing surprises can help preserve relationships. But occasionally they happen, and any temporary relationship dents can be repaired as shown in two examples.

H. Pat Ritz, CEO of Footwear Specialties International of Portland, Oregon, says, "What frustrates people most on the job is not overwork. It's when they are blindsided—when unexpected things happen. This can occur when the company is not clear about who is to do what. A systems breakdown can take place. Then everyone gets mad because they don't know what to do. So they blame."

For example, one Friday, shoes scheduled to be shipped were not shipped to customers. Pat, the CEO, asked the shipping department, "What happened?" and worked back through the chain. It turned out that several large orders were held by the credit department until 11:45 a.m. and then sent to the shipping department all at once. The shipping target might have been met if (1) the credit department had communicated to shipping that a high volume of orders was coming later that day, and (2) sales had alerted credit to the need to ship the orders that day.

Pat says, "Unfortunately you can't rely on the workers to pass the information up—it's management's job to alert people as to when things will happen. Workers in this situation don't have enough knowledge—they're task oriented. Management is at a level where it can see enough to predict trends."

"Work flows through your company like the tide," Pat continues. "It ebbs and flows. As an order for shoes passes through the company it touches a lot of different spots. Management has to communicate all up and down the line what's happening with the ebb and flow. If guys in the warehouse know there's a surge in orders, they can mentally prepare for it. Stress accumulates if the orders pile up and then get dumped on them all at once."

"I may need a new employee or a new procedure to deal with business," Pat says. "The point is to *deal* with it and not wait and blindside people. The same thing applies to predicting trends like cash-flow problems, running out of shoes, and so on. It's management's job to look ahead and not surprise people. That creates confidence within the workforce that management knows what it is doing."

Interdepartmental communication is a challenge in many industries—one department may not know how its action or inaction affects another department. The managers may incorrectly assume that other departments understand what they need and why. Even if they work on the same project, often groups do not know the impact of their team's work on the company timeline. For example, in a creative company I worked with, Fred, the head of manufacturing, reluctantly attended the first of a series of mandatory leadership trainings. He was reluctant to spend time in training because his group had tight deadlines to meet.

Fred's job was to get the product built and shipped on time so the product could be installed on-site at events with fixed dates. Manufacturing's completion dates were set in concrete. So every time sales accepted a customer modification or the design group came up with a new idea, or engineering found a new and better way, what happened to Fred's department's schedule? His group experienced the crunch. They could not make paint dry any faster than paint will dry. Yet they were required to ship the product on schedule so it could be installed before the event opening date.

The first few times at the weekly training sessions, Fred expressed anger and frustration and others conveyed annoyance at his complaints and seemingly rigid adherence to policy, procedure, and process. I complimented Fred on his process and organization skills and urged him not to give up.

Throughout the interactive training, the different departments disclosed their challenges and why they worked the way they did. They learned to listen to each other and they developed relationships and trust. They understood and committed to common corporate goals instead of turf objectives. Fred became a cheerleader for the training. He leapt to the whiteboard to articulate ideas of benefit to everyone and explain how the process would assist everyone. Other leaders learned of his frustrations and what manufacturing needed in order to construct and ship products on time. They began to appreciate his strengths in process and scheduling and now viewed him as an asset. Communication and getting to know each other triggered enhanced cross-functional teamwork. They built relationships.

What dependencies do the departments share? In Fred's case, he depended upon engineering's final say in order to build the products. Within his own team, there were many dependencies. Painting could not be done until quality control had checked the constructed items. Fred's own department scheduling was meticulous and even built in flexibility for delays. But the unintended blindsiding from other departments had, in the past, thrown his schedule into a tailspin and caused stress on his staff. This impacted his relationships with other managers and their direct reports. When all groups were cognizant of each other's constraints and needs, surprises could be kept to a minimum and communication to a maximum.

Managers proficient in communication will drive relationship building with other groups or departments. They will initiate meetings with peer managers to discuss how each unit's work interrelates and how to best work together toward common goals. Taking the initiative to understand peer managers' goals and needs can contribute significantly to forming healthy work relationships. And relationships can help get things done.

Building and Preserving Relationships

The first step in developing and sustaining relationships at work is to decide that relationships are important in creating a productive and motivational environment. Once that value is in place, acknowledge that building relationships takes time and effort. What are some tips for forging work relationships? Let's look at three ways that managers communicate their intent about working with people: (1) communicating with words, silence, availability, and absence; (2) spending quality time with direct reports; and (3) creating laughing moments to lighten the environment and let people save face.

Communicating with Words and Silence, Availability and Absence

Managers communicate continually, whether or not they intend to. Everyone knows we communicate with words. But what do we communicate with silence? It might be perceived as good listening and trust or caring about the person. Or, if a trusting relationship does not exist, staff might interpret silence as a lack of knowledge or concern, arrogance, anger, or even indifference toward the work or the person. It depends upon the context, but silence communicates something. It may not be the intended message, but employees will interpret the manager's silence through their own points of view, based on their backgrounds, experiences, and the types of relationships they have with their manager.

If managers make themselves available, they communicate that the work is important and so is the person. Availability lends credibility to managerial statements that they want to help employees succeed and accomplish their goals. Many managers have told me, "I have an open-door policy, but nobody comes." Showing availability might mean putting yourself physically in neutral territory, such as walking around, hanging around the coffeepot a few extra minutes, or eating in the employee lunchroom. An employee who is hesitant to breach the proverbial open door might feel more comfortable approaching you in a casual way "out in the open" rather than behind the "open door."

If the manager is not available, again the employees interpret the absence through their own viewpoints. Such unavailability might convey trust that employees can handle the work on their own or, alternatively, be perceived as lack of involvement in the work, or it might spark other reactions similar to the responses to silence.

Spending Quality Time with Everyone

Some managers wonder how to be perceived as treating all staff fairly. One way is to spend quality time with everyone. As a manager, I used to have a weekly one-on-one meeting with each of my direct reports. These were scheduled on the same day at the same time each week so we all made the meeting a priority. We used the time to discuss progress on the project milestones, the employee's future plans on the project, expectations, and any help he might need removing obstacles or obtaining resources. One consequence of these meetings was to build and sustain relationships. We each knew what to expect and how we could work better together toward the goals.

Spending quality time with staff does not mean you have to go to lunch or socialize after work. It means everyone gets the same treatment and support for the work at hand. You and they get continual opportunity to clarify expectations and to reduce surprises on the assignments. They get regular feedback on performance toward goals in a routine meeting and thus a better chance to perform well. You each get a chance to get to know each other better.

Encouraging Laughing Moments

Craig Amack, director and co-owner of BodyMAX Physical Therapy and Sports Training in Pleasanton, California, is an extraordinary communicator with patients and athletes. As an experienced physical therapist, Craig educates and encourages people throughout the healing process. He also creates a positive, humorous environment, which motivates patients and athletes to deliver their best efforts toward their goals. Once I reported to Craig something a friend had done that had annoyed me. Craig asked me, "Did you laugh?" "No," I said. "I got angry." "Oh," Craig said. "That was a laughing moment."

Craig and his wife, Dana, co-owner of BodyMAX, are the parents of five children, usually have one or two foster children with them, and own a thriving physical therapy business in two locations and an athletic training facility. As busy as Craig is, he laughs his way through his days at work with his patients and staff. You can hear him through the walls, and his laughter is infectious. After Craig taught me about laughing moments, I got to thinking of the wisdom of his message. It would be fantastic if people laughed more at work in good times and especially in tough times. Many of us have read that laughter is physically and emotionally good for us. So why not laugh?

Can we recognize laughing moments when we see them? Do we look for them? Can we laugh through problems? Sometimes when driving, another driver makes a mistake. If I laugh, they laugh too. I've also appreciated when I've made mistakes driving and the other driver laughs along with me as I shake my head or motion with my hand over my head that I know I'm in the wrong.

If it's not a safety issue, project crisis, or a major error, mistakes can be laughing moments instead of times to get hot under the collar. Most of us would rather be around a humorous person than an angry one. Emotion can be contagious and we'd rather catch laughing and happiness. If we create "laughing moments" in which we lighten up the unexpected or even mistakes, we can help people save face and realize that mistakes can contribute to learning. Laughter creates a more relaxed, pleasurable environment in which to work. It can also endear us to employees and help them use their passion to support the objectives, their managers, and their teammates. People who laugh together have more fun and a good shot at building a strong, trusting work relationship.

On an August flight to Orlando, our plane hit extensive turbulence on our descent. I clutched the armrests. I furrowed my brows. I breathed in deeply. Then I heard loud laughter throughout the plane. How we were viewing the turbulence varied. Most people saw it as a laughing moment—much to my surprise. Now let's look at context. My frame of reference was desire for a safe landing so I could get to a family funeral. The many kids on the plane were probably on their way to Orlando theme parks and looking forward to the attractions. Riding the clouds like a bucking bronco was a laughing moment for them. I laughed aloud as I thought, "Why not?"

Enjoying Personal Relationships at Work

Even without out-loud laughing, a more personal and close relationship between workers helps create a more pleasant and effective working environment. For example, while eating dinner at a restaurant in Jupiter, Florida, I noticed our waiter seemed to enjoy his work. When I asked him about it, he said the current owners had bought the restaurant and kept on the staff. He said, "I like being with the people I worked with before. It's not just a job. We have worked together as a team for a long time."

A Florida banker who had moved from Connecticut said, "In the Northeast people have more family around. But in Florida, people hang out more with people they work with." This was also the case when I first moved to California. Many of us were transplants and wanted to make friends. The manager was our friend, too. The entire group, even those who had been with the organization thirty years, enjoyed socializing at lunch and parties. This led to workplace cooperation, fun helping each other, and a comfortable working environment. When it came to teamwork, we were there for each other.

When You Don't Like Someone

It is highly likely that you will need to develop a working relationship with someone with whom you feel uncomfortable. A manager must assign work, follow up on performance, and give feedback every day. How can you deal with someone you would rather avoid?

Once, during a ten-week supervisory certificate program I was leading, it became apparent that one participant did not like one of her direct reports. Nicole complained every week about Matt's shortcomings. Each week there was new "data" to substantiate why he wasn't a good employee. However, much of it was not factual. It was primarily judging and opinion.

One week, after she blamed Matt for his latest transgression, I asked in a neutral tone, "Do you like him?"

"Of *course* I like him," she said, as the rest of the participants shook their heads left to right. Some turned to her and said, "No, you don't."

"I *do* like him," she said.

"Does *he* think you like him?" I asked.

"Of course he does," she said. "He knows I like him." Again the class disagreed with her.

"Your other employees know you don't like Matt too," one participant added.

We had developed trust in the group so people gave and heard feedback quite well. Nicole was surprised but eager to hear why the class gave that feedback. So we held a discussion of what happens when employees sense you don't like them or are judging them in a negative light. It is hard for them to escape the judgment and be seen as performing well. They may feel unconfident and uncomfortable coming to work. They may avoid tasks in which they might make a mistake. They might even avoid the manager, which makes the relationship impossible to repair.

Nicole had never stopped to think about whether she liked Matt or not. She had just gotten into a habit of looking for the negative and blaming him for it. And she hadn't thought about the effect her constant faultfinding with Matt had on the rest of the team. Fortunately, the training participant group had built a good team relationship with lots of trust and she knew we were trying to help her. Not liking people is only human. But as managers, it's not how we feel, but how we act that matters. We turned the class conversation to what we can do when we don't like someone. I recommended that Nicole follow six steps. She tried it and she changed her behavior toward Matt over the next week and reported positive stories about him in our next training sessions. If there's someone you don't like, or feel uncomfortable around, try the six steps.

What to Do When You Don't Like Someone

1. Hunt for the positive. Find one thing good about the person. Maybe he has technical expertise in one area of the job. Or he gets along well with a coworker. Or he always meets deadlines. Or he asks provocative questions that can save the company problems later on.

2. Concentrate on this one positive thing until you accept this positive trait or behavior. This might take a day, a few days, or even a week.

3. Compliment the person on something job-related that he is doing well and specify why it is important.

4. Once you've accepted one good characteristic, pick another positive trait or behavior and focus on that. Don't allow previous bias or preconceived notions to interfere.

5. Have coffee or lunch with him and seek to understand him as a person.

6. During weekly checkpoint meetings, ask for his opinion on the work and *listen* to what he says. Paraphrase and clarify. Think about what the opinion offers rather than rejecting it.

Try these steps for three to four weeks and see if it works for you. That's about how long it takes to ingrain a new habit. If you truly *intend* to develop a better relationship with the person, you will change your habit from seeking negative information to seeking positive work behavior and results.

Following these steps can enable a manager to act fairly toward everyone by viewing the job performance objectively and without bias. It usually improves the relationship with the direct report and, by the ripple effect, with others on the team. When there is trouble between an employee and the manager, the whole team experiences discomfort and stress. They look to the manager to fix the problem, not instigate it.

Summary

This chapter has introduced the importance of building and sustaining healthy working relationships with all staff members. Relationships help drive the work because of the commitment and enjoyment associated with good relationships. Strong work relationships invite trust, open communications, and positive interpersonal interactions.

The next chapter targets crystal clear expectations. When employees know what to expect, they can deliver. Thus trust grows, and so do relationships.

CHAPTER

2

Setting Expectations with Turbocharged Clarity

Communicating expectations is the basis for all management communication. You need to very clearly communicate unambiguous expectations to your staff. All other management functions fall into place when you lucidly communicate expectations to your team. Clear-cut expectations are the reference point for employee performance. You have to refer back to the expectations in order to deliver effective feedback and compelling coaching. Name any management function—motivating, planning, progress management, performance management, teaching, decision making, and so on—they all depend on determining definitive requirements in the beginning.

Once you decide the course you want your direct reports to follow and tell them, you enable them to perform their duties at an acceptable or exceptional level. They cannot achieve success without knowledge of your performance expectations.

This chapter offers tips on why turbocharged expectations are important to your success and that of your staff. This chapter also explores the impact that defining expectations has on creating and sustaining relationships, including building trust. When blindsiding and surprises are kept to a minimum, trust and relationships increase. Trust means your group can depend on you to make decisions and assign reasonable expectations.

To ensure you are on firm ground when you decide expectations, you need to "manage up" and be clear on what your own boss expects of *you*. To be viewed as a strong leader, you must link with and be on the same page as your manager. When you communicate expectations to your staff, you must be sure that your boss is not going to change such expectations later. This would dilute your authority, slow down work progress, reduce trust, and damage relationships. To help you clarify your boss's expectations, we include a sample worksheet later in this chapter (see Figure 2-1 on page 35). After you and your boss agree on *your* responsibilities and levels of authority, you can use a similar worksheet with your direct reports as a communication tool about your turbocharged expectations of them.

Communicating Expectations

Expectations are the written and unwritten outcomes, or methods of achieving outcomes, that a manager hopes will be accomplished. The more explicitly expectations are delineated, communicated, and understood, the more likely they are to be achieved. Assumptions that a direct report knows what the manager wants delivered, or how, might end in disappointment for both parties. A decisive manager states what success should look like—either in the end result or in the method to reaching the result.

The starting points of expectations are job descriptions, performance standards, and goals. These written requirements are essential communication tools. They have great merit. Formal job descriptions and goals are, however, only the beginning of setting expectations. They are the skeletons on which skilled managers flesh out the rest of the expectations.

Many managers assume that providing written job descriptions and goals or expressing expectations verbally one time means that staff know how to proceed. If you find yourself thinking, "the employee *should know*," try substituting the words, "the employee *probably does not know.*" The word *should* implies that the manager is unsure if he and the employee have the same understanding of the task at hand. Where there's lack of certainty, the employee probably does not understand the expectations to the manager's satisfaction.

Even the best employees interpret what they hear from their manager through their own experience and previous expectations of their current and prior managers. This interpretation may or may not line up with what the manager intended to say.

Many managers do not take time to crystallize their own expectations. They take the approach that they'll "know good performance when they see it" or they'll "make it up as they go along." Often these managers dole out mediocre ratings on performance appraisals because no one can measure up to a nonestablished expectation. They use phrases such as "there's always room for improvement," or "no one is perfect" as excuses to avoid awarding an outstanding rating and to distract from their inability to explain why they gave a rating that was not outstanding.

Purpose of Clear Expectations

Managers who articulate their expectations and ensure that their direct reports understand the expectations make achieving the expectations feasible. Managers who candidly state requirements can get what they want and need: quality results delivered on time and according to budget and specification. This prevents the common miscommunications that arise when expectations are not transparent.

Consistent clarity gets the work done appropriately, with minimum errors and rework. It builds trust because the work is not a moving target. It builds relationships because employees are less stressed and they are able to succeed when they know specifically what is required. Clarity shows the decision-making and communication adeptness of a manager, and this enhances support from all directions: upper management, direct reports, and peers.

Skilled managers guide their teams to accomplish work and grow the teams to meet new demands. These managers set a clear direction that aligns with corporate vision and goals. It's the domino effect: clear expectations equal easier performance follow-up, feedback, and coaching. Once expectations are understood, managers can confidently provide the resources their team needs to produce high-quality products and services. Managers then increase the effectiveness of feedback and coaching because these functions relate explicitly to the stated expectations. So direct reports always know where they stand in relation to what the manager needs. Competent managers increase the odds of getting what they want: outstanding results, motivated employees, and a cohesive team that is happy enough to stay with the organization. For managers to get what they want, they must define exactly what the desired result will look like with turbocharged clarity. Then they need to communicate that desired outcome to the staff.

This seems so logical and yet it is not easy. Everyday there are managers who do not know how to decide on and/or communicate their expectations. This poor communication leads to decline in morale and support for management. Let's look at two examples of how lack of clear direction (1) keeps managers from getting what they want and (2) teaches employees that to survive, they must disregard their manager.

The Impact of Not Setting Clear Expectations

Not being clear about the expectations costs the organization time, money, relationships, and quality results. It costs the manager her reputation and sometimes her job. Two true stories of the loss of employees' productivity and commitment, due to lack of clear expectations, follow. These are the stories of Tom and Kristen (not their real names). In Tom's case, his manager cannot set expectations. This causes rework and last-minute scrambling to complete projects. In Kristen's case, her manager doesn't set expectations at first, rather only when she observes behavior she doesn't like. Expectations after the fact come across as punitive. In both cases, work relationships and communication are strained and stressful.

Tom, an engineer, works for a consulting firm and is an expert in both construction management and claims resolution for construction disputes. Think bridges, tunnels, hospitals, airports, radioactive site re-mediation, power plants, highways, and public transportation. His work affects safety, so Tom's projects should be well planned in advance and in concert with management. Yet, for two years, Tom struggled to get direction from his boss on how to proceed on a multibillion-dollar proj-ect. Fifty percent of Tom's time was allocated to this project.

Tom's manager insisted that they work in the same office site, yet despite the proximity, the manager was not able to provide the guidance needed to get the job done. Tom would ask his boss for direction and get no answers. His manager could not explain the expectations. So Tom did his best with what he imagined he was supposed to do. He mapped out proposed plans and recommendations for the client and submitted them to his manager to see if he was on target. The boss would act as if he were grateful, then leave the documents in a pile on his desk—where they stayed. No amount of leverage could budge the manager to make a decision on the direction of the work. There was always something else that took priority. People began to show up late for work because the work didn't seem to matter.

Since the manager did not perform the day-to-day operational work, decisions became last-minute crises. It turned out that crisis was the environment in which the manager thrived. The manager stepped out in front as soon as deadlines loomed, but the team grew frazzled. He dic-tated orders and the work got done on time at his employees' expense. What a waste of talented engineers' intellects, client money, and time that could have been paced properly to develop the highest quality work. Eventually, the boss was fired, but team trust, loyalty, and morale had already eroded.

Do you know people like Tom who face this uncertainty at work? Have you ever had a manager who kept you guessing? Unfortunately, Tom's experience is not unique. Many people, even managers, go to work every day not knowing what is expected. They have a general idea of what to do, so there is activity. But often they don't know what the manager's performance expectation is and therefore cannot excel in the manager's eyes. They take the blame for lackluster performance even though the manager was responsible by not articulating the desired performance. Managers cannot get what they want if they cannot identify it in specific terms.

Tom's example involved a manager who ignored both his staff and opportunities to set and clarify expectations. In the second example, we look at Kristen and her manager. This manager also does not set expectations up front. Unlike Tom's boss, who ignores the employees, Kristen's manager seeks "teaching moments" whenever she sees something she doesn't like. She explains her expectations only after something goes wrong.

Imagine people keeping a low profile and staying below the radar. You have seen them do this to prevent getting "dinged" by their manager. Managers who do not specify what they expect up front are often the same managers who nitpick the negatives later rather than focus on the whole performance picture.

Medical imaging technician Kristen said, "My manager dresses to the nines. She wears Gucci and all the right clothes. But she doesn't know what I do, so it is really hard to take direction from her. She doesn't thank us for working long hours or recognize our efforts. Instead, she identifies the one thing that is wrong. For example, she came into our work area the other day and noticed an open cup of water. Instead of just putting the lid on it or rolling up her sleeves and asking how she could help, she chastised us, saying that the cup of water should not be there. With her punishing tone and interruption, she irritated us as we were running around trying to get our jobs done."

Tired and thirsty, a medical technician accidentally left the water out. The manager missed an opportunity to build morale by assisting the busy team or at least observing their dedication to work long hours. The few times this team hears from the manager regarding expectations are when something goes wrong.

In Tom's case, no expectations are given, no matter how often the employees seek them. These engineers cannot do the project without knowing the expectations. In Kristen's case, expectations are learned in bits and pieces when an employee misses the mark. In both cases, the managers do not build a trusting relationship with employees. Instead, they inadvertently generate unnecessary stress, decline of morale, and fear of failure. How can employees produce quality products and services under these conditions?

A Model Example for How to Set Great Expectations

Fortunately, there are managers who are expert at delineating expectations. The ideal situation is when the organization ingrains setting and reinforcing expectations as part of the corporate culture and everyday operations. A spectacular example of this is the Balboa Bay Club & Resort (BBC&R) in Newport Beach, California.

When I delivered a three-day seminar at the BBC&R, the service from every employee was extraordinary. No matter their job, they extended exemplary hospitality and sincere friendliness if you so much as passed them in the hallway or outside on the grounds. They worked in collaborative teams to freshen up the seminar room during breaks. I ate several meals at the restaurants and the teams of servers and servers' assistants anticipated our needs and replied to every "Thank you" with "My pleasure." They seemed to enjoy both their work and their coworkers. When I asked a few employees why all the workers seemed so happy, they said the view was terrific and the people they worked with were wonderful.

I was astounded by the outstanding service. For the first time ever, I felt like I was on vacation while on business. Because of the exceptional experience I enjoyed, I knew two things were happening behind the scenes here: management was setting very clear high expectations and management was providing regular feedback.

So when I returned to my office, I phoned BBC&R to find out exactly what management was doing to achieve such high performance and happy employees. Cynthia Goins, who oversees training and quality, confirmed what I had surmised: Managers maintain turbocharged clarity on their expectations and they give clear, immediate feedback targeted at those expectations. They consistently reinforce the expectations through feedback. Although this book separates the topics of setting expectations and giving feedback into different chapters, they are intertwined. Think of them as a pair. You can't perform either one of these management responsibilities well without the other. I will include Cynthia's comments in both this chapter and in the feedback chapter to show how expectations and feedback link together.

Not surprisingly, it begins with selecting friendly applicants in the hiring process, a tradition at BBC&R since 1948. Since the BBC&R is selling service and experience, it initially looks for the first impression of friendliness, dress, and smile. Then applicants are screened with prepared behavioral questions that will determine how well they have worked with fellow workers and customers in the past. Past work behavior is used to predict potential buy-in on the mission statement and the "15 Legendary Service Basics." Choosing employees who can deliver on the mission and service is so crucial that successful applicants must make it through three to five interviews, including one with the president and COO, Henry Schielein. The concept is that the organization can teach people how to make drinks or make a bed, but applicants have to be friendly before they get hired.

Once people are hired, they must attend new-hire orientation, where the organization immediately begins to set formal standards and expectations. The uniform expectations of the entire organization are covered in the luncheon orientation, which includes talks by the president and executive committee. Specifically, the orientation covers the history, mission statement, who does what in all areas of the organization, the 15 Legendary Service Basics expectations, and the expected customer engagement behaviors, including greeting all guests by name. Human Resources conducts role-plays to ensure that new hires are knowledgeable about and practice the "BBC&R Service Culture and Engagement." They practice scenarios with props, for example, using maps to be able to tell guests how to get to theme parks, since staff is trained to go above and beyond what guests ask for. Orientation is used as a check and balance to be sure corporate expectations are done right.

After orientation, the responsibility for delivering the next set of expectations, which are position specific, is turned over to individual department heads, who make sure the supervisors train using the job descriptions. The supervisors also train employees to show gratitude, such as thanking guests for staying and inviting them back. They are trained to focus on "One Guest at a Time" and anticipate needs. When I stayed at BBC&R and the employees anticipated my needs, I felt that the employees had to have been empowered to make their own decisions.

Three weeks after the orientation session, Human Resources follows up on how well expectations are understood and seeks feedback from each new employee on the job. Did we paint an accurate picture during orientation? Do you have a correct understanding about uniforms? Any concerns? Are you getting trained? Are you happy? The new employees fill out a form and Human Resources addresses comments on it right away with the division and department heads.

Each week, one of the 15 Legendary Service Basics is reinforced with all staff. One week it is using proper vocabulary when communicating. Managers tell employees they can use their own phrases on their own time, but while at work they must use proper verbiage such as "my pleasure" instead of "no problem." Language sets a tone consistent with organizational exceptional service goals. They teach the staff how to shape the greetings and to give eye contact. Reinforcing the 15 Legendary Service Basics on a regular basis highlights their importance. It also ensures that everyone has the best chance of meeting them.

The expectations for managers are also clearly stated and continually reinforced. Managers are held to high standards. President and COO Henry Schielein says, "If your department is exceeding expectations, it's because of you. If not, it's because of you." Managers are told they must be role models and make it a priority to lead by example.

Managers are trained quarterly on leading people. Human Resources conducts seminars, which include role-playing to practice the concepts. The group addresses turnover. It uses Hiring Batting Average (HBA) as a metric to measure management performance. When managers hire, they are expected to be sure employees are trained and happy so they pass the six-month performance review. If the employees don't pass, the manager is held accountable for either not training properly or not having the right leadership skills. If an employee cannot meet the standards, it affects the manager's HBA. BBC&R found that by implementing HBA, it decreased turnover by 28 percent.

Leadership Performance Report Cards are also used on a regular basis to give continual feedback to managers. As head of quality, Cynthia carries these cards in her folder all the time as she walks around. They measure managers' achievement of no accidents, turnover last quarter, their HBA, how happy the newly hired employees were when HR interviewed them three weeks after orientation, and if there are any new hires who were not sent for orientation. Another measurement is how many employees a manager nominated for awards. If a manager had no employees outstanding enough to nominate, they examine why not. Since communication is of top importance, managers are expected to hold departmental meetings with their entire team for 1½ to 2 hours at least quarterly. Continual improvement is measured on the number of good ideas submitted *and implemented* by both employees and the manager, so the manager is expected to encourage and empower employees to propose ideas.

From a quality aspect, BBC&R monitors problems on guest comment cards on a quarterly basis. If there is a trend, the resort addresses it, sets a goal of better performance by the next quarter, and then follows up to ensure managers are addressing the goal.

Continual reinforcement of expectations is a daily habit at the Balboa Bay Club & Resort. The managers use a Daily Information Line-Up Sheet when they hold morning and evening meetings to set expectations for each shift. They tell the team about the groups that are holding in-house seminars or parties, and mention any VIPs. They also talk about comments written by guests who were not happy with their stay as well as remarks about exceptional service. They continually mention standards and discuss whichever Legendary Service Basic is the weekly topic. The managers are constantly checking to see if employees are aware of all expectations and that they know why they are important. Teamwork is relentlessly reinforced. Managers ask the staff, "What can we do better than yesterday?" The quality manager attends as many meetings as she can. She knows if a manager has skipped a line-up meeting if she asks employees a question and they say, "uhhh." It probably means the manager didn't communicate the message at a daily line-up, so she calls the manager.

Managers and the quality manager mentor and lead by example and give immediate feedback to reinforce expectations. For example, if they see an employee not greet a guest, they say something right away to constantly reinforce expectations. The same holds for when they observe excellent examples of employee adherence to expectations. For example, while I was interviewing Cynthia for this book she asked me to hold on a minute while she wrote down something she had just observed. She overheard a room reservation agent anticipate a guest's needs. Cynthia wrote down specifically what she heard so she could compliment the employee when she got off the phone.

When all managers in an organization define expectations with turbocharged clarity and give continual feedback, employees can relax because they know they will be guided to stay on track. They get the opportunity to develop skills and relationships and do their best work. This heightens confidence, trust, relationships, and, thus, communication.

The Power of Trust

Working relationships are built on trust. Trust establishes the framework for delegating, giving feedback, and coaching, because if people think you have their best interests at heart and you know what you are doing, they will put themselves out to help the team succeed.

Trust is the result of consistent, respectful, and factual interaction. A manager who is precise about expectations and who helps employees achieve those desired results earns trust. People want to know that their task is not a moving target and that their boss is upfront about their progress toward meeting the goal.

When trust exists, a manager can assign work and converse regularly with direct reports about performance with greater comfort. Regular feedback and listening helps everyone to know whether work should continue on the current path or be redirected. Discussing task and project status becomes an opportunity for growth for all parties as well as for enhancing the work and the relationship.

Cynthia Goins at the BBC&R says, "Recognition builds trust—getting to know your people. Asking 'How's the family?' shows genuine interest and relationship. Trust building is an ongoing process. We train our managers to ask employees how they are doing and 'What else can I do to help you?' We want them to be hands-on managers. We train them to 'keep your promises, find time for your employees, and treat your employees the way you treat your guests.'"

In fact, one of the guests observed that philosophy in action. He told me, "I saw managers ask employees 'How is it going today?' in a very surprising way. I got the feeling they'd drop everything and run and get pencils if the employees said that's what they needed." Helping people do their best work does build trust.

A 360-Degree Look at Responsibilities and Levels of Authority

Upper management support is key to helping managers develop trusting relationships with their employees. When employees know that the expectations are clear and that their manager has upper management support, it is easier for them to follow their manager and do what is asked. When their manager is aligned with organizational direction, employees can trust that the expectations will be realistic. It is less stressful for everyone because the tasks most likely will be stable. Assignments that change frequently create stress and distrust and therefore undermine a manager's *personal* power. Stable tasks enable employees to believe that the manager knows the direction and is there to support the employees achieve the goals.

In short, to set clear expectations for others, you must first know clearly *what is expected of you.* Looking at your managerial role from the points of view of your boss, staff, peers, and upper management will help you feel confident about the breadth of your scope and the extent of your authority. This 360-degree look at your responsibilities illuminates what others need from you. Used well, this knowledge can prevent misunderstandings and translate into achieving results through positive working relationships. Transparent understanding of your entire suite of responsibilities—written and unwritten—can result in gaining support from all directions and levels of the organization. It also points you to a bigger picture of where to contribute to others in supporting corporate goals.

Using a recommended worksheet will help you to communicate in a logical manner with your boss. It is critical for your success that you comprehend your roles as your boss and others see them. To effectively lead and manage your group, you and your manager must agree on your responsibilities and depth of authority. Once you solidify what your manager expects and what level of authority you have for each project or task, you can confidently delegate to and follow up with your staff. If you live in the dark, your staff will too, and they will not see you as their leader.

Expectations are frequently unwritten and often unspoken or undefined. Yet you will be evaluated on these unwritten expectations. It is your job to take the initiative to clarify your manager's expectations so you can succeed.

Many managers ask, "Shouldn't this conversation be initiated by my boss?"

"Has it?" I ask.

"No," they reply.

"Well then?" I ask.

"Point taken," they say.

Request a meeting with your boss in upper management and thoroughly prepare for it. This is a chance to show your strengths in organization and planning as well as your desire to partner with your manager.

Clarifying Your Manager's Expectations of You

Communicating with your manager about what he expects of you is an ongoing process. First you analyze what you think he expects. Then you meet with him to discuss these responsibilities and levels of authority. It may take more than one meeting for you to both agree. After meeting, you must continually dialogue with your manager to be sure you are on target and to include changes as they occur. Let's look at each of these three activities. Figure 2-1, "Clarifying Expectations Worksheet," is a worksheet to help you analyze and clarify your boss's expectations of you.

Use this worksheet to define your understanding of your responsibilities and what level of authority you have for each responsibility. Use the ideas in the worksheet to jump-start your list of responsibilities. Add other responsibilities and delete those that are not applicable.

1. **Responsibilities.** List all your responsibilities and goals, as you know them. Besides those from your job description, include unwritten responsibilities that you think you have so you can get confirmation from your manager.

2. **Performance Expectations.** Record performance expectations you have of yourself and those you think your boss has for you. Define what you think the expectations mean for this particular assignment. For example, instead of writing "team player with sales department," specify *what you would do to demonstrate* that you are a team player, such as "Provide information on customer complaints on same day received."

3. **Level of Authority.** Next to each responsibility, goal, and performance expectation, write what you perceive to be your level of authority: H (High), M (Medium), or L (Low). *High* might mean complete decision-making and implementation ability—let your boss know what you have already done. *Medium* might indicate you can make recommendations but need your boss's approval before taking action. *Low* could mean check with your manager before starting a task or project for clear definition of what your manager wants. You and your boss need to define exactly what H, M, and L mean in your work situation. Expect that your level of authority may differ for each responsibility, goal, or expectation.

4. **Who expects this of me?** Check off the responsibilities *you* expect of yourself in the "I Do" column. Then put checkmarks in other appropriate columns based on who you think expects that responsibility: your boss, your staff, peers, or senior management. There can be multiple checkmarks for each responsibility.

Explain to your manager that to ensure you meet her expectations, you have prepared an analysis of what you think your responsibilities and levels of authority for each duty are. Tell your manager the worksheet is a "talking document" so you can get her ideas and collaborate. Ask for a meeting—in person, or if not possible, by videoconference or phone.

Depending upon how collaborative your relationship with your boss is and how he deals with written information, you might decide to e-mail your completed worksheet ahead of the meeting. This gives your boss an opportunity to think about his expectations, whether he agrees with what you've written, and what to add, delete, or modify. With both people prepared for the meeting, you might have better results in a shorter period of time. However, if you think your boss will e-mail it right back to you with a pithy note to avoid a face-to-face meeting, you may not want to e-mail it. For the ideal communication, you should persuade him to review it ahead of time and meet in person to discuss his expectations.

(*Text continued on page 40*)

Figure 2-1. Clarifying Expectations Worksheet

Responsibilities	Level of Authority	Who Expects This of Me?				
		I Do	Boss	Staff	Peer	Sr. Mgmt
Set Clear Expectations						
Define goals for my work situation						
Carry out department goals						
Prioritize tasks and projects						
Provide leadership						
Create/implement business plans that will succeed						
Share the same goal as other groups Specifically:						
Support joint tasks effectively						
Drive change initiatives						
Meet compliance issues						
Get team member buy-in						
Develop Work Relationships						
Foster a good work environment for my peers and coworkers						
Support different departments						
Advocate for my employees						
Be fair, honest, and trustworthy						
Maintain peace/harmony						
Set an example of following "rules"						
Set example of good customer service						
Boost morale of group						
Support my staff/management						
Trust staff/management						

Figure 2-1. (Continued)

Responsibilities	Level of Authority	Who Expects This of Me?				
		I Do	Boss	Staff	Peer	Sr. Mgmt
Show respect for everyone						
Build a strong team to support the company						
Be a positive role model						
Communicate Expectations						
Communicate department goals						
Communicate high-level goals/expectations to my team						
Get the work done on time and within budget						
Consistently enforce rules/expectations						
Ensure staff understands expectations						
Use Process Skills & Technical Knowledge to Meet Corporate Goals						
Produce quality products/services						
Provide organization						
Complete tasks that will help company obtain goals						
Ensure staff is trained and able to perform job						
Eliminate quality issues						
Ensure bills are paid on time without exception and without error						

Figure 2-1. (Continued)

Responsibilities	Level of Authority	Who Expects This of Me?				
		I Do	Boss	Staff	Peer	Sr. Mgmt
Identify more efficient processes/workflow						
Ensure safety of staff members						
Provide tools and resources to do the job						
Plan						
Prevent & Solve People Problems						
Make employees/company/teams successful						
Resolve and manage HR issues						
Maintain smooth operation of department/ group						
Create teamwork						
Delegate						
Set deadlines & progress check-in dates						
Provide employees with the tools to do jobs						
Provide guidance and support						
Tell "big picture" about "why" and "what" they need to do						
Mentor staff						
Trust staff						

Figure 2-1. (Continued)

Responsibilities	Level of Authority	Who Expects This of Me?				
		I Do	Boss	Staff	Peer	Sr. Mgmt
Monitor progress on regular basis						
Give Feedback						
Meet deadlines						
Make sure job/task is done effectively						
Provide regular feedback						
Hold people accountable						
Coach						
Guide individuals						
Help get staff involved in problem solving						
Ensure department goals are met and obstacles are overcome						
Effectively train						

Figure 2-1. (Continued)

Responsibilities	Level of Authority	Who Expects This of Me?				
		I Do	Boss	Staff	Peer	Sr. Mgmt
Hire Talent						
Recruit, interview, and hire						
Listen						
Listen to staff point of view						
Assist staff with their issues						
Support others' ideas						
Be a sounding board						
Accept feedback						
Motivate Talented Staff						
Motivate employees						
Set positive, comfortable environment						
Ensure I am a positive role model						
Keep turnover low						
Boost morale						
Create good days for staff						

Figure 2-1. (Continued)

Responsibilities	Level of Authority	Who Expects This of Me?				
		I Do	Boss	Staff	Peer	Sr. Mgmt
Other						
Fulfill boss's duties when he or she is not available						
Meet sales and/or revenue goals						
Ensure safety						
Evaluate performance						
Plan career development						
Plan succession						
Increase profit						
Educate self on current trends						

Lead the Meeting(s) with Your Boss

Open the meeting with a recap of the purpose of this communication on expectations and responsibilities. The purpose is to ensure that you meet your manager's expectations so that you can better lead your team and meet all goals. Explain why it benefits him, you, and your staff.

Review each responsibility and get agreement on what authority (H,

M, or L) you have for each of the responsibilities. If this seems too time consuming, think about how long it takes when you and your team have to change directions because of not meeting what your boss expected.

Add, delete, or modify items on your list according to your manager's comments. Make sure you ask targeted open-ended questions to elicit any unwritten expectations your manager has that are not yet on your list. Discuss any disagreements as you go, so that you both concur with the final list. Set up additional meetings as necessary until you and your manager complete and agree upon the final list. Finalize the worksheet and e-mail or give your boss a copy of the finalized "Clarifying Expectations Worksheet."

Keep an open mind during the meetings and recognize that it may take more than one meeting to come to a final agreement. This is especially true if your manager has trouble specifying expectations. This conversation will be of enormous benefit to both of you in working in partnership. It should also prevent situations in which your boss might go directly to your staff or undermine your decisions with your direct reports.

Follow Up Continually to Ensure You Are in Agreement

Ask for and schedule a weekly meeting to review your progress and plans. The weekly meeting is one of the best communication tools you can use to ensure you and your boss continually see eye to eye. If your manager does not see the necessity of a weekly meeting, do not give up. Persuade him that it will help you be better able to meet his expectations and to communicate. You can save your boss time by saving up the little matters and handling them all at once. You can be sure you and your team are always aligned with the organizational goals. You can discuss anything that has changed, including priorities, and stay in alignment with your manager's expectations. When you work cohesively with your manager, you demonstrate how you want your staff to work with you.

Setting Turbocharged Expectations for Your Staff

Once you and your boss finalize the "Clarifying Expectations Worksheet" (or your version of such a worksheet), it is time to trickle the communication over to your staff. You need to clearly set expectations for your staff. They need to be crystal clear on their responsibilities and levels of authority so they can meet your expectations.

If they are managers, you might ask them to use the same worksheet that you did. If they are individual contributors, ask each direct report to make a list of what they think their responsibilities and performance expectations are. Ask them to indicate what level of authority they think they have for each of the responsibilities. Then follow the same steps as you did with your boss. Meet with each person and discuss areas of agreement and what must be modified, added, or deleted. Set up a weekly meeting to stay in continual communication about how well the performance expectations are being met.

Establishing transparent expectations and using the communication techniques recommended in this chapter will enhance your direct reports' ability to obtain quality results on time. You will also forge and bolster trustworthy working relationships and prevent people problems.

How Performance Expectations Link with Delegating, Giving Feedback, and Coaching

Since performance expectations are what you are trying to attain, they are the basis for any conversations you have with employees when delegating. To perform well, the employee must understand the assignment being delegated. He must know whether he has full authority on all aspects of the task or project or if he needs approval. He needs to know when you both will meet to discuss the checkpoints.

At the checkpoints, or whenever it is appropriate, you give feedback on progress. Feedback should relate back to the performance expectation—what the employee was asked to do.

When you coach, again, the topic is optimal performance—so you revisit performance expectations. Therefore, the foundation of these vital management functions is to gain turbocharged clarity on performance expectations so *you can get what you want* and need to be done.

Summary

Powerful managers have comprehensive knowledge of their organizations, the goals, and what they need to accomplish. They ally themselves with their managers, upper management, and the results that need to be achieved. They also work with their staff to ensure that the direction and expectations of the organization are understood as they apply to direct reports' jobs.

This chapter has covered how to specify unambiguous expectations. Chapter 3 offers suggestions on how to communicate those expectations to employees and ensure that they are understood as intended.

CHAPTER
3

Communicating Your Expectations: What to Say and How to Say It

Once you have defined your clear-cut expectations, you need to communicate them in a way that creates and sustains energized relationships. How you introduce your expectations impacts how your staff perceives your credibility—can they trust that you will treat them professionally and give them the support they need to succeed? What you say, how much you say, and how you say it will influence whether they achieve the needed results and whether they take ownership of the task.

In this chapter we are going to look at the day-to-day expectations that employees receive on an ongoing, ad hoc basis. This chapter assumes knowledge of the basic expectations such as goal setting, job descriptions, and performance standards. For a refresher, or if you are not familiar with them, they are covered in Appendix A.

Importance of Communicating Expectations

You can use the worksheet provided in Chapter 2, your own list, or project documents specific to your organization to create turbocharged expectations. The more definitive the expectations, the greater the chance of achieving the desired outcome. That is the beginning.

Next comes how you communicate those expectations. The conversations when you communicate the expectations will seal the employee's understanding and commitment. How you communicate—what you say, how you say it, and how much you tell—will impact your working relationship for the imminent task and for future work with this employee. At one end of the spectrum is a manager who relinquishes all responsibility and authority to the employee. At the opposite end is a manager who micromanages. Neither of these approaches is balanced. It is important to energize, empower, and support direct reports, and also to give them just the right amount of guidance and direction that they need to get the task done.

Stating Performance Expectations

Even unwritten expectations need to be decided upon in a specific way and then communicated, because employees cannot meet vague, unspecified requirements. If a manager instructs employees about the standard *after* they have erred, it is punishing and damaging to the relationship. It provokes fear in employees of making more mistakes because they don't know the rules.

Every day managers make assumptions that employees are like them or know what to do. When the employee doesn't deliver on the assumption, many managers get upset and/or blame the employee, or label him with a word like "slacker," or say he has a poor work ethic. Often it is just a misunderstanding that could easily be handled as a one-off instead of lumped under a pile of transgressions and used as an excuse to label someone. Managers make mistakes when they make assumptions. They can fix these mistakes. When managers are surprised by behavior or lack of action, it is an opportunity to acknowledge to themselves that they need to take time to delineate what they expect and communicate it.

If we don't clearly think through our expectations ahead of time, we can end up upset and create communication problems. Before my husband and I had children, we planned for our thirteen-year-old niece to come spend five summertime weeks with us. We were excited. We were the cool aunt and uncle in the family. Kids loved us because we were so hip.

"What are your expectations?" a friend, who was a family counselor, asked us.

"We don't have any," I replied.

"Yes you do," she persevered. "You have rules."

"We don't have rules," I said. "We are supportive."

When our niece arrived, we were surprised by her actions. One night she went out in the dark to skateboard down the hill of a nearby mildly busy street. We realized we had expectations. When she visited a twenty-something bachelor neighbor friend's home by herself, we were startled. We had rules after all—we just hadn't thought about them in advance. One day we three sat calmly in our car in our driveway for fifteen minutes until she finally complied and put her seatbelt on for our road trip. Again we discovered we had expectations. Over a decade later, our niece called us up to thank us for the seatbelt rule. She had been run off the road by an eighteen-wheeler and the police told her the seatbelt saved her life.

Guidelines and expectations are beneficial to people. Being supportive actually means letting people know the boundaries and expectations ahead of time. It is not supportive to avoid defining expectations and then watch people make unnecessary mistakes. When you tell them your expectations after they have erred, it comes across negatively and can create tension and defensiveness.

We do not do anyone any favors by not getting clear on our daily expectations. If managers don't spend the time to think about expectations ahead of time and ensure they are stated and clearly understood, performance cannot soar. Relationships get injured. Trust declines. Resentment and tension escalate. Work suffers.

Impact of Unclear Expectations

When a manager either doesn't state any expectations or discusses them in an ambiguous way, the direct report does not know either the expectation or what to do to achieve it. If the expectation is a change in behavior, the employee does not know what to change or how to do it.

Recently, Lindsey, a manager with over ten years of experience, but no management training, told me her boss had given her a management book to read on dealing with people. She didn't like the book, even though she knew that all the senior executives were reading it as a group.

"You're supposed to sugarcoat everything these days," she said to me. "You can't just tell them what to do. I don't get it," she continued, "it's their job. My boss told me that my problem is that I have such high expectations of myself that I then have those high expectations of my staff. Doesn't he want them to meet high standards? I don't understand why that is a problem."

Can you see the big question mark that lurked over Lindsey's head as she walked away from her boss, book in hand? She felt confused and wasn't sure what message the boss was conveying. She did not really know why he wanted her to read the book.

The message that Lindsey has high standards sounds like a compliment. But what was the boss really saying? That she doesn't know how to deal with people? That she should cut back on her standards? The problem was not identified, so how is she to fix it?

The real point was not about how high the expectations were. It was about being clear about *what* those expectations actually were and determining whether they were appropriate. For example, did Lindsey expect her staff to stay until 8:00 p.m., like she was doing every night for weeks? One of her staff was out on extended medical leave. Did she expect the other staff to do all of that person's work? Did they sit down as a team and discuss what they could and could not accomplish as a group? Were specific tasks assigned and agreed to, or was it assumed staff would know what to do?

What were the high expectations Lindsey's boss referred to? Did he take the time to specify them and help her set up a realistic plan? Did he simply tell her his expectations? No, he gave her a book in the hopes she would figure out what he was unable or unwilling to specify.

The boss made common errors. He missed an occasion to coach Lindsey and make a strategic plan for her development. He made ambiguous statements instead of giving specific feedback about a particular issue. He dodged an uncomfortable conversation instead of being honest and telling Lindsey exactly what was not working and what he expected her to do. Part of the plan should be management training for Lindsey. How can she perform well as a manager when she has to learn on her own without benefit of training? Another section of the development plan should be regular coaching meetings, with specific feedback, support, and comments on progress. Communication and managerial goals could be set up, with checkpoints to determine how well the goals are being met. Listening to Lindsey's challenges, point of view, and suggested solutions for next steps at each coaching session is essential. But the first step is for Lindsey's manager to nail down his specific expectations. He intended to help Lindsey better communicate with her staff. His intentions were admirable, just not effective.

Communicating Expectations Is an Opportunity to Get Buy-In

After managers recognize their precise expectations or standards, these are set in motion by how the managers state the expectations. A manager's success depends on how advanced his influence and persuasion skills are. Employees in today's workforce expect to have a say and to be heard. Most want to be told why the work is important and why it has to be done certain ways. They want to see the benefits to themselves as well as to the organization. Recognizing such benefits focuses the work and enlivens it with meaning. Today's employees expect to be treated as colleagues and want to work shoulder to shoulder with their manager.

The belief that "it's their job, they don't need to know why" is not practical thinking. Management responsibility is about communication, which is how we say things. If people feel they are choosing, they feel more in control of the work. Even if there is a nonnegotiable way that a project is expected to be done, managers can explain the benefits to the employees of doing it that way. Explain how it helps them successfully reach the goals so the conversation can be viewed as supportive and collegial rather than as "bossy." Use your intuition about tone of voice and word choice. How would you like to be treated?

Managers know they are supposed to motivate direct reports or at least provide a motivational environment. That's what influence and persuasion is about—providing motivation. Strong managers persuade people to be committed to deadlines and a high level of quality. Telling people why their participation is important is an essential part of maintaining relationships and getting quality work done. Managers can get compliance in the short run with or without a good relationship, but they might get sabotaged in the long run. If people are not allowed to express their opinions or if a relationship is not valued, a manager may get what he wants done right now but lose collaboration in the future. Collaboration occurs when people work together to try to meet the needs and best possible outcomes for all parties. This benefits quality and productivity.

The way managers communicate expectations can motivate or de-motivate as an unintended consequence. Management communication skills are key to stimulating top performance. How well the work gets done is dependent on the staff. How well they work together to align personal interests with corporate interests is dependent on the manager.

How to State Performance Expectations

What are your expectations? If you were to ask your direct reports to tell you their understanding of your expectations, what would they say? Would their understanding be the same as what *you* think the expectations are? What are the unwritten expectations many employees have to discover and wrestle with by themselves?

Typically, a manager is keenly aware and careful when discussing performance essentials during hiring interviews, new employee orientation, role and responsibility clarification, job description review and revision, and goal setting. But, more often, expectations are mentioned in passing. Managers may not even realize that they are setting expectations. As a result they don't take the time to be deliberate and think carefully about the best way to set and communicate everyday job needs.

Management activities such as work assignments and follow-up, delegation, process and project management discussions, weekly progress meetings, giving feedback, and coaching demand thoughtful consideration and consistency in message. It is also important to use paraphrasing and to ask employees to explain their perception of the expectation so you can be sure you have the same understanding.

Use your intuition about how to state expectations based on your knowledge of the work, the relationship you share with the direct report, and what the situation requires. Trust yourself. If you are prepared from the business side and you have a good working relationship with the direct report, you will know how to phrase the expectations.

When stating expectations, it is essential to tell the individual whether or not she has discretion in *how* to do the task. Whenever the how can be delegated, greater ownership of the task ensues. But sometimes, there is only one way to do the task because of policy, procedure, regulation, or communication needs of groups. It there is only one way to do the task, be clear about it. Following are two scenarios with suggested steps to follow and an example of each. The first scenario applies when there is a required way to do the task and the second scenario is for when the employee can decide how to do the task. When there is only one way, you tell the employee both *what* you expect her to do and *how.*

When There Is Only One Way to Do the Task

Task: Organize the Work

1. Describe specifically what kind of organization is required and why. For example, let's say customer information needs to be organized a particular way so that several people can access and use it.
2. Explain the importance and implications of organizing the work the required way.
3. Check the employee's understanding of how to do the task to be sure that she understands what needs to be done. Ask her to explain the key points: "So just to be sure we have the same understanding, what is it you think I'm asking you to do?"
4. Ask what support the employee needs from you or others to meet the expectation.
5. Get agreement that she will organize the required way.
6. Set up a supportive check-in date so you can give feedback on the employee's progress.

That's fine when setting up expectations that need to be done one way. What about when there are *options* as to *how* the work gets done? When reflecting on how to set performance criteria, it is important to think of the level of expertise a direct report has developed as well as the processes that are in place to guide the work. Maybe he will do the work a different way than the manager would, but the employee's way will get the end result. If he has the experience and ability, tell the employee what you expect and let him decide the *how*.

When the Employee Decides How to Do the Task

Task: Create a Newsletter

1. Describe the end result and the performance standards or parameters. For example, "We need to create a newsletter to inform customers about our services. What I need from you is your recommendation on how to do that.

> Some parameters to consider are content, layout, frequency, required staffing hours, production, and distribution. The budget for the newsletter is $_____ over your current budget. This fits with our division goal to increase customer service."
>
> 2. Explain the importance and implications of creating a newsletter. Who originated the idea and why? What problems is the newsletter intended to solve? What are the foreseen opportunities and problems?
> 3. Ask for ideas on what other considerations should go into the proposal. Listen and discuss.
> 4. Ask the employee to summarize what you both have agreed the proposal parameters are.
> 5. Ask what support he needs from you or peers to do the assignment.
> 6. Agree on a deadline and any check-in dates.

How Much to Say When Stating Performance Expectations

How much you say when communicating what you need done varies depending on the situation. A sign on I-5S from Seattle to Tacoma reads: "Uneven pavement surface." The sign states the fact and drivers are assumed to have the intelligence and experience to know what to do. A sign further up the road gives more information. A flashing sign reads, "Caution. Uneven pavement ahead." This sign tells drivers to be careful up ahead. Why the difference? The conditions were different in each of those sections of highway. Sometimes conditions at work will vary from task to task or from day to day or from employee to employee. Managers may need to state expectations with more or with fewer directions depending on variables.

When stating performance expectations, deciding how much to say and how to say it fluctuates. The amount of detail and way to talk to your direct report depends largely on the task, the delegatee, and the process. How much elasticity does the task offer for determining *how* to accomplish it? What is the experience and track record of the delegatee on this or similar projects? What is the grade or rank of the position the delegatee holds in the organization? How much required process or structure must be incorporated in getting this assignment done? Is the delegatee familiar with the process? Other variance factors include your company's or the customer's budget, the financial health of your company, and/or the general economy. Other crucial considerations are the time window for accomplishing the task as well as the flexibility or rigidity of the deadlines. The following two examples show distinct variance factors that dictate how much or how little the manager must say when setting expectations.

Example of Stating Expectations and Empowering

Let's look at an example of a manager who hires experienced professionals to do creative work.

Rob Rankin is vice president and director of Brand Development for Clarity Coverdale Fury (CCF) in Minneapolis. The American Association of Advertising Agencies named CCF one of the elite creative agencies in the United States several times, so it has a reputation for outstanding results, which comes from fostering a spirit of collaboration and creativity.

When asked about the process CCF uses for stating expectations to innovative team members, Rob explained that there are many tiers. "Generally speaking, what we are doing as account services managers is pulling together a multidisciplinary team to accomplish specific goals for our client brands," Rob said. "We do this through very well-thought-out and well-researched strategic business plans that outline our objectives and strategies. These plans are developed with the client and an internal team we call the 'core team.' Each person on the team from CCF is a more senior team member representing a specific discipline within the agency. The strategic plans are designed to achieve very specific goals."

After the strategic plans are developed, the next tier is the tactical.

Rob says, "The tactical aspects of the process involve a broader group from our internal team. That group is responsible to develop the media plans and specific creative elements to achieve the strategic goals. It also handles the purchasing and production of those tactics."

However, according to Rob there is more to setting expectations than just drafting strategic plans and handing them off to the team to execute:

"It starts with the people we hire. We look for an individual who is naturally motivated—a self-starter who is passionate about the communication business and tends to be more entrepreneurial. It is this type of person who is more likely to be accountable to themselves, our clients, and to others on the team. They self-police so we do not need a constant check-in process to make sure individuals are doing their jobs. We check in periodically during the process, offer advice and suggestions, and then let the team concept work with the counsel we have given them.

"It's not that there isn't a specified process involved—there is. We have a kick-off meeting for an initiative where we brief the team and have a formalized creative brief or media brief that is presented to the team. We establish goals, budgets, and timing. We have midpoint check-ins to be sure the work is focused and on track and conduct what we call stand-up meetings, which are intended to pull the team together on short notice to be sure everyone is aware of what progress is being made and where individual teams are. These stand-up meetings are designed to be brief, no more than fifteen minutes. This way, everyone can get a quick status on the project or come together to quickly solve a problem. But meetings are not time consuming so that people can get back to their workloads. Premeetings are also scheduled before a client presentation to ensure that everyone is properly prepared and to be certain the work meets the set of deliverables we established with the client."

Rob continues:

"While we do have a process and we have meetings, we try not to hover. We empower individuals and the team to do the work and they appreciate that freedom and take their responsibility seriously. We check in, but don't micromanage. Often team members won't wait for a midpoint check-in if they have questions. They want to keep things on track so they ask right away or seek an opinion. They also then tend to become good at empowering others, too.

"Another expectation of the account services groups is that we ask these individuals to set their own career goals and strategies for achieving those goals. They are responsible for their own career plans. And a larger part of their evaluation is a self-evaluation. Because they are the ones setting their goals, they tend to take these very seriously. And the plan they write is theirs and their responsibility. We also have other team members evaluate their performance in what we call a 360-degree review. This process helps further develop the sense of accountability we foster here at CCF."

Rob's example works well when working with experienced professionals with technical expertise in their fields. Some examples would include engineers, IT professionals, scientists, artists, analysts, writers, medical professionals, designers, and others who have the education and background to get the job done independently and need breathing room. Generally speaking, the work is enriched by the ideas of such employees. Most managers have expectations for the quality and timeliness of work and expectations that employees will cultivate their skills and abilities. Managers still initiate and oversee the expectations regardless of the level of professional.

Example of Stating Expectations and Partnering

Sometimes managers have more subtle expectations that they need to state and manage. Kenneth W. Paulin is former senior vice president of commercial real estate lending at M&T Bank, a highly regarded regional bank in western New York State. In his position, Ken had the expectation to always have the loan committee approve the loans presented by his direct reports. Ken also made it clear to his lending officers that he expected to never be surprised by them in loan committee meetings.

Ken clearly stated these expectations, then he partnered with his staff so they would be able to provide answers to all committee questions. This enabled the committee to approve the loan in the same meeting. In addition to having discussions about expectations, Ken prepped his direct reports on all the parameters. When they thought they were totally prepared for the meeting and ready for all questions, they made their presentation to Ken. He then asked questions the loan committee might ask to help the employees prepare. Inevitably there were some questions that, despite their preparation, they hadn't thought of. Through this process, they learned how to be more thorough in their preparation.

By reinforcing expectations and providing support for his staff in this manner, Ken built collegial relationships and a sense of team accomplishment. Everyone won because the committee approved the loans. His employees won because they were successful. So Ken won, too. The committee saved time and was confident in its decisions because it had all the necessary information to weigh risks and benefits and make appropriate decisions.

To E-Mail Expectations or Not?

When talking with the COO of a client company, I learned he was upset because he had e-mailed out new job descriptions and had not heard back from his direct report managers. He did not know the implementation status. He wondered if his managers had implemented the revised job descriptions and if they had then written descriptions for their own direct reports.

E-mail alone is not a good communication vehicle when introducing new expectations. Since people receive large volumes of e-mails, the e-mail may not receive the attention it deserves or might even be missed. Expectations are best introduced face-to-face so the direct report can react and discuss them with the manager. The manager gains the chance to clarify and be sure about the agreement going forward. If in-person discussions are impossible, the next best thing is voice-to-voice.

E-mailing first so that the direct report has a chance to read and think about the new responsibilities and prepare for the meeting can enhance communication. It is also effectively used to confirm agreements after the meeting. But e-mail augments the conversation rather than replacing it.

Understanding the Expectations Across the Organization

On a grander scale, successful managers take the initiative to discover other organizational expectations. Although many communication misunderstandings arise from unstated and unclear job responsibilities, performance standards, and goals, many other challenges emerge from the informal, unwritten expectations that occur at work. These expectations can be those of the manager, coworkers, other departments, or the organization. When not met, these expectations lead to confusion, lack of communication, and blaming, and can affect the quality of the work, interdependent deadlines for customers, and relationships. Differing expectations cause communication problems.

Six Communication Problems Arising from Unmet Expectations

In my work with various companies, leaders cited several organization-wide communication issues. These communication problems were identified only when staff members noticed that their expectations were not met. In other words, staff members did not state the expectations they had of other departments ahead of time. They expected certain actions of those groups or managers that did not occur. Instead of initiating conversations with others to clarify mutual expectations, they made assumptions. These assumptions led to disappointments now cited as communication problems.

Each of the six generic organizational communication problems includes a bulleted list of specific problems the leaders mentioned. Since these issues are common to many organizations, suggested solutions are also listed.

● ●

Problem 1. Lack of Clarity in Delivering Information

- Not communicating clearly enough with information so other groups can understand.
- Not giving a specific deliverable date.
- Not being clear on what action should be taken.
- Assuming the information is clear to others.
- Not giving consistent information.
- Giving incorrect information.

Solution: Deliver Clear Information

It's important to verify the facts before delivering information. Always state the information as briefly and simply as possible. Then ask your direct reports to restate what they think they heard you say. Then ask them what they think it means to them. Ask them what action they plan to take. If you disagree on the action, discuss it right away—don't avoid it. Ask them to e-mail you their written understanding. If it's different from yours, talk (don't e-mail) to them again. Avoid "hallway delegation."

Problem 2. Management Priorities Need Clarification

- Individuals' priorities are in conflict.
- There are different objectives from group to group.
- People don't see the big picture—they're focused on their own jobs.

Solution: Resolve Conflicting Management Priorities

Review the priorities of all your team members to ensure that individuals' priorities are not in conflict with each other. Change any conflicting priorities by ranking tasks and projects in the order of importance to the organization. Consider the impact on organizational as well as group goals, customers, costs, launch dates, deadlines, employees, inventory, shipping, and financial health of the organization. When there are different objectives group to group, tell your boss about the effect this has on your group's progress. Unless there are political ramifications that your boss tells you about, talk to peer managers to see what you can work out together. If you and peer managers have incompatible objectives, create a mutual proposal recommending how the objectives could be aligned. Keep working with your boss and negotiate with the necessary approvers to get the priorities in sync. Your manager may have to work with higher management depending on the scope.

To help your staff see the big picture and prevent them from focusing only on their own jobs, continually talk about how each person's contribution relates to the team, and how that relates to the organizational goals. Don't assume they remember this. To show that their work is relevant to the whole, keep mentioning how.

Problem 3. Organizational Obstacles

- Physical location of team members is an obstacle. There are communication challenges due to the layout of the building.
- There is no unified information system.
- There are too many forms that don't all work together.
- People do not know what other people are doing.
- There are inconsistent or absent work orders.
- Cross-departmental chain of command isn't clear.
- File management systems are lacking.

Solution: Remove Organizational Obstacles

If you do not have authority over the obstacles, research the facts on all sides of the issue, come up with potential solutions, and discuss with your boss. Persuade your manager with facts about cost, the bearing on performance and morale, and the benefits of changing the way things are currently done. Keep your staff informed about what is being done or not done regarding these organizational issues and why. Let them vent. Lead them to voice opinions about how to improve their work situation given the reality of organizational constraints.

When you do not have control over the issue, work with others who do. Make recommendations and persuade them to take action. Define what obstacles stand in the way of your team's performance. Is it the layout of the offices? In the case of one client, there were offices on both ends of a large plant where the final products were constructed and prepared for shipping. The long walk inhibited people who would have benefited by face-to-face communication with other groups across the warehouse. An expensive solution would be redoing the physical layout. A middle-of-the-road solution would be swapping offices so that interdependent groups, which interact the most with each other, would have offices on the same end of the building. The easiest, least-disruptive, and least-expensive investment would be to leave all offices alone and buy bicycles, scooters, or golf carts so people could travel quickly from one set of offices to the group on the other side of the plant. What solution is appropriate for your office is up to you. The point is to thoroughly investigate the facts of the problem and compare the costs of doing nothing to alternative solutions.

If the lack of a unified information system is hindering the work, recommend that the appropriate group research the need and options for a unified information system. Be sure they coordinate with other groups during the research as well as with senior management.

When people complain that there are too many forms and the forms don't always coordinate, determine the purpose of each form and exactly how all the forms do or don't work together. This is a study of process and workflow. What information is truly necessary to convey to whom on a task or project? Forms are meant to be communication aids, not obstacles. Who needs what information and when? Can some forms be eliminated or revised to be simpler? Are there similar forms that could be converted to one form that would travel from group to group? What are the time constraints of delivering information? What forms can be eliminated or put online?

If there are inconsistent or absent work orders, what can a manager do? This relates to process and workflow. If there are inconsistent and absent work orders, why? How many people or groups are not completing the work orders? What is the effect? If there are ineffective forms or procedures, get clear facts from direct reports on why they think the process could be improved and what they recommend. Then work with the appropriate managers whose groups are touched by the flow of the work orders and procedures. If needed, get senior management approval for any major changes in process and workflow.

If you do have control over the organizational issues, remove the obstacles. You probably have authority to resolve the last two obstacles on the list.

Clarify the chain of command across departments. It is essential that managers look into who is responsible for what part of a project—for flow of information and/or materials. Who has the authority as interdepartmental interaction is needed? If there is no authority, what are the best influencing strategies, and do your direct reports need training on getting results without authority?

Create a file management system for your group. Can you determine what the needs are or delegate the research to a direct report? What would be the simplest, least-expensive, and most-accessible file management options? What are the benefits and constraints for each alternative? Who else needs to be part of deciding if a new file management system is necessary and what would be the best choice?

Problem 4. Management Timing

- There is slow response to requests and inquiries.
- There is a lack of timely information.
- There is too little help that is too late to be useful when it is finally given.

Solution: Demonstrate the Importance of Timing

Give a quick response to requests and inquiries from direct reports so they can stay on schedule. When they thank you, reinforce the value of fast turn-around with a comment about how you also value quick turnaround from colleagues.

If the lack of quick response is from other managers or groups, be like an octopus with eight legs stretching out to other managers and upper management to collaborate on solving this issue. If there is slow response to requests and inquiries or lack of timely information, meet with the appropriate peer manager and explain the situation and how it affects your group and the mutual goal you share. What is that manager's point of view on the problem? Develop a timeline together and give/get commitment to established timelines.

Problem 5. Management Lack of Follow-Up

- Managers do not check employee progress.
- Employees doubt the importance of assignments and deadlines.
- Employees are reluctant to approach manager for guidance.

Solution: Follow Up on Project Progress

This management action influences much of a manager's credibility with staff. If a manager follows up, it is a statement that the work assignment and the deadline are important. This leads to being able to trust that the next assignment will be significant, not just another flurry of activity with no follow-up. With follow-up, a manager can be viewed as consistent, organized, and trustworthy. In addition, people are more likely to ask questions of their managers when their managers approach them about progress on an assignment. This helps keep a project on track.

Problem 6. General Communication Issues Throughout the Organization

- There is a lack of communication in terms of sharing project information.
- People often say, "I have a better way" rather than collaborating.
- There are trust issues.
- There are personality blocks.

Hidden behind or underlying these complaints are informal and unwritten expectations that people have of one another at work. They expect clear communication and are unhappy when it is not achieved. Teams of leaders and managers up to C-suite in one company made the above observations. But they are universal dilemmas. And they can be handled with the intention to be great communicators. Let's go through the list of problems and look at how a manager can contribute to solutions.

Solution: Examine General Communication Issues Throughout the Organization

Lack of communication in terms of sharing project information will improve when the organizational obstacles are resolved. Perhaps implementing a companywide online project management system would help. This is worth investigating in terms of needs, cost, time, payback, and staff time compared to what the cost is of not doing it.

If people say, "I have a better way," ask yourself, why? Do organizational obstacles such as forms and workflow create it because of the confusion? What are the ideas for a better way? Perhaps create a method for opinions to be aired, such as an invitation to submit ideas in writing when an organizational issue is going to be examined and a change might result.

Trust issues will improve when interdepartmental processes and conflicting priorities are discussed and peer managers work together toward common goals. Each individual manager must still work on open communication and relationship building.

When staff members mention that personality blocks are interfering with their work, it is an opportunity to increase understanding of and communication with others. Every workplace has a diverse array of personality types with behavioral preferences in terms of how they deal with data and people. Human Resources can help with behavioral style assessments. Participants score their answers to behavioral assessments and recognize how varied people are in terms of thinking, analyzing, taking care of other people's interests, and taking action. Many times differences and lack of communication between people are suddenly explained in a logical way. Managers can choose to flex their own style in order to work better with people who act in a different style. Work with your Human Resources department to identify an assessment and an approved way of using one in your group if you want the group members to understand each other better and to behave with greater understanding toward each other.

Ideally, clarifying expectations and working together across the organization should be handled at the top echelon of the organization. But realistically, attempts to resolve issues at other levels may preclude the information from getting to top management. Grassroots efforts are every manager's responsibility. Each manager needs to be responsible for listening to and resolving organizational and communication issues as much as possible. This starts with preventing problems in the first place by keeping direct reports informed with clear expectations and information about why their tasks and projects are important.

Elevating the Importance of the Expectations: Why Should They Care?

Help your staff understand why the work they do individually and as a group makes a difference. Be sure all expectations are transparent to everyone. Have regular team meetings so that direct reports can describe their roles and project progress to each other. This keeps everyone informed. Communicate the *what* and *why* of tasks and projects. Within your own group, what are the department goals and how do they align with corporate goals? Ferret out information that will help your direct reports see the reason their work makes a difference to them and to the corporation.

The second part of elevating the importance of expectations involves working with other teams. What groups are interdependent with yours? What is the greater corporate goal that you share in common? Take it upon yourself to be the clarification expert. Go to the other managers and ask how your group's work affects them and the workflow. Ask their advice on how your team could make changes that would make their work easier. Tell the other managers how their group's work impacts what your team does. Ask for changes that would simplify your team's work.

Summary

Communicating expectations in a clear way enhances relationships because direct reports learn they can consistently rely on the manager to think through, decide on, and say directly what they expect. This clarity eliminates time-consuming guesswork. It prevents the employee having to do rework or getting blamed for not meeting unclear or changing expectations. When expectations are communicated with the right amount of direction or delegation depending on the person and the situation, buy-in and employee ownership are developed. Relationships grow because employees can trust the manager to both be clear and treat them according to their level of experience and expertise.

Once expectations are set and communicated, the direct report moves on to getting the work accomplished. Workflow process and project management are communication tools that help with how the work gets done. These are addressed in Chapter 4.

P A R T

II

HOW TO USE YOUR PROCESS SKILLS TO PREVENT AND SOLVE COMMUNICATION PROBLEMS

P art I of this book reinforces the importance of creating and sustaining energized relationships. Relationships are essential to preventing and solving communication problems. They induce a mutual exchange of help, information, courtesy, and cooperation.

Part II introduces workflow structure, which is equally important in preventing and solving communication problems. Part II covers workflow process and project management as communication tools. A structured process creates common understanding of vocabulary and the steps to accomplish a task. This part contains chapters on using process steps to stop the habit of judging people, solve common people problems, and use questioning techniques as part of problem-solving.

Process and Relationships Are Partners

So how does Part I on relationships dovetail with Part II on using process steps to prevent and solve people problems?

Work relationships (emotion, trust, intuition) and process (facts, steps, logic) partner to amplify effective communication. At first blush they may seem diametrically opposed concepts. But they are inextricably linked if you want your communication skills to top the charts. You must pair relationship and process to be the ultimate communicator.

Sometimes a nonbusiness analogy helps clarify the point. Everyone can relate to math and theater. Let's look at how one author paired fact (mathematics) with emotion (theater).

Danielle Carroll united these two in her master's thesis, "Performances of Truth in Theatre and Mathematics" (Tisch NYU, 2007). Carroll writes:

> With math set up as purveyor of fact and empirical truth and theatre positioned oppositionally in the realm of fiction and emotion, the decidedly irrational, these two systems occupy very different spheres in academic discourse. However, by placing theatrical performance and mathematics in dialog with one another, I find that the two are more similar than I had previously thought.

Putting relationships and process "in dialog with one another" lifts communication to a more enlightened level. Pairing these two broadens and deepens our experience both with the person and with the process. People who separate relationship from the work process often have distant, stilted work conversations. An employee working with a manager who does not blend relationship and process might be uncomfortable asking questions or admitting he is unclear about an assignment. This can lead to work performance or people problems later on. But integrating relationship and process can prevent and solve problems more quickly and satisfactorily for both parties and lead to collaborative goal attainment.

Carroll also asserts:

> Even parts of mathematics, a discipline known for its systematic nature, must be intuited. Once, in a sophomore-level math class, I approached a professor about how to create a system that could tackle all of the problems that we were doing. He responded, "there is no system. You just have to feel it out." I recall feeling abandoned; after all, I had begun my study of mathematics for its structure and certainty. Since then, however, I have learned to enjoy letting go, occasionally finding the answers to problems by accident or I suppose

acknowledging that they find me. In order to discover truth, one must carve out a space in structure and system for intuition.

So it is with process and relationships. You have to "feel them out." We may want certainty, but that does not exist with either relationship or process. Both grow and change shape. One informs the other.

The Role of Intuition

Processes support the search for better relationships, and relationships support the quest for better processes. Effective managers focus on both, letting one give information about the other. Intuition springs from this information.

Confident managers trust their intuition. They listen and clarify the other person's meaning, and also intuit the person as both a professional and a human being. They use intuition to frame their speech on the listener's level of expertise and interest. They also use intuition to knit together relationships and structure to make it easier for direct reports to do their best work.

CHAPTER

4

Workflow Management: Communication Tools

This is a chapter about formal workflow process. A workflow process helps communication because it has a set number of steps. Everybody knows what the steps are. Within each step of a process there may be some flexibility, but everybody still knows the goal of each step.

What about project management (PM)? The same rules apply. The only difference is that the steps are not for an ongoing workflow process, but for a one-off project. The business of sales is a process. Opening a new sales office is a project. Both require a series of steps.

The unique point of this chapter is that process and project management are communication tools that can be applied to preventing and solving people problems. This chapter lays the foundation for how to do this.

Getting the Work Done

This chapter presents a high-level view of process skills and project management, both of which improve communication by ensuring common understanding about the work. A bird's-eye view helps us gather sufficient knowledge to apply this business approach to preventing and solving people problems. If you want to dive deeper into these topics, there are many classes, books, and websites that cover them in detail.

Process and project management frame the work in business terms understandable to direct reports, peers, and upper management. They also facilitate setting expectations, monitoring progress, giving feedback, and coaching. Everyone knows the original plan and can compare it to the actual performance. The vocabulary is common to all and is work related rather than subjective and judgmental. When expectations are documented, information can be dispersed consistently.

Most jobs have a process, or methodology, which is a logical arrangement of tasks leading to achieving an end result. This is true for sales, engineering, manufacturing, finance, scientific fields, and IT, although the processes differ from discipline to discipline.

In fact, most managers are promoted because they are expert at the technical process demanded by their job function. As managers, they are then expected to oversee the processes and coach others to become proficient in the job process. Ironically, their managerial work will no longer be evaluated on their own outstanding process skills but on how well they communicate, work with people, and help their direct reports deliver results. Success in these responsibilities is achieved through process and relationships.

Everybody has process skills. They may be formal or informal. Using yours in day-to-day communication produces wonderful results because it gets everyone on the same page.

Process and Communication

What do process skills have to do with communication? How can process be applied to working with people? What has project management to do with preventing and solving interpersonal issues?

When people talk to each other, they often embed emotion into the conversation. Tempers can flare based on past experiences with a particular coworker or issue. When people don't get what they want, they may or may not take the time to clarify each other's meaning and work it out. One might say, "I can't believe you thought. . . ." Or they might just jump to, "That's not at all what I meant." Yet in reality, setting and gaining understanding on managerial expectations is just business. And the more process we build into setting and clarifying the expectations, the less personal it feels to everybody. Documented process helps clarify expectations upfront, saves time, and prevents disagreements later on.

Process is systematic and logical so it is easily learned. In fact, since most folks use process in their technical areas, they can transfer that skill to dealing with coworkers. Just change the content from technical to interpersonal relations.

Handling the interpersonal aspects of the job requires blending relationships, intuition, and process. Since process focuses on using observable facts to prevent, determine, and solve problems, process is a reliable pivot point when dealing with performance issues. Referring to process can help neutralize potentially difficult conversations.

Some companies have formal processes, especially for engineering or manufacturing. Standardized process is helpful because the regular patterns make it easier for people to repeat the process next time. It saves time negotiating the way teams solve future problems or make decisions. Process provides common vocabulary and promotes clear communication because all team members use the same methodology and know what to expect and how to proceed.

Lack of process and project management can cause organizational communication problems and confusion about priorities. Sometimes lack of structure promotes miscommunication among senior management, which ripples down to the rest of the company. It can create "camps" within the company. For example, in a small company growing larger in products, revenue, locations, and staff, the CEO and president disagreed on certain strategic directions. Some departments lined up behind the CEO and others behind the president. Much of this taking sides was based on previously developed relationships. When the company was small, things got done because relationships were leveraged and there was smaller scope to agree or disagree on. Now that the company was expanding rapidly, naturally it was more difficult to stay united. More structure was now required.

These same phenomena can occur on a department or team level as well. Often managers are surprised by communication problems that erupt as growth occurs. One seminar participant said, "When our group was smaller, we just knew what the other person needed and when and we provided it. And vice versa. Things just flowed. Now we have a lot of new people and they don't get it. They don't know how we get things done." For better or for worse, the more the growth, the more the need for structure to solidify communication and thus reach the objectives. New people do not have the background or intuition to know what the team needs and how people previously operated together. They do not have the history of relationship nor the informal process that took place.

Defining Terms

Here are definitions of the terms *workflow process* and *project management* as they are used in this chapter. After this brief description, later sections provide more detailed explanations.

Workflow process is a series of interdependent steps that have a logical sequence from beginning to end and produce a result. The steps are best documented to make them repeatable and consistent for all employees. They are semipermanent and repeatable.

Project management organizes one particular project. There are also steps that must be followed. PM specifies who will do what by when and then tracks the progress for one particular project.

Example of Workflow Process

One example of process is the sales process. This process is similar from company to company although there may be minor differences. Chuck Carroll, a former sales executive, says, "A sales process is a set of sequential tasks to provide a product or service to a client in exchange for money. Sales is getting the prospective customer happily involved with the benefits of owning and using the product or service."

Chuck adds: "From the first time a potential customer hears about your product or service until long after buying, you want him to have no surprises. Consistency in message before you talk to the client, throughout the sales conversations, and postsale is critical. You want a sales process that continues to support the client, makes them happy—Nirvana. It doesn't happen by accident. You have to figure it all out ahead of time and follow the steps of the sales process."

Here are the steps of a typical sales process:

1. Presales
2. Initial contact
3. Agreement on how the customer's buying process and the salesperson's selling process will dovetail
4. Definition of value
5. Demonstration—proof of the value
6. Agreement to buy and negotiation of the contract
7. Postsale implementation of product and customer service

Within each of the process steps, there is flexibility for *how* to achieve that step. This may vary from company to company or even from individual to individual. The manager must decide how much flexibility to delegate. Can you let the direct report decide *how* to accomplish each step? Or do you need to direct her on the how? How much authority are you delegating for each step?

Project Management Overview

Project management includes identifying project stages in the development cycle, estimating how long tasks typically take, and initiating a formal scheduling system that can easily be modified as multiple projects are managed across departments or functions. The system should have the capability to track accountability for meeting task deadlines. Accountability develops people and clarifies who is responsible for what.

Benefits of Project Management

So what are the benefits of using project management? It reinforces communication about who is responsible for what, when, and with whom they interface. This planning from the beginning to the end improves productivity, reduces redundancy, and minimizes rework. Project management shows the interrelationship of tasks, drives project schedules, and eases oversight of budget, risk, and quality. Project management decreases stress and miscommunications because all concerned have the same expectations and information about progress and/or delays. Let's look at a situation that could gain from formal project management.

One growing company faced the challenge of moving most of its manufacturing overseas, remote from the staff. This arm's-length manufacturing created major challenges and was a critical issue the company had to address. Almost 90 percent of its top products were now produced in Asia instead of the United States. This impacted every corporate function and required special attention from each function. The company now needed to bridge communications among finance, purchasing, engineering, product development, sales, and quality control with more structure, including formal project management.

When a company requires increased attention from every department, this calls for a new way to manage the interactions among the groups. Formal project management generally replaces informal project flow as organizations expand.

Another stimulant to implementing formal project management is expansion of product or service menus. In response to increased product demand and competition, a company concurrently upped the array of new products it developed and manufactured. This proliferation of new product types upset many employees because of their swelling workloads. Management needed to tackle new project and personnel realities due to these unintended consequences.

Some companies formalize project management to shorten product development from original definition to market. This helps new product team members know how long particular tasks in the product-development cycle should take. It is easier to estimate and track the required person-hours for each task. This means timelines and schedules that coordinate with multiple functions can be accurately developed and communicated with minimal confusion.

Formal project management limits impromptu decisions being made with inadequate information or consultation. Project management drives decision makers to gather enough specifics, from all people affected, to take appropriate action. When the determined action is well thought out, it avoids rework and employee frustration with ever-changing directives.

Project management also prioritizes tasks so that individuals are not left to set their own priorities. Communicating priorities keeps employees safe and productive as they work on important tasks. Employees can also be confident that there are formal dates for project milestones and overall deadlines. This eliminates blaming and miscommunication that can occur when dates are informal or unwritten.

Management Workflow Processes

It is easy to see that process and project management ease communication for tasks and projects. Managers also need to set up ways to ease communication with and among their direct reports. You need to create management processes so that you can get work done with and through other people. These processes help your staff know what you expect. They also routinize communication so that everyone can depend on regular information exchange. Two important management processes are meetings and status reports.

Using Meetings to Optimize Communication

Well-structured meetings are recognized as a productive use of time. They can enhance understanding of responsibilities and build relationships. They can save time in the long run if people are clear on roles and level of authority as well as due dates. Here are some tips to increase communication during meetings you control:

- ▶ Weekly status/progress meetings, consistently done, contribute to two-way communication and benefit both direct report and manager. One purpose is to update the manager on progress made toward objectives, problems and how they are being fielded, and the employee's plan for the next week. This weekly checkpoint provides an opportunity for positive and redirective feedback and thus keeps the work on track. When the manager and employee talk weekly about the work, they are more likely to stay in sync and avoid surprising each other. Weekly meetings also improve time management because the employee and manager can save up nonurgent questions and reports until the meeting rather than constantly interrupting each other.

  Another purpose of a weekly meeting is that employees have regular access to their manager to build a relationship, gain clarification on expectations, and get needed resources. The employee can work independently between meetings and not be micromanaged because the manager is regularly kept informed.

- ▶ For project, product, or business strategy meetings, decide who should attend meetings to enhance cross-functional communication. Ensure that invitees are included by functions that need to be there, since staff time spent in meetings is expensive. Be sure all invitees know in advance what they are expected to contribute.

- ▶ Train and coach people to actively participate in meetings. Attendees should be held accountable for contributing information about their functions. Coach the person who remains silent in meetings and then complains later or waits until problems emerge. Sometimes these people are trying to avoid conflict. Help them learn how to address concerns as a business issue during the meeting to prevent larger conflicts and problems with others later on.

- ▶ Some individual contributors may have been raised in a culture that taught them not to express their opinion if more senior people, or people of higher education level, are present. Helping these individuals, whose contribution is so needed at meetings, to speak up may take some one-on-one conversations. Privately explore their reluctance to speak. Reinforce how important their ideas are to other team members. Ask them what you can do to make it more comfortable for them to have their thoughts included in the meetings. Be patient as they transition.

Using Status Reporting to Maximize Communication

Institute routine status reporting. This offers opportunity for mutual feedback to flow continuously. Weekly status reports can be online or e-mailed or brought to the weekly progress meeting. A high-level summary of goals and status is submitted with whatever level of detail the manager requests. This helps trigger regular positive and redirective feedback and coaching. These reports also create a record to which the manager can refer when assessing formal annual or semiannual performance reviews.

The reports create a sense of urgency on a weekly basis for employees to meet targets. They also reassure employees that they are heading in the right direction. Direct reports benefit from timely, job-related feedback and have an opportunity to give feedback to their manager.

To elevate the importance of timely status report compliance, a measured objective could be added to goal setting on each individual's performance appraisal. Communicating status to management is a vital part of the employee's job. It is also a key management responsibility to know status as a part of effectively delegating.

Setting Expectations, Giving Feedback, and Coaching

Processes are common communication tools in companies. Standardizing the way a group does a job saves time and questions. Streamlining how work gets done saves money and reinventing the wheel. Processes provide the group with consistency and shared terms to discuss the work.

Project management affords the same benefits on a different scale. Effective PM drives project goals, schedules (including other groups' roles in the schedules), budget, and milestones or checkpoints. This planning takes the past into consideration in terms of planning for the future. By knowing how long various pieces of the work have taken in the past, a project manager is able to estimate how long similar tasks will take on the new project. The project is broken down into these tasks, which are sequenced and then scheduled.

The project plan is a wonderful communication resource for the team because everyone knows what is needed by when. It also aids managers in monitoring and controlling the workloads, work progress, and deadlines. These formal plans communicate project status to the team as well as to upper management. Strong project management can preclude misunderstandings and problems that crop up with people.

One successful company that I worked with ran like a spinning top on the manufacturing side of the business. Why? Because it had procedures and processes in place. The employees knew exactly how to assemble the products and how long each part of the job should take. They knew who was next in the chain of getting the product built and why it was important to give it to them on time. However, on the engineering, sales, and product design side of the business, there were communication problems. It is true that these functions are more creative in nature and offer more discretion to each professional in how to accomplish tasks. Perhaps that is all the more reason to formalize project management. Without formal interdepartmental project plans in place, they experienced classic miscommunications such as complaining instead of problem solving. Conflicts intensified among departments and finger-pointing began. Groups blamed other groups. "Us-versus-them" thinking erupted. Time was wasted because a department would wait for information instead of being able to access it on a project management system.

Processes and project management plans help prevent these typical communication problems. And when they do occur, they are easier to describe in a factual way. Ideally an organization as a whole will have processes and project management in place. If so, learn them. If there are formal plans in place, you can develop and use project management within your scope of responsibility. If you already possess PM skills, they will serve you well in setting expectations, developing fair relationships, and following up on achievement. PM assists in giving feedback because it enables a manager to stay focused on the work issue instead of the person. In coaching, you know what skills to help with. Using process and project management focuses conversations on the business issues and away from emotions, opinions, and personalities.

Project management starts with detailed scope definition and helps fend off scope creep. When the scope of the work creeps larger and larger, morale and productivity can dive. When scope is clearly defined and agreed upon upfront with upper management, there are business and relationship reasons for staying on course. If changes are requested, they can be discussed in terms of the impact on the whole project. Project activities are identified and clarified before the schedule is set. Project scheduling may include a critical path diagram showing interdependencies with other groups and specific timelines for passing the baton to them. This heightens the importance of meeting deadlines as everyone can relate each task to the project as a whole.

Delegating, observing performance, giving feedback, and coaching can be targeted directly to ongoing project documentation and status reports regarding specifications, budget, and timelines. Having processes for feedback, coaching, delegation, and listening is equally important, and that is addressed in Part III of this book.

Summary

People often think of process as being a systematic approach to a technical way of doing things, an arm's-length approach to getting work done. It is just business. Exactly. That is the same analogy to this book's unique way to prevent and solve people issues.

Process and project management steps reinforce expectations in a clear, dependable way. The more employees know clearly what is expected, the greater possibility they can trust that the task will stay stable. Teammates and managers can share vocabulary and understanding of who is doing what within what time frame. This shared perception of expectations prevents miscommunications among team members.

Using process steps is logical and common practice with functional and technical work. But what happens when people problems emerge? Whenever people are involved, emotions can vibrate. If a machine fails, managers do not blame it and say it has a bad attitude. They usually do not get angry at the machine or try to avoid it. As quickly as possible, people gather data and analyze the observable facts dispassionately to determine the root cause of the machine failure.

Finding the root cause of a problem rather than using a bandage leads to determining a lasting treatment. This prevents future breakdowns. The same is true for working with people. In order to help them succeed and realize their best work, use process to prevent and solve people problems. Be clear on expectations, observe actual performance, give regular feedback and coaching, and find the root cause of any problems. And, as we will see in Chapter 5, using questioning techniques in all of these management endeavors enhances communication.

Top-Tier Questioning Techniques

Managers use questions in interviewing, delegating, giving feedback, coaching, problem solving, decision making, and developing employees. This chapter examines various types of questions and the purpose of each. This chapter shows how to ask questions to get vital information to meet business objectives and preserve relationships.

Why do managers need to master asking appropriate questions? What has questioning to do with management communication? Asking questions of oneself and others is part of finding the *content* information necessary for any *process* to work. Whether the process is sales, engineering, hiring, delegating, giving feedback, coaching, or anything else, skilled questioning techniques are imperative to gather facts and opinions. In addition to aiding process, well-constructed questions contribute to reciprocal relationships, as we see in the next section.

Purpose of Questioning

Questions help move the work forward. Raising questions can help people to conceptualize groundbreaking products and services, to discover innovative processes, to follow established process, to determine a new technique, to analyze the root cause of problems, to analyze decisions, to plan for the future, to staff projects, and to gather facts for any situation. Questions get people to think about concepts and alternative routes. They challenge people to go deeper to find the optimal or new idea rather than the status quo, check for accuracy, and examine the comprehensiveness of their thinking. Questioning assumptions and presuppositions can lead to higher quality work and job satisfaction.

Questions can also help people build and sustain healthy work relationships. Thoughtful questions can demonstrate trust and interest in the employees' intellectual capacity. These questions can be a factor in expanding employees' development and ability to take on more stimulating assignments. Asking questions shows attention to employees and their ideas, demonstrates that the manager has the competence to know what to ask to advance the task or project, and helps the employee enhance professional skills and knowledge by widening the scope of possibilities.

Managers adept in questioning techniques enable employees to take ownership of their work challenges. Questions assist direct reports in thinking about and solving their own problems and making their own decisions. This leads to enhanced employee competence and independence on tasks and projects. Thinking independently fortifies employees' proficiency and confidence.

Questioning is an important part of setting expectations and delegation. Since individuals' perceptions may vary considerably, questioning is used to clarify goals, assignments, action steps, and progress so that the manager and direct reports have a common understanding. Managers state expectations that are perfectly clear to themselves. They then use questions to clarify what the employees actually heard, which might be quite different from what the manager intended.

During follow-up progress discussions, questioning assists a manager in learning about his direct reports' points of view and thinking throughout the task or project. Asking appropriate questions can help employees stay on task and focused on business goals and increase ownership of the work since the employee is the person with the answers to the questions.

Benefits of Questions

There are numerous benefits to knowing how to ask targeted questions. When I was a manager, questioning skills enabled me to galvanize others to create groups, departments, products, and services where none previously existed. Questioning techniques advance collaboration, fact-finding, and innovation. They enable others to find ways to step up to new directions.

Questions involve others in a collaborative discovery process. Accomplished managers facilitate learning and engage others every day. Getting top results with and through other people requires setting the climate for learning and engagement. Questions pull information from capable people instead of pushing information at them. This reveals the leaders' trust in employees' abilities and it helps build constructive relationships.

Mastering the technique of asking questions in an empathetic way boosts the manager's credibility. This questioning ability is essential to successful listening, and listening shows consideration for others and their contributions. Properly framed, empathetic questions advance management communication goals.

However, questioning because managers think they are supposed to ask questions has the opposite effect. Instead of enhancing a work relationship, it can injure it. If managers don't want to listen to the answer, they should not ask the question. When the manager asks questions but already has a preferred answer in mind, this can also dent trust and increase stress. Who wants their time and energy wasted? The next time the manager questions the employees, they might shrug the question off rather than invest themselves in a futile conversation.

When managers' intentions are to build relationships, gather ideas, and honestly collaborate for the best work result, questioning is a top-tier tool. Using this tool, managers can communicate better and reap rewards by developing their staff's ability to fully contribute strengths to the team.

Managers who use appropriate questioning techniques also benefit employees in many ways. Employees learn how to ask questions by observing their managers do so effectively. They learn to work out interpersonal conflicts they have with coworkers by questioning and listening. Employees learn to use process skills and think in factual terms. They know they will be expected to present their opinions and data during feedback and coaching and learn to better formulate questions to get the information they need. By watching their manager, employees learn how to express their ideas, listen to other ideas, and synthesize ideas for practical solutions to working with coworkers up, down, and across the organization. They broaden their perspective by asking questions themselves and listening to others and learn about leadership. Direct reports also may feel supported and valued for their contributions and be energized and empowered.

Making Friends with Change

When I was a little girl, my mom called me "The Question Girl." My curiosity compelled me to constantly ask questions. I wanted the details on just about every person, place, thing, idea, and situation I came across. Mom encouraged this insatiable desire for continual learning. Her nurturing of my natural inquisitiveness led me to believe that I do not have to have all the answers. I can successfully collaborate with others to explore ideas through questioning techniques. I can live in uncertainty and thus be partner to change and innovation.

On the other hand, Dad did not discuss the topics with me. "Look it up," he would say. He referred me to books. Since there was no Internet yet, I had to identify specifically what my question was so I could look in the right part of the right books. I also learned to research for facts and analyze for myself.

The combination of working with others to answer questions and the research approach honed my searching abilities. The questions burned and the answers always created new questions. Is this the way your work takes you—to a new twist constantly? Managing change is a daily happenstance in most workplaces. Sharpening questioning skills can prepare a manager to take on any new challenge with confidence.

Questions—Barrage or Communication Tool?

How can you work questions into a conversation without sounding like you are interrogating a witness? Managers are influencers and facilitators in their quest to get results. They need to facilitate daily work discussions that *include* staff rather than put them on the defensive. How best to do that?

Put the questions in the context of why you are asking. For example, "To make a good decision about selecting new software, I would like to learn more about your research on the needs the various divisions have. Is this a good time to ask you some questions?" Or, "Let's ask each other some questions about this new product proposal so we can advance the ideas to the next level." Or, when a person comes to you for advice, "I know you can solve this problem yourself so instead of saying what I would do, I am going to help you think through your own solution by asking you some questions. Sound good?" Context gives the rationale for the questions and also the benefits of answering. When people know *why* they are being asked questions, they are usually more forthcoming and willing to converse.

Another way to avoid coming across like you are cross-examining a witness is to listen carefully. Listening to the person's answer puts time and space between the questions and makes for a conversation rather than a barrage of questions. Reacting spontaneously to what the employee says in between the series of questions also creates a normal conversation.

Use a neutral, friendly tone of voice, and open, relaxed body language. Make sure neither one of you is in a hurry. Take enough time for the person to be comfortable if you have a list of questions to ask.

Four Types of Questions: Open, Closed, Behavioral, and Situational

Let's talk about four different types of questions and the purpose of each: open, closed, behavioral, and situational. When deciding which type of question you need, reflect on "What information do I need back?" Each type of question will steer the person answering the question in a particular direction, so it's important to know the purpose of each question and how to word it.

Your questions educate employees about what is important to you and the company. Are your questions high-level, or detailed? Are they process-oriented and fact-finding, or opinion-based? Are they job-related, or personal to you? Are they related to goals? Are they supportive, or accusatory? Do they relate to budget, timetables, and specifications? Do they direct the employee to think one way, or do they open the possibility that the employee is capable of solving the problem and deciding? Do they teach?

The questions you ask demonstrate your professionalism and competence as a leader as well as a coach for technical expertise. The level of your question shows how much knowledge you have about the technical aspects of the job and how well you know this employee's ability on this particular task or project. Your query also signals how important the relationship is to you, based on the words and tone you choose. You also unveil the breadth of your management expertise by being able to flex your style based on the style and needs of the employee.

With all that looming in the wings, the importance of word choice and selecting the right type of question is elevated. Having a handle on questioning techniques is indispensable for successful managers.

1. Open Questions

An open or open-ended question broadens the opportunity for a wide array of responses. This type of question provides a chance for the person answering the question to assess and state what he thinks is important, express his opinions, expand upon facts, suggest alternatives, and apply his knowledge in varied ways. Open questions are useful for creative and collaborative problem solving and decision making.

Open questions elicit others' ideas and assessments. Because employees' ideas are considered and more ownership is invited, they may bring a higher degree of motivation to the task or project.

Since these questions generally open the conversation to a number of possible answers, you get more information than with closed questions. However, the challenge is that the person answering is free to answer in many divergent ways not controllable by the questioner without interrupting. Also, while the answers may help the manager to form a general impression, the employee may not give specific examples or sufficient detail. Such answers may require follow-up questions to probe deeper. Another disadvantage is that answers to open questions may lead to conversational detours, and the manager must be skilled to bring the focus back to the issue at hand.

When to Use. Open questions can be used during interviewing, delegating, project follow-up, monitoring progress on tasks and performance, giving and receiving feedback, coaching, getting employees to assess their achievements and performance, brainstorming, getting new ideas, working collaboratively, listening, clarifying your understanding or theirs, employee development, projects, assessing milestones, project debriefs, and planning for future projects.

Open questions encourage the direct reports to explore an issue or challenge them to analyze situations. They require more thinking than closed questions. Process questions are the ones most professionals wrestle with daily. They are mostly open-ended questions dealing with problem solving, analysis, synthesis, comparing and contrasting, creating, and thinking.

Benefits to Manager. Open questions are used to gather facts about the work, learn about your employees' process skills and approaches to the tasks, discover what motivates and is important to them, and get a more well-rounded picture of events by listening to their sides of the story. They help employees develop competencies and confidence, which in turn leads to better work production. Open questions are also used to discover employees' feelings, knowledge levels, skill needs, and views. Use these questions to find out information about employees so you can connect with, understand, and build a relationship with them.

Downside. It takes longer to listen to the answers because you can't control the direction of the answers. The purpose is to allow expression and broad-based, wide-ranging responses. You might have to sift through extraneous information.

How to Formulate. Typically open questions start with What, How, or Why. Nonquestion statements that serve the purpose of an open question start with "Tell me about . . . ," "Describe . . . ," "Let's talk about . . . ," "Compare and Contrast . . . ."

Examples of Open Questions

What is your opinion about . . . ?

What happened that caused you to suddenly miss this deadline?

What will you do now?

What do you think about . . . ?

What projects could be delayed if the budget were cut by 10 percent?

What could we use this extra material for?

What would happen if we did . . . ?

What is this similar to that we've done in the past?

What did you observe?

What is the value of doing the project this way?

What would successful installation of this product look like to a customer?

What does this software update mean to our clients? To our competitors?

What information do you have on . . . ?

What new opportunities does this information offer us? What potential problems?

What did we learn? How can we apply that to the future projects?

What went well? Why?

What would you do differently next time?

What did our team learn that was unexpected?

What are your goals for personal development next quarter?

What is the impact of the restructuring on our Latin America employees?

What do you think about our new project parameters?

What else do we need to consider?

What strategies do we need to consider to increase our customers in the Eastern region?

What are the benefits of opening a site in Europe?

What are the key alternatives we need to discuss?

What is our best alternative? Why?

What do the test results mean?

How will we know if the project is successful?

How else could we do this?

How can we fix this?

How does this differ from . . . ?

How do you think we could . . . ?

How should we negotiate this deal?

How could we approach this project?

How will your team interact with team x on the new task?

How does that compare to our top three customers' visions of product installation?

How do you explain the fact that the part failed on one machine and not the other?

How does this change in direction affect you and your team?

How is the manufacturing division affected by the new OSHA regulation?

How does this hiring freeze impact the project?

How do you feel about this deadline?

If we take on this project, how will it impact your current priorities?

Why do you feel that way?

Why do you think this occurred?

Why are we considering Tokyo for our factory site?

Why should we choose this vendor over the other one?

Why did the machine fail?

Tell me how this works.

Tell me about a typical project life cycle.

Tell me about our market share and what we need to do to increase it.

Tell me about your key concerns with this deadline.

Tell us about our alternatives.

Describe how you see this project unfolding.

Describe what happened.

Describe the key features of our competitors' products.

Let's talk about the differences between version 2.0 and version 2.1.

Let's talk about your understanding of senior management's directive.

Compare and contrast the two top alternatives.

2. Closed Questions

Closed questions invite a yes/no or a short answer. The purpose is to elicit facts, to open a conversation, or to serve as a bridge to move the conversation along. They are used when you don't need background information, detail, opinion, or theory.

When to Use. Use for the same management situations as for open questions.

Benefits to Manager. Saves time if a short answer is all the information needed.

Downside. Improperly used, they can come across as curt or cutting people off. They can also direct someone to agree or disagree, and the manager may miss an opportunity to learn about the person's true thinking.

How to Formulate. There are several ways to ask a closed question. Typically, closed questions start with directive words such as Where, When, Who, Will, Would, Did, Do, Could, Can, Should, Are, Were, and sometimes the word What.

Examples of Closed Questions

Where in Europe are we looking for possible office sites?
Where did you get your experience in operations?

When did you send the report to Engineering?
When will the distributor deliver the parts?
When should we check progress again?

Who is the project manager?
Who called about the part breaking?

Will we open a factory in Australia this year? Where?
Will you submit that form to Quality Control by Thursday?

Would the customer buy our service if we gave a 5 percent discount?
Would you prepare a proposal for the senior executive committee?

Did Accounting reply to your e-mail?
Did we meet our deadline?
Did you get the announcement of the change initiative?

Did you complete the monthly report?

Did you give the customer the handout on our service policy?

By what percentage did our market share grow last year?

Do you work at home on Fridays?

Does our competitor sell this product?

Could we meet on Monday?

Could we come up with three options by Thursday?

Can your team meet the deadline if we add this new task?

Should we give gift certificates as a performance reward?

Are you CPR certified? When does your certification expire?

Are you ready to give your presentation to the executive committee?

Are we within budget?

Were you in our Paris office last week?

What is the budget for this project?

What is the address of the New York office?

What department do you work in?

3. Behavioral Questions

Behavioral questions use past behavior to predict what a person might do in the future. Behavior is what a person does or says. It is the *observable* manner in which a person acts or performs under specified circumstances. Behavioral questions refer to actions others can observe by using the five senses. In most offices, actions you can actually *see* people doing or statements you can *hear* them saying can be described as behavior. In libraries, stores, labs, manufacturing plants, restaurants, and other environments you may be able to apply the other senses of touch, smell, and taste.

When to Use. Most often behavioral questions are used in interviewing to discover what applicants have accomplished in the past and the way they did it. The idea is to project how the candidate would handle a similar situation on the job the manager has open. Some of my clients have also used behavioral questions in team training meetings. The manager asks teammates to answer a behavioral question about how they have handled a challenge. Several coworkers might answer the same question. As the colleagues listen, they learn a variety of ways to handle similar situations. Behavioral questions can also be used in coaching sessions to help employees build off a foundation of their past successes.

Benefits to Manager. Allows manager to zero in on specific work scenarios and target how a person has dealt with them in the past.

Downside. Their use is limited primarily to interviewing, unless the manager creatively finds ways to use them in progress discussions, training, and coaching.

How to Formulate. There are three elements of a behavioral question: The manager asks the question in the past tense and then asks the candidate to give a specific situation or example and tell exactly how he handled the situation.

Examples of Behavioral Questions

Describe a difficult problem you had with a customer and how you handled it. (As opposed to open questions, such as "Are you good with customers?" Or "Tell me about your customer service problems.")

Tell me about a specific time when you had to deal with a gray area because there were no policies and procedures to follow. How did you handle it? (As opposed to "How well do you work when there are no established policies and procedures?")

What was the last dangerous situation you faced on the job and how did you resolve it? (As opposed to "How safely do you work?")

Tell me about a typical day when there were a moderate number of interruptions and how you handled the situation and balanced the work. (As opposed to "How closely do you concentrate when there are interruptions?")

Describe what specifically you did as a team leader that made you excel. Please give a specific example. (As opposed to "What are your strengths as a team leader?")

Please give me an example of a time on a project when you thought you might go over budget and how you resolved it. (As opposed to "How do you handle project budgets?")

Examples for Monitoring Progress and/or Coaching

Tell me about your greatest achievement this past quarter and how you accomplished it.

Describe exactly what process you followed that enabled you to exceed quota this month. How did you go about it?

Tell me about your biggest organizational challenge on the project so far and how you handled it.

What was last month's most important scheduling issue, and how did you resolve it?

Describe specifically what your department has done this quarter to contribute to the XXX corporate initiative in light of the budget cuts and how you went about it.

4. Situational Questions

Situational questions invite a person to think about how they would handle a situation that might arise in the future. These are "if/then" questions. They are designed to ask what a person *would* do, given a specific situation. They are hypothetical in nature and always asked in the future—"Suppose X happened. What would you do?"

When to Use. Use situational questions during interviewing, delegating, feedback, coaching, training, role-playing, rehearsing, or preparing for tough situations that might occur. You can use situational questions to do a practical run-through of potential problems and opportunities.

Benefits to Manager. They are useful when interviewing senior executive candidates and others to learn about their creative and spontaneous problem-solving and decision-making skills. On the job, such questions help a manager understand how a direct report would handle a situation of concern to the manager. They serve as a jumping-off point for discussion on alternative approaches to the work. They are a great coaching tool. Such questions help people think through how to solve their own problems and make their own decisions. They let employees know you trust their capability to handle situations. They reinforce your expectations that the employees plan and practice in advance and that you are there to help. Situational questions emphasize that you need to be kept in the loop, although employees are the *owners* of the situation.

Downside. You have to be sure to get agreement that the employee's statement of how she *would* handle the situation is in fact going to be the approach she will follow.

How to Formulate. The questioner provides the specific scenario, as opposed to behavioral questions, which request the person answering the question to provide the example. It asks *how* a person thinks they *would* handle it in the future, not how they've done it in the past.

Examples of Situational Questions

Since you have not handled national accounts before, how would you handle X difficulty with a nationwide customer?

Let's say the CEO asks you "X" in your upcoming presentation. How would you answer?

If you were to sell the new software to our top account, how would you handle the technical aspects?

If you were asked to increase productivity by 10 percent on your team, what would you do?

If you had to cut your budget by 6 percent, how would you handle it?

As head of HR, how would you plan and manage a downsizing if we have to go that route?

As marketing director, how would you handle the advertising of our new product if our customer base diversifies and grows by 25 percent?

If the other department has a conflicting priority with your project, how would you resolve it?

If your staff told you there is a quality problem with the new product due out this month, what would you do?

Using Questions for Problem-Solving and Decision-Making Processes

Chapter 4 discussed process as a formal, step-by-step approach to work. Successful organizations have processes, or systematic approaches, to manufacturing, sales, engineering, quality control, and so on.

Management activities can also benefit from having a systematic approach. For example, every day managers solve problems and make decisions. What can managers learn from engineers who analyze problems to find the root cause? Engineers might look for the exact reason a component failed or why there were variations in production instead of all products meeting the expected standard. They typically have a standard approach to finding root causes of problems. Part of this step-by-step, precise process is asking questions to ferret out accurate data.

Every day managers solve problems using analytical skills. They ask themselves questions in order to find the root cause of a problem before making a decision on what to do about it. The problems can relate to any function of the business within the manager's span of control. Maybe there is a problem that a marketing campaign did not succeed and the team needs to know why. Or maybe a project is over budget and the manager needs to find the cause.

Some of the process questions often used to find root causes of problems are included here:

What is the exact problem to be solved?
How do I know?

Who else can shed light on this?

Why ask those particular people?

When did the problem first occur?

Why didn't it occur earlier?

What else was going on at that time? What changed?

Is the trend getting worse, getting better, or staying the same?

How big or small is the problem?

What is the impact on the rest of the task/project/machine/team?

How does it change our time frame?

Who else needs to be notified?

What exactly is wrong?

Is the pattern of the problem intermittent, or constant?

Are other projects/tasks/machines/teams experiencing the same problem?

Why or why not?

What are the differences and similarities between our projects/tasks/machines/teams and theirs?

What are some potential causes of the problem?

How does each of those possible reasons fit with the observed facts?

Just as for finding the cause of a work problem, an analytical decision-making process also requires questions. Questions can help the manager uncover information to make an informed decision on something as relatively straightforward as "What desks should we purchase?" to more complex, intricate decisions, such as "Where in Asia should we locate our factory?"

Some typical decision-making process questions are included here:

What is the decision to be made?

Why is it being made?

What is the need for the decision?

Who should help make this decision?

At which point in the decision-making process should each person be brought in?

What are the criteria?

Which criteria are "essential" and must absolutely be met (budget, timelines, specifications)?

Which criteria would enhance the solution and are "nice to have," but are not required?

What are the alternative solutions?

How does each alternative compare to the list of criteria?

Which alternatives are eliminated because they don't meet all "essential" criteria?

If an alternative meets all the "essential" criteria, how well does it meet the specified "nice to have" criteria?

What are the risks associated with choosing each alternative?

How well can the team manage each of those risks to prevent potential problems?

How serious would it be if a problem occurred despite our best prevention efforts?

How can problems be resolved it they do occur?

How can the team best leverage possible opportunities?

What is the best decision?

Determining the best questions to ask to solve work-related problems and make decisions will be your call based on your situation. The important point is for you to collect an array of questions and become an expert using them at appropriate times.

Using Questions to Prevent and Solve People Problems

When managers use expert questioning techniques in delegating, monitoring work progress, giving feedback, and coaching they will prevent problems with people. However, despite best efforts, misunderstandings and conflicts will occur. Managers can be most effective if they use questions to prevent and solve people problems. Managers should remain neutral and ask questions to find root causes of the problem, just like they would do if there were a variation in performance of a machine or functional work situation. If managers identify the source of the problem, and use it as a learning opportunity, they are positioned for a more lasting solution that also preserves the relationship.

The list of questions to ask when problem solving or making decisions for functional work issues (covered in the section on using questions for problem solving and decision making) can be applied to situations involving people too. If a person did not meet a deadline, it is more useful to find out why than to label the person a "poor performer." A manager can more easily solve the problem by staying with the issue at hand and the observable facts when evaluating performance and giving feedback. At a checkpoint meeting, if the milestone was missed, an opening question (asked in a friendly, supportive tone of voice) might be "What happened?" or "What's going on?" These open-ended questions do not assess blame, so they help the employee save face. The employee can then open up and answer the question in a number of different ways. You might find out there is an organizational obstacle, a supplier didn't meet the agreed-upon timelines, or another department did not deliver when it had agreed. A new opportunity might have evolved. If the delay is the employee's responsibility, you might learn about a skill or motivational concern. In any case, you are better prepared to ask more questions.

Often at this point, a manager will say, "What can I do to help?" which moves right to a solution. If an employee is "stuck," it might be more useful to coach with process questions so the employee can solve his own problem. These questions aid employees in discovering more about the problem and enable them to develop their own process skills.

For problem solving or decision making, you can ask open-ended questions from the list in that section of this chapter. Other questions to help the employees tap their own resources might be:

What parts of the project are working well? Why? How could you use that as a basis for the part you are working on now?

> What tasks have been successful? What did you do that made them work? What could you apply from what you did in the past to the task at hand?

> What are the obstacles to meeting this goal? What have you done to remove similar obstacles in the past? What needs to be done to remove the present impediments?

> What else do you need? How best to get that?

> Who else is/what other groups are impacted? What is the best way to work with them on this? What trade-offs need to be made?

> What are the alternatives? What other choices are there? How do they compare with the criteria we need met?

> What support do you need from whom? What is the best way to get the support or resource? What do you need to do to support someone else?

> What do you need to do differently? What do you need to change? How can you improve the situation? When will you do that?

> Given all we've talked about, what is your current plan of action? How will you keep me informed?

> What questions do you have?

Summary

Expertise in asking questions leads to more organized, collegial, and productive conversations when delegating, monitoring progress, giving feedback, and coaching. The more adept the manager is at using questions in these management processes, the more each direct report will be working to his or her potential and contributing to team development.

Planning ahead and developing effective questions can boost your confidence as well as your competence. Prepared questions can help you analyze and evaluate situations factually and follow logical steps. Asking questions also draws in the direct report's opinions and expertise and thus enhances the working relationship. Asking well-framed questions advances your direct report's competency and confidence and thus prevents people problems while increasing collaboration.

In Chapter 6, we address how to unravel judgments when people problems do occur in spite of a manager's best efforts at prevention.

How to Break the Judging Habit

This chapter tackles the cause of many communication problems: judging, sometimes called labeling. This common habit is when people form an opinion of someone and put a label on that person, such as "slacker" or "know-it-all" or "lazy." This kind of judging has a negative impact on management communication because it prevents problem solving and can actually produce greater problems. Judging stops a manager's rational discovery process and creates tension within relationships. This chapter discusses many of the most frequent examples of judging/labeling and shows a process for how to turn these opinions into facts with solutions. When managers substitute the process described in this chapter for judging, they improve communication and dissolve bad feelings that deter achieving results. Managers who develop the process skill offered in this chapter also expand their ability to prevent people problems.

What Is Judging?

Judging is defined here as categorizing a person by labeling, or describing him or her with a word or term. Characterizing people with a name, or label, classifies them into vague groups, such as "the lazy people." People may or may not agree on what "lazy" means, but one thing is for sure—a manager cannot fix "lazy." Sometimes judging is referred to as "name calling" or "tagging" or "giving a negative descriptor."

Judging reflects a person's opinion. It is not fact. Labeling someone causes tension between you and the other person and with others who may be aware of the tag. So why do we judge? Judging is a shortcut to communicating because it assumes others have the same definition of the label. That may or may not be true, but judging is a dead end when trying to address a performance issue and help people succeed.

Judgments can be positive or negative. Isn't it interesting that we are aware of when other people are judging us? Have you ever been "labeled?" Sometime in your life someone may have branded you with a descriptor that was repeatedly mentioned—usually to other people. It may have been something you liked, such as "prez" (for president), "the family writer," "the artist," or "the smart one." Or it may have been something you didn't like, such as "the scrag," "clumsy one," "idiot," "a klutz," or "self-absorbed." In this chapter, we address the latter type of labeling or making judgments—the kind people do not like. These judgments are impractical for team building and productivity. They cannot be solved logically as stated and they damage relationships and teamwork.

Negative Judgments Mean Unresolved Conflict

A clue that interpersonal conflict exists is when people judge someone in a negative light. When there is labeling or name calling, it is a fair bet that communication is not taking place and neither is conflict resolution. Oftentimes managers are upset or even angry with employees when they judge.

Some typical comments from managers include: "She's got a self-esteem problem," "The younger generation has no work ethic," "The older generation has no technology expertise," and "She's Mt. Vesuvius." (We talk about Mt. Vesuvius in Chapter 9 on coaching.)

Employees also make negative judgments. They may complain and blame their managers and coworkers. They often lament that their managers cannot, or will not, help them with their coworker problems. When they give up on their managers, they tell their friends.

A common employee comment is that coworkers bully them and the manager won't do anything about it. Or perhaps they think the *manager* bullies them. But what does that "bully" label really mean?

California children's author Elizabeth Koehler-Pentacoff received two frantic calls on the same day. Why? Liz's two friends stated the same problem—their coworker bullied them and their manager was useless. Both of her friends wanted to meet with Liz immediately to vent and get advice about whether to quit their jobs. Upon some questioning, Liz found out what "bullying" meant to each of them.

One friend, a local librarian, said, "Liz, my coworker is taking over my job responsibilities. I'm the book buyer, not her. But she's buying books even though she's not supposed to. She's using my book budget for her purposes and my manager won't do a thing about it. This woman intimidates my manager and me."

Liz's other friend, a medical secretary, had a malingering coworker. Liz's friend had routinely done her colleague's work in addition to her own. Her manager shrugged her shoulders and did nothing about it. Eventually the medical secretary developed carpal tunnel syndrome. She finally sought medical help, and the doctor gave the advice her manager should have: to just do her *own* work and let the coworker suffer the consequences.

Typical Judgments

There are a number of judgments that are commonly used to indicate that the manager is not getting expectations met. Here are some labels I have repeatedly heard managers call their direct reports:

- Dr. Jekyll and Mr. Hyde
- Slacker
- Old dog (older worker)
- The kids (younger workers)
- Lame duck (getting ready to retire)

- Moron or idiot
- Jerk

Or sometimes managers use adjectives or other descriptors to allude to the problem they are experiencing with their employees. Here are some that are frequently mentioned:

- Short tempered
- Low self-esteem
- Bad personality
- Not committed
- Difficult
- Doesn't respect me
- Bad attitude
- Lazy
- Obnoxious
- Unreasonable
- Complacent
- Has tunnel vision
- Disinterested or doesn't care
- Overbearing
- Insecure

Unfortunately, some managers go as far as to use medical diagnoses, which they are not qualified to make, such as referring to direct reports as schizophrenic, bipolar, or depressed. How does this make the staff feel? What if the person they are labeling or some other coworkers actually suffer from these illnesses? It is never acceptable to call people by these terms, and it is not acceptable for managers to laugh when others do so.

When people judge each other, as in the above examples, the descriptions are vague and the problems unsolvable. The labels they call each other perpetuate their current perceptions. These self-fulfilling prophecies generate blame. Change in behavior is not possible if no factual discussion takes place. Blaming prevents identifying and solving the *real* problem. It also can lead to managers feeling disappointment in or anger toward employees. This blaming occurs every day in the media, in politics, at work, and even in our personal lives. So if you find yourself blaming and judging, don't worry. It's a common habit and you can change it.

Did you drive anywhere or take a cab this week? By any chance did you call another driver a name? Driving is the simplest example to use because it is commonplace to get angry with other drivers occasionally. This happens when other drivers do not conform to communication symbols such as stop signs, double yellow lines, and even red lights. Or when they surprise you by changing lanes in an unsafe way. In short, the action they take doesn't meet your communication expectation (that they follow the rules of the road), or it surprises you (and maybe scares you).

What has driving got to do with workplace communication? It's an example of how people habitually and quickly respond when performance expectations are not met or when they are surprised or feel unsafe. On the job, when expectations are not met or there is a deadline looming, managers might worry that the work will not be done correctly or on time. That could threaten the security of the manager's main job—to get work done through other people. It's a common reaction to blame the other driver or, at work, the employee, because all the facts are not yet examined. You, and other managers, are not alone if you judge others. It's a widespread response.

Judgments hinder communication, relationships, and progress. They also inhibit managers from discussing the problem with the employee, because the judgment is not factual and not useful. Judgments also take managers off the hook—"there's nothing I can do; the person is 'like that,' that's all."

Many managers refrain from fixing the problems because they fear confrontation or disagreement. Sometimes they worry that they do not have the skill to handle an unpleasant situation. This is because they have not been trained to clearly state expectations and assess performance in a factual way. They may feel uncomfortable discussing undesired performance and giving appropriate feedback. Managers may feel vulnerable if they get into a conversation and are unprepared to handle potential opposition. We address these concerns later in this chapter. There are simple ways to analyze and handle these situations.

"Don't Judge Me"

Many TV comedies have had a character say to another, "Don't judge me." It is funny because judging is so common and most people have experienced it. So we laugh when the character says that. But in real life, most people do not appreciate being judged. They dislike being saddled with a name they can't shake. They bristle at being misunderstood. And they resent being labeled as "always" or "never" doing things, rather than having each specific action on each different day evaluated separately. Judging is not useful to managers or employees because it skips over the facts and leaps to name-calling.

When a manager labels a person, the manager may see the employee consistently through this lens ("slacker," "lazy," "poor work ethic," and so on). Then the manager may hunt for proof that the judgment is correct rather than trying to help the employee succeed.

What is more useful and solvable is to examine little chunks of the employee's behavior rather than putting employees in boxes from which they cannot escape. Judgments are too vague and large to solve. But a problem that is stated as observed behaviors, rather than judgments or opinions, is solvable. It is a bite-sized problem to tackle rather than an overwhelming, infinite problem that erodes relationships.

Communicating performance discrepancies is simply a business transaction that needs to take place. It is easier to discuss performance when focusing on facts, not judgments. Having a factual discussion can cause an employee's behavior to change because the manager has identified observable behaviors and an achievable path.

Analyzing judgments and turning them into facts can also have surprising effects. Sometimes a manager sees that the judgment is off base when the facts are examined. Oftentimes a manager learns that the organization itself has prevented performance. Sometimes the manager has been the obstacle, by not setting clear expectations, not properly discussing changes, not giving regular feedback, or not asking process questions.

Judgments are common and the skill to deconstruct them can be easily mastered, helping you to be confident of your facts, learn the employee's point of view, and determine alternative courses of action.

Why Is It So Easy to Judge?

We live in a judging world, so it is easy to fall prey to judging first and thinking later. One may not see very many excellent communication role models. Television is a medium that has the power to influence millions of people. This medium could teach viewers how to communicate well. The irony is that fiction and story require conflict to keep a reader or, in this case, a TV audience interested. Television news, commentary, coverage of political speeches, and even sitcoms frequently depict judging behaviors, and these become role models for how to act and how to communicate.

Millions of people worldwide watch TV news channels. It is easy to see how the news channels judge the people they report on. The commentators use a tone of voice tinged with amazement, disappointment, shock, or some other emotion that is supposed to be contagious to the viewer. Their choice of words shows their bias and tries to pull the audience to their point of view. Interviewers ask loaded questions that lead the interviewee in the direction the news station wants to portray—all to convince the viewer to judge the person on whom they are reporting.

Politicians choose words carefully to put their opponents in a bad light. They skillfully use semantics to sway their constituency to fall in line with their own feelings or with what will have the best marketing outcome. Instead of describing factual behavior, many politicians cherry-pick certain quotes or deeds to back up their judging phrases. They might say something all encompassing like "she is a failure" instead of citing observable actions that resulted in one failure on one issue. Sometimes differing points of view are judged in a negative light instead of regarded as opportunities to look at all the facets of an issue.

Some of our funniest TV shows are satires with characters that demonstrate communication skills that are not helpful in real life. Without conflict, a story is boring. But in real life, conflict needs to be managed with skillful communication, or unhappy consequences can occur. At work, interpersonal conflict can lead to stress and lessen teamwork. Teams might experience discomfort, leading to missing deadlines or to not accomplishing the highest quality work. One man told me that he always avoided people who were demanding or who were overbearing to try to get their way. Part of a manager's responsibility is to help employees work out the best way for the company, instead of letting them "run over" or "avoid" each other.

Strong managers who can step up to conflict, without judging direct reports, increase their credibility, solve problems quickly, and set up employees for success.

How to Untangle Judgments: A Four-Step Process

Why use a process? A process helps you discover the underlying problem you are trying to solve, which is not apparent when judging/labeling. When judging, perception becomes the reality and the employee being judged is seen through only one lens—the label. No person performs every action the same way, and when we see him or her unilaterally as "a slacker," the true business problem may not get solved.

If you want to break a judging habit, you must first analyze the judgments you make. That will lead you to the facts of the situation and help you discover the real cause of the problem you are encountering. Only when you deal with observable actions or behaviors and facts can you dispassionately solve the problem. So how does one untangle judgments and solve the real problems?

At first we state the problem "as is," even if it is judging. It is important to capture the first impression. We then peel back the layers. Here is a four-step process you can use:

1. State the problem "as is"—your original definition of the problem (slacker, not committed, doesn't respect me, overbearing, old dog, etc.).
2. Identify observable behaviors and facts—what did you see and hear? Recheck those "facts" and eliminate any judgments. Keep rechecking until you have identified facts and observable behaviors—not opinion.
3. Brainstorm a list of alternative solutions or action steps.
4. Decide preferred solution/action steps.

Eight Real-World Examples Using the "How to Untangle Judgments Process"

These eight examples are actual work problems (judgments) and solutions. The names of the managers have been changed to protect their privacy. Their stories may be different from yours, but you have probably heard other managers use the same judgments. Maybe you have even thought these judgments yourself. Your analysis and alternative solutions might be different because your situation differs. However, if you follow the four-step process, you will have a great chance at management success. This process will help you form the *habit* of sticking to facts and thus doing a better job of following up on employee progress, giving feedback, coaching, building relationships, and achieving your goals.

At first the managers specified their problems in these common judgmental, unsolvable terms:

A. Lazy lead analyst
B. Old dog foreman doesn't like change

C. Nitpicky and insensitive boss

D. Lame duck awaiting retirement

E. Weak link—employee or manager?

F. Controlling senior director

G. Hostile engineer

H. Employee milks assignment

When one creates a negative judgment about someone and gives him a label, it is easy to forget the details that led to the judgment in the first place. The solving is in the details, not in the label. Peel back the layers. Analyze the facts of the situation rather than targeting the person. This leads to discovering the root causes of the people problems. Once root causes are uncovered, logical action steps emerge. Solutions involve both following a structured process and preserving the relationship, or rebuilding it if damaged.

Now let's walk through the four process steps using the content provided by the eight managers about the A through H judgments. These examples of judgments will be redefined as facts. The alternatives and solutions that the respective managers decided to implement are also included. Perhaps you can get some ideas so you can untangle the judgments that plague you.

A. Lazy

1. **State the problem "as is."** The manager, Eliot, originally stated the problem as, "Lead analyst is lazy." To analyze what the judgment "lazy" means to Eliot, we move to Step 2.

2. **Identify observable behaviors/facts—what did you see and hear?** This step can be tricky. Sometimes what seem like facts are really more judgments. So you may need to keep peeling the layers. For example, Eliot said he observed the lead analyst abusing company time and not working to full capacity. But those are still vague judgments. When we kept asking, "What do you see and hear that makes you say that?" the real facts emerged:

> ► She takes extended lunches and breaks, which are not reflected in her work hours' time sheet.

> ► The capacity charts do not reflect the amount of work that should have been done in the hours worked (e.g., charts show she has completed 20 percent of the workload, while other employees have completed 80 percent). As a lead person, her percent of the workload should be higher than the other employees.

Now we were getting somewhere. It is much easier to deal with these facts than with the judgments. Eliot's next attempt to describe the employee's behaviors without calling her "lazy" resulted in calling the analyst "dishonest" and stating that the other employees were picking up the slack. Again, vague. So we kept digging, and Eliot got to the facts:

> ► The lead analyst delegates tasks that she is supposed to do herself and falsely claims to do work she's not doing. Capacity charts show proof of her lower productivity. She takes credit for those delegated tasks, claiming to have completed those tasks herself (the other staff dispute this).

> ► Other managers witnessed extended lunch and breaks. After facts have been presented to her, she denies them.

3. **Brainstorm a list of alternative solutions or action steps.** Eliot came up with this list:

> ► Pull the job description and capacity standards information.

> ► Review job expectations of this employee. Gather the capacity charts and other facts. Now give feedback to the employee.

> ► Meet with employee to review policies (i.e., lunch hours), job expectations, and actual performance observations.

> ► Clarify the lead analyst's understanding of job requirements by asking her to state what she thinks is expected of her.

> ► Make sure expectations are the same as the manager's.

> ► Set up action plans to meet expectations. Ask, "What specifically will you do to meet these expectations?"

> ► After she states her action steps, then ask, "What can I do to help you do your job?"

> ➤ Identify consequences for not meeting expectations. Document the conversation and use it as a baseline for future performance issues.

> ➤ Set up and hold twice-weekly job check-in meetings to make sure employee is on track with performance expectations. Discuss issues and build rapport.

4. **Decide preferred solution/action steps.** Eliot decided to follow all the action steps in Step 3 and then observe subsequent performance. Follow-up steps would depend on whether the analyst met expectations.

> ➤ If the lead analyst meets expectations:
>   • Employee keeps job and grows in skills and expertise.
>   • Job check-in meetings might become less frequent.

> ➤ If she does not meet expectations:
>   • Document facts.
>   • Consult Human Resources.
>   • Counsel and begin disciplinary action according to company policy.

Eliot felt better once he had a plan instead of an unsolvable judgment. It may be difficult to converse about these issues with the employee, but it is a whole lot easier than confronting the employee with the word "lazy."

B. Old Dog

1. **State the problem "as is."** In this case, David, the manager, stated the original problem as, "The old dog does not like change."

2. **Identify observable behaviors/facts—what did you see and hear?** David said he was dealing with an older foreman who will only do what he wants to do. David continued that this foreman is an experienced person who only likes to do the "fun work." The foreman doesn't like to do housekeeping tasks, and he "milks the job," David reported. When we teased this information apart, we got to the facts.

- The experienced foreman spends 85 percent of his time doing his familiar construction tasks (roadwork) at which he has expertise rather than new duties (industrial).
- He should spend 80 percent of his time on the industrial work. Instead, he defers the industrial work to other employees (laborers). He doesn't finish the industrial work that he begins. He does complete roadwork assignments.
- The foreman states, "I was hired to do the roadwork, not the other work," and "I don't like that other type of work."
- "Milks the job" means he does roadwork almost full-time but does not do industrial tasks.
- Industrial tasks are a new assignment in the last few months.
- The foreman has not had any training in the industrial tasks.
- The foreman, who had been a star performer until a few months ago, was getting blamed because the new assignments had not been fully explained and the foreman did not know how to do them because of lack of training.

3. **Brainstorm a list of alternative solutions or action steps.** David's list of options was to first determine if it was important that the foreman do industrial work instead of delegating that work to his direct reports. David needed more information to decide this. If it was only important that the industrial work get done, and not necessarily by the foreman, David would just confirm that new expectation with the foreman.

If it turned out to be important that the foreman do the industrial tasks, then David listed these action step options:

- Update the foreman's job description and David's expectations.
- Acknowledge that the foreman was originally hired to do only roadwork and explain to the foreman that the job has changed now.
- Discuss duties and expectations going forward.
- Tell the foreman *why* it is important that he personally does industrial work rather than delegating all of it.
- Tell him what percentage of time you expect him to do roadwork and what percentage is to be industrial. Tell him why each of these percentages is important and the impact on others.

➤ Arrange dates for training on industrial tasks.

➤ Get ideas for solutions from the foreman.

➤ Get agreement on what he will do from now on.

➤ State consequences of noncompliance.

4. **Decide preferred solution/action steps.** David decided to follow all the action steps and to start to document behavior if the foreman refused to meet new expectations or attend training.

C. Nitpicky and Insensitive Boss

1. **State the problem "as is."** Kathy, the manager, said her boss is, "insensitive and nitpicky about performance."

2. **Identify observable behaviors/facts—what did you see and hear?** When we got talking about the situation, the behaviors and facts fell into two categories: The boss is new in his position, without adequate help from his own manager, and the boss needs help on how to deal with people.

The fact that the boss is new in his position cast a different light on things. Kathy began to empathize with him instead of thinking he was insensitive. Maybe he did not have bad intentions, but lack of knowledge and skills. So Kathy listed these facts about the boss being new in his position:

➤ He is inexperienced as a manager of managers.

➤ His new management roles and the roles of his direct reports are not clearly defined.

➤ Unclear reporting relationships—no organizational chart or system.

➤ Unclear expectations—we don't know what he expects of us managers.

➤ He acknowledges the organizational problems, yet no solution has been determined.

Kathy realized that the boss had not received adequate preparation and organizational support for his newly expanded responsibilities. Managing managers requires broader communication abilities. She figured out that he needs help with how to deal with people. The observed behaviors and facts were:

> ➤ He has poor feedback skills: He criticizes staff, yells, and does not give specific information about his expectations and what he wants the direct-report managers to do differently, and why.

> ➤ Managers have not observed him giving positive feedback to any of them when they do meet his expectations. They need to hear that they are on the right track—especially since there is so much uncertainty about the roles and expectations.

> ➤ He undermines the authority of direct-report managers with sarcastic remarks at staff meetings in front of our employees.

> ➤ He does not acknowledge employees. He passes people in the hall and gives no greeting.

> ➤ He rejects my ideas without giving his reasoning (he says, "I don't think it is important").

> ➤ He says, "You are paid to do the job."

> ➤ He disregards authority boundaries, criticizes tasks and employee performance for which he is not responsible (our staff).

> ➤ He needs higher-level management and communication training.

3. **Brainstorm a list of alternative solutions or action steps.** Once Kathy quit labeling her boss as "insensitive" and examined the facts, she decided to take the initiative to improve the relationship. This would improve the work situation for the whole team. Kathy's list included:

> ➤ Meet with him one-on-one to formally discuss issues.

> ➤ Tell him of direct-report managers' needs for clarity on roles, reporting relationships/organizational charts, expectations, and feedback delivered in a constructive way. Tell him how the clarification will impact the productivity and help him get his goals met.

> ➤ Give him feedback that direct reports want to improve working relationship with him and tell him of issues listed under Step 2 "observable behaviors/facts."
> ➤ Ask him for a meeting to clarify roles, responsibilities, and level of authority. (See Chapter 2 on turbocharged clarity.)
> ➤ Ask him to commit to identifying and solving the problems his direct-report managers are having with him.
> ➤ Tell his boss he needs direct on-site coaching by his own boss.
> ➤ Ask his boss to get him higher-level management and communication training.

4. **Decide preferred solution/action steps.** Kathy decided to start with all the action steps she brainstormed except the last two bullets, which deal with going to his boss. She might do that if she has to, but she chose to start with her boss in an effort to solve the problems effectively and build the necessary relationship with him. However, if he is not receptive to working with her to resolve these issues, Kathy will:

> ➤ Tell him she is going to talk to his boss and invite him to join her. She will put it in positive terms of enhancing the working relationship of all team members.
> ➤ Suggest he invite all direct-report managers and his boss to a meeting to discuss and clarify expectations. She will get consensus in the meeting and document the decisions and results.
> ➤ Involve HR to mediate if they cannot resolve it.
> ➤ Check other positions within the company if it does not improve.

D. Lame Duck

1. **State the problem "as is."** Alexandra, the manager, first described the problem as, "The employee is a lame duck just waiting for retirement."

2. **Identify observable behaviors/facts—what did you see and hear?**

> ➤ The employee is leaving in six months.
> ➤ He is bored with his job.

➤ There is no back-up person for his responsibilities.

➤ He is a good employee—completes all work and does it well.

➤ He has worked for company for over twenty years.

Alexandra agreed that she could not validate that the employee was "bored" with his job, since the employee never mentioned he was bored. "Bored" is a judgment. What was more useful were the observed behaviors that led her to say he was bored: Comes in late once every two weeks, leaves early once a week, and takes long lunches every other day. Now Alexandra had something she could work with—the employee was not complying with work-hour performance standards.

3. **Brainstorm a list of alternative solutions or action steps.**

➤ Meet with employee and express her concern about how he ends his long-term employment with the company. Tell him she wants him to end his time on a successful note and that she will help him do that.

➤ Set expectations about work-hour policy to be fair to all employees.

➤ State consequences of not complying with policy and express her hope that he will comply.

➤ Work together to create an exit plan that includes having him mentor people in his last six months so his institutional knowledge can be preserved.

➤ Have him train one or two employees as back up on his job ASAP. These people will take over his responsibilities when he leaves.

➤ After his years of contribution to the company, she will help him enjoy and celebrate his last six months.

➤ Plan a retirement party with coworkers, if policy permits it. Otherwise, set up a lunch date.

4. **Decide preferred solution/action steps.** Alexandra decided to:

➤ Follow all above action steps unless employee does not follow policy and expectations.

> ► Treat him as she would any other employee by monitoring and documenting performance according to company policy if he does not comply, or if performance declines.

E. Weak Link (Employee or Manager?)

1. **State the problem "as is."** Ling said his problem was, "How to deal with the weak link in the group when at least some members of the group know the employee is the weak link."

2. **Identify observable behaviors/facts—what did you see and hear?** When Ling tried to state observable behaviors/facts, he realized he had been calling the employee the "weak link," but that maybe he as the manager was the "weak link." He had not provided the employee with sufficient information to succeed. His list of what he had observed was vague. If he tried to talk to his employee, it would be like discussing cotton candy. It might look like a big problem, but if he and the employee bit into the problem, it would quickly disappear. He did not have concrete facts. Let's look at what he said so his action steps will make more sense:

> ► Scope—it takes this employee the longest of all employees to absorb instruction.
> ► Manager sets expectations and clarifies, yet the employee still misinterprets them.
> ► The employee does not ask questions; he pretends to "get it."
> ► When there is a definite deadline, he adheres most of the time.
> ► Quality of output compared to others—he does not contribute as much as the other employees do.

3. **Brainstorm a list of alternative solutions or action steps.** Ling decided he had some homework to do. Here is his list:

> ► Determine clear definition of expectations for this employee and put them in writing.
> ► Tell employee the expectations. Ask him to restate what he thinks the manager expects of him and by when. Ask him to send the

manager an e-mail stating those expectations. Ask him to write exactly what he will do to meet those expectations.

- Get specific data on how long it takes the employee to absorb instruction. What do employees do to demonstrate they have absorbed instruction? What is the performance standard on how long it should take?

- Meet with employee and express the manager's desire for him to learn the job and achieve the objectives. Tell him the manager will add more structure to help him.

- Provide training or a buddy, if needed.

- Set milestones/check-in points for the work and dates to follow up on each milestone (project planning).

- Meet with employee on daily or twice-weekly basis depending upon his needs for help and the manager's needs to be sure he is on track.

- Explain impact on the team when quality is insufficient or deadline is not met. Do other workers have to cover for him?

- Keep up the regular one-on-one meetings.

4. **Decide preferred solution/action steps.** Ling decided to:

- Try all of the above action steps.
- If they don't work, he will begin the formal counseling process that the organization has in place.

F. Controlling

1. **State the problem "as is."** Mary Beth said, "Our senior director is controlling."

2. **Identify observable behaviors/facts—what did you see and hear?** Mary Beth was specific about the facts:

- Three years ago her company had an audit that required corrective actions.
- There were 1,200 open complaints three years ago, but they now have only 400 complaints.

➤ The goal is to close complaints within thirty days of opening them, and the company is at thirty-nine days.

➤ Senior management wants thirty-four days to be the maximum, and eventually for the company to meet the goal of thirty days.

➤ The senior director calls every day to see how Mary Beth's department is doing regarding this goal. She also stops Mary Beth's staff in the hall, and even e-mails them asking for a progress date.

➤ It took forty-five days to close complaints three years ago. Mary Beth's department has made significant improvement from three years ago, but the corporate image is not healed because complaint closings are not at thirty days. So instead of emphasizing the progress they have made, the senior director constantly points out that they are not at the goal.

➤ Currently, the closings are more than the openings, so throughput is over 100 percent. Mary Beth thinks that should count for something, but the senior director says the priority to look at is only to get the closings down to thirty-four and then thirty days.

➤ The average closing takes twenty-four days, but the European region pulls the closings off average. So, the current average is thirty-nine days to close.

➤ Quarterly Trending Report is by product complaint and cause. They tend to be the same problems.

➤ The senior director constantly contacts Mary Beth and states that her team is not performing to the expected standard.

3. **Brainstorm a list of alternative solutions or action steps.** When Mary Beth got clear on the facts, she realized that she and her team wanted credit for improvement over the last three years but indeed they were not meeting the goals in front of them. The senior director was emphasizing the importance of what goal Mary Beth's team must attain, rather than looking back at what they had accomplished in the past. Mary Beth decided to discuss the situation openly with the senior director. She planned to:

➤ State to the senior director that she and her team are onboard to meet the goal of thirty-four days and then thirty days to close. State what she and her team were prepared to do to meet that goal. Ask the senior director's opinion of what she thinks they could do differently to meet the goal. Tell the senior director she wants to work collaboratively with plans and follow-up on progress.

▶ Set up frequent meetings with the senior director to discuss stat sheets.

▶ Ask the senior director to work with the European region to solve the problem they have with slow closings, since Mary Beth does not have the organizational power to do that.

▶ Print a *progress* report showing progress percentage by quarter. On the quarterly report, show the *regional* breakouts, to show that the European region is not complying and is dragging down the average. Compare current closings to past periods. Use bar charts (visuals) to highlight what the team did differently in each period.

▶ Prepare and deliver a quarterly formal presentation to the senior director rather than just e-mailing her the quarterly report. Discuss progress and plans for the next quarter during that meeting.

▶ Identify team training needs and organize the training.

▶ Invite the senior director to team meetings.

▶ Keep the senior director informed on a weekly basis of progress.

4. **Decide preferred solution/action steps.** Mary Beth decided to follow all the alternative action steps.

G. Hostile

1. **State the problem "as is."** Javier said the problem was "an engineer, who doesn't like to be questioned, becomes hostile and goes around the person he disagrees with."

2. **Identify observable behaviors/facts—what did you see and hear?** At first Javier's observations were judgments, so we kept defining what he saw and heard until he could describe observable behaviors and facts.

▶ "Poor work ethic." This means the engineer comes in a half hour late and leaves fifteen minutes early twice a week.

- ➤ "Violent outbursts." This means he shouts profanities.
- ➤ "Hostile when questioned." This means he rolls eyes, sighs, and walks out.
- ➤ "Unprofessional behavior toward coworkers." This means he uses sarcasm or refuses to respond to them and forces his way into conversations.
- ➤ "Not a team player." This means:
  - Peer engineers object to working with him.
  - He seeks advice from others not involved with the project.
  - He is critical of others—offers negative feedback but not positive.

3. **Brainstorm a list of alternative solutions or action steps.** Javier's list:

- ➤ Ask Human Resources' counsel on the employee's behavior related to shouting profanities to see if it is considered to foster a hostile work environment and to be harassment. Ask them whether to provide feedback from other engineers on how he is perceived. Take any action Human Resources advises.
- ➤ Review expectations of work-schedule tasks and projects.
- ➤ Review relevant company policies with him.
- ➤ Review expectations of acceptable behavior toward peers and manager with him.
- ➤ Discuss expectation for open dialogue and working with team members.
- ➤ Discuss his observed behavior, contrasting that with expectations.
- ➤ Explain impact of his behavior on workflow and morale.
- ➤ Try to find root cause of his behavior.
- ➤ Offer coaching and communication training classes to help him find proper ways to express ideas.
- ➤ Discuss consequences of continued behavior, including company counseling process.

4. **Decide preferred solution/action steps.** Javier decided to start with Human Resources to discuss the shouting of profanities. He would

then discuss the other bullet points with them and, if they agreed, follow all action steps brainstormed in Step 3.

H. Employee Milks Assignment

1. **State the problem "as is."** Deborah stated the original problem as, "the employee doesn't take the initiative. She only does what is asked of her and 'milks' assignments."

2. **Identify observable behaviors/facts—what did you see and hear?** This is what Deborah had noticed:

> ➤ The employee closes Windows (computer applications) when manager walks by.
> ➤ The employee meets all deadlines. However, she takes double the time needed to complete a task.
> ➤ The employee takes one day to complete tasks that should take only a half day. Deborah previously did this job, but has not told the employee that this task should take a half day.
> ➤ Employee does not inform Deborah when tasks are completed.
> ➤ Employee does not ask for additional assignments/projects when she completes a task.
> ➤ Employee transferred from a subsidiary company.

Once Deborah completed this list, she realized how many assumptions she had made about how this new employee should perform. Deborah had not set clear expectations about how long jobs should take. Deborah needed to examine whether it was realistic to want the task completed in only a half day. After all, the employee did meet all deadlines. Also, the employee is new to the organization and needs to be told about the expectation that she come to Deborah and ask for additional work. It may not have been an expectation where she worked before.

3. **Brainstorm a list of alternative solutions or action steps.** Deborah's list:

> ➤ Determine how long tasks should realistically take. Just because Deborah did the task quickly does not mean that should be the measure.

➤ Talk to employee about the length of time the project should take. Get her side of the story. She's a new employee so does she need training? More structured guidelines?

➤ Discuss expectations that she get the task done in projected time allotted.

➤ Discuss all other expectations about informing Deborah when tasks are completed and asking for more assignments.

➤ Give shorter check-in times and follow-up at half day until no longer necessary.

➤ Assign more work/tasks if employee needs more work.

➤ Discuss adding a more challenging assignment.

➤ Set up regular, periodic meetings/checkpoints/goals/status reports/deadlines.

4. **Decide preferred solution/action steps.** Deborah decided to follow all the action steps.

Through following the four-step process, you can replace judgments with facts and then easily determine a path toward a solution. As you saw in the examples, many times an employee was blamed when the manager was the organizational obstacle. It is common for managers following this process to realize that they may not have set clear or realistic expectations. The managers may need to provide resources, including training, in order for direct reports to meet the goals.

In the case of managing your manager, the same concept applies. Judging is frequently a misunderstanding. Once you examine the facts, it is often the "judge" who stands in the way of solving the problem. People who work with this process quickly and honestly examine who needs to do what in order to collaborate, achieve work objectives, and preserve relationships.

Word Choice

Once managers follow the process to discover the root of the judgment, they need to speak to the person they are having the problem with. Picking the right words can make the difference in whether the message is heard. The right words can also generate enthusiasm for collaborating and moving forward together to get the work done.

Words convey specific meaning. Managers are responsible for what they say. Since managers exert so much influence, whether or not they intend to, they must choose words carefully. It is important to be factual and friendly.

Words can include or exclude people, make them feel good or rile them up, and even assert dominance or invite collegiality. Selecting words appropriately and positively is one of the most essential decisions we make when we speak. The words we use can advance or impede communication about the work and the relationships. They show respect and courtesy, or the opposite. Consider the words in each of the following pairs and the connotation of each: smile/smirk, senior management/the suits, business trip/boondoggle, famous/notorious, economizing/cheap, curious/nosy, experienced/over-the-hill, and youthful/immature.

Poor word choice (including judgments and labels) builds walls instead of bridges. Picking words ineffectively can make people feel discounted and unvalued. It can create or contribute to conflict, and be interpreted as insensitivity or lack of caring. It can lower employees' confidence and self-esteem. Words can place blame, create distrust, and shut down communication. And the person choosing unpleasant words can be viewed as being closed-minded.

Careful word choice can prevent people problems and establish an atmosphere of trust and respect. Neutral words or words with positive connotations show empathy and caring, create open communication, and facilitate conflict resolution. Positive words make it easy for the employee to hear your feedback and to feel welcome to give you feedback. When the relationship hits a roadblock, employees are more likely to work through the misunderstandings if they feel that, by and large, the manager is collegial and trustworthy, as demonstrated by his use of neutral and positive language. A trustworthy manager does not use judging terms or labels to describe anyone, up, down, or across the organization.

How to Handle Body Language Judgments

Besides using words, people can use their bodies, facial expressions, and tone of voice to insinuate judgments and put other people down. Imagine you and another speaker are up on the platform debating an issue in front of a large audience. You are seated next to each other. Every time it is your turn to speak, the other speaker lowers her head and shakes it slowly left to right. She scrunches up her nose in a way that brings her eyelids closer together rather than being open all the way. She smiles showing her teeth. She sighs audibly. We see this behavior every day on news panels on TV, and you may see this in your office or at a meeting.

Even though it was not this person's turn to speak, she took the audience's attention away from you and your words by using body language. How do you react? Perhaps it rolls off your back and you don't care. Perhaps it upsets you. How do you interpret the body language? Do you say she disagreed with your message? Do you say she was rude? She smirked? She dismissed and discredited you?

One might have any of those opinions and they are just interpretations or judgments. They are not facts. The only facts are what we actually saw and heard happen as described in the first paragraph. The judgments may or may not be the purpose that person had in mind when she chose to react to your words using nonverbal communication. Acting on body language judgments will not advance relationships or get your message heard. You will have greater success staying with observed facts.

You have options while you are on the platform. You can ignore the nonverbal behavior of the other person. This is what many managers choose to do with their direct reports. Sometimes it is appropriate, and sometimes the behavior escalates until it bothers the audience (other teammates).

Let's assume you decide to address the nonverbal behavior of the other speaker on the platform. If you choose to speak about your opinion/judgment, she will probably deny it and you will end up looking petty.

"Why are you being so rude?" you might say.

"I'm not being rude," she answers.

"Yes, you are," you continue. "You're smirking."

"You're wrong. I am *not* smirking. What's the matter—are your feelings hurt?"

Notice that you are not talking about the content of the debate, but the topic has now switched to your feelings. By now you might be plenty angry and easily distracted from the importance of your original message. You will not be winning the support of your audience. You will look like you do not exhibit grace under pressure. You may think people see you as a "victim" who can't handle the communication challenge.

Another option is to address the behavior using only observable facts. This might get some information about *why* the person is using the body language and get an honest discussion going. Perhaps it will get you both back on track and focused about the work at hand.

"I noticed you shook your head 'No' and smiled when I made my point."

"Did I?"

You use neutral, open body language and silently wait for her to continue.

"Well, what you said about X was totally ridiculous," she says.

You ignore her tone of voice and concentrate only on the words she spoke. "What exactly did you find ridiculous?" you ask.

"I totally disagree with your comment about . . . ."

"I'll present my research in a moment," you say. "But first let's talk about why you disagree."

Now you are back to debating ideas because you have facilitated a nonemotional discussion based on observable behaviors rather than being judgmental or letting the other person's judgments control your behavior. You have stayed on message and can get results.

Summary

Judgments and labeling can escalate problems with people and thus block productivity and quality. Judging—even done jokingly—damages relationships because there is no clear communication about the meaning of the label or what to do to change behavior.

When you use the process for untangling and solving people problems, suddenly "people problems" become factual business issues that are unemotional. Once you are able to unravel them and get to the bottom of the situation, you are able to analyze and work it out much more easily. The emotion gets washed out and the problem becomes an arm's-length issue. You can confidently handle these problems using process skills, just as you would handle any other of your managerial responsibilities.

Stating facts and observable behavior is a very important skill to use in all work discussions. Whether delegating, following up on progress, giving feedback, or coaching, it is imperative to untangle any judgments and speak with words both parties can agree on—facts.

Chapter 7 addresses many common management communication problems. Just as in this chapter, the facts of these problems also need to be analyzed so that solutions/action steps can be determined.

Common People Problems—
A Handy Reference

Chapter 6 offered a process for untangling judgments so that people problems could be analyzed and handled as business issues. Besides judging or labeling people, there are other common people problems that are prickly for managers. Several of the most common ones are discussed in this chapter, using real-world examples. A simple process is offered here to help you handle these types of problems. If you develop this simple skill for solving people problems, you will form a habit that will help you invigorate relationships and work collaboratively. This habit will help you achieve work results through others.

People problems *can* be solved, and it is the manager's job to handle these problems. Sometimes what seems at first to be a "people problem" is an opportunity to explore differing points of view. Multiple viewpoints can contribute to innovative and better products and services. Having different perspectives can help the team develop conflict-resolution skills, which strengthens the team. When coworkers are able to honestly state their views on the work, they develop trust in the working relationship and confidence that misunderstandings can and will be worked out.

Defining People Problems

"People problems" is a shortcut term many use to describe unresolved interpersonal conflicts, as opposed to mechanical, technical, or other work problems. Sometimes managers who are quick to resolve other work-related problems procrastinate about resolving work problems that they perceive are related to people. A manager might not like a direct report, or might judge him, as discussed in Chapter 6. Or a problem might exist between coworkers who report to the manager.

Sometimes there are elements of emotion involved and the manager isn't sure how to properly tackle the issue. Perhaps the manager wants to avoid confrontation or an unpleasant conversation. Or the problem is with the manager's boss or peer. The manager isn't sure how to approach a person she perceives as having equal or more organizational power because the stakes are higher. Oftentimes the manager just plain does not know how to define "people problems" as logical work performance issues to be solved by a rational process.

Conflicts can be about differences in opinion, traits, or beliefs. Sometimes a person thinks he is right and refuses to explore the other person's viewpoint. On the other hand, a person may lack confidence in his own ability or opinion or lack the capacity to defend his position without escalating conflict. Sometimes people fear looking bad or losing their jobs or reputations, so they choose not to be honest communicators. Others overlook the value and necessity of developing strong working relationships.

Causes of Problems Among People

Misunderstandings and other communication problems among people at work are probably as old as work itself. How could it be otherwise? People have backgrounds and viewpoints that differ from those of others. Because of this, it is difficult to articulate meaning in a nonemotional way that others can understand dispassionately. This section will examine many factors that can cause communication problems.

Too Much Togetherness

The old adage "familiarity breeds contempt" means that it is quite common for people who are together a lot—at home, at play, or at work—to become upset with each other. When people work closely together, there are bound to be misunderstandings and communication problems among them. Too much in-person contact might just be annoying, especially if a coworker has a habit we don't like. It is to be expected that people may become impatient with one another if they see each other frequently. Or they may take each other for granted and not make enough effort at communicating properly. They may misinterpret a message based on what it meant in the past when they worked on something similar.

Didier's cubicle is next to Pierre's. They have worked on projects together for over three years. Pierre has been the team leader and, from Didier's perspective, has imposed his way of approaching the project every time, supposedly because of time constraints. Today, Pierre asks Didier, "What are some alternative ways to approach this project? What do you think we should do here?" Instead of answering the question directly, Didier might use his past experience with Pierre and be cautious. Will he waste his energy if he spends time analyzing the best approach and then Pierre does what he wants anyway? Has Pierre changed his leadership approach and does he truly want Didier's opinion?

Not Enough In-Person Contact

The opposite of too much togetherness is not seeing each other in person enough. Not being together in the same location contributes to many communication problems. Today many managers have direct reports who work at remote locations—at home, at a coffee shop, or at another office location. Other office locations can be in other cities or in other countries—even on other continents. These remote workers are connected to coworkers via the Internet. They work virtually, meaning technology links them together regardless of the geographic location or the time zone. Virtual teams collaborate and can be in constant contact worldwide.

If Ron works in Toronto and his direct reports work in Tokyo and

London, he must develop a top-notch ability to manage by results, because he cannot observe what his team is doing on a day-to-day basis. Ron must also hone listening skills, because he will be working by phone when voice-to-voice communication is needed. Without seeing people in person, Ron will not have the benefit of observing nonverbal communication like body language. Most communication will be done via the Internet, which presents many opportunities for misunderstandings.

When the Message Sent Is Different from the Message Received

A typical communication problem is often categorized under "the speaker sends a message but the listener receives a different message." Why? There are many possibilities. Our life experiences frame our point of view, and our listener's life experiences form his outlook. Let's say Soula explains something to Kyle. Soula thinks she is perfectly clear, but Kyle hears a different meaning. Soula might be using jargon or vocabulary that Kyle is not familiar with. Or Soula might have a generational frame of reference (music, literature, historical events, technology, terminology, and so on) that differs from Kyle's orientation. If Soula has done the job a long time and Kyle is new at it, they have a different perspective on the work. There are many other reasons for this message sent and not being heard problem, including cultural differences and traumatic or major events that shape how a person sees things.

We could include e-mail under the category of a reader assuming a different message than the sender intended. Words and tone in e-mail messages are frequently misunderstood, and tempers flare. Sometimes the e-mail thread goes on too long, when a phone call could have straightened out the misunderstanding.

Not Knowing the Context

Sometimes we understand the vocabulary but not *why* people say what they say or do what they do. Their behavior may seem out of place or it may not fit with the rest of the behavior we have seen from them. For example, in one class I led, no matter what the team exercise was, "Send them to an anger management class" appeared on the wall charts as part of the team solution. I observed who was offering that as a solution and casually sat next to her at a break. When I engaged her in a general conversation, she quickly told me that, two weeks before, her son had been at Virginia Tech when a man murdered so many students. In fact, her son had been in the very building at the time of the crime. No wonder "anger management class" was on her mind. We often don't know the context for a person's remarks until we converse with him or her.

In another class, a woman, who had been a major class contributor for one and a half days, was daydreaming during the second afternoon of the seminar. When we ran into each other in the ladies' room, she volunteered, "I know I've been daydreaming and I'm sorry. I got a call at lunch that my friend is dying and if I want to see him alive I've got to get there tonight. My husband is picking up our baby from day care right now and driving two hours down here to pick me up. Then we need to drive an hour and a half South to see our friend." Who would have guessed she had so much going on? We find out only when we don't judge people and offer a compassionate, gentle car. Then, they *may* choose to include us in their concerns.

Not Listening

Another reason for miscommunication is lack of listening. It is easy to miss a person's meaning if one doesn't focus on the message. Listening is covered in Chapter 11.

"Personality Conflict"

Some people say they have a "personality conflict" with certain other people. They might say there is "bad blood" or "ill will" between them. Frequently these problems are just preferred behavioral styles and easily solved. Often in my classes we use assessments so people can learn about their own preferred styles and those of others. The assessments are lists of questions about how you act in certain situations or words that best describe you. Then the assessments divide up behaviors into quadrants that give more information about why a person acts and responds to work, other people, time, and the world the way he does. It is amazing to see the proverbial lightbulbs go off when managers have an explanation for why they have conflict with other behavioral styles and receive advice on how to solve it.

Downsizing Effects

When an organization is downsizing and running lean with fewer staff to do the work, it causes people to be stressed. They may worry about the quality of the work they can produce. Or they may be concerned about lack of time to accomplish their tasks or insufficient time to give appropriate depth in the analysis they need to provide for a task. The same thing can happen when companies are expanding with limited assets. Stressed managers managing frustrated employees can trigger miscommunications and problems among people who previously got along together.

When there is turnover or downsizing, personnel changes impact staff, who may have to learn to work with new people. If people leave, there is lost expertise and lost momentum. The people remaining may have to quickly learn new responsibilities and not be allocated time or resources for training. Stress can cause finger-pointing and lack of patience with each other.

Requests of Other Groups

Any time a manager makes a request of other departments for resources or to do work, the manager might not understand how the request impacts the other group. There may be a conflicting process or priority that needs to be ironed out. Both managers need to talk frankly about their needs and how they can work together to achieve the overall goals.

Uncertain Priorities

Organizational priorities that conflict and change rapidly cause miscommunication, hallway gossip, and uncertainty. This leads to stress and further communication problems.

General Tips for Preventing People Problems

What should a busy manager do when faced with miscommunication, regardless of its cause? Besides using the process detailed below, there are some generic pointers a manager should keep in mind. Focus on the positive and assume peer managers and other colleagues have the best intentions. This will help shore up communication. Communicate frequently and consistently from team to team to create trust and reduce uncertainty. Tolerate others' stress and help them find a process to address their own concerns. Helping them can buoy up the relationship. Some managers need to remind themselves to step back, breathe, and not judge others or be quick to say, "That's not right/fair." This time for reflection can provide the space for logical problem solving. It is also important to accept that having people listen to you does not equal getting your way or the way you wanted it to happen. One of the key ways to prevent problems with people is to be specific about observed facts and behaviors versus labeling/judging them (as covered in Chapter 6). Labeling can escalate people problems and cause new ones. It is indirect, ineffective communication and can be hurtful to people and their reputations. During times of stress, there is all the more reason to focus on preserving relationships and analyzing problems in solvable ways.

Solving People Problems: A Three-Step Process

Why use a process? A repeatable process helps you to develop a routine habit and saves you time whenever you encounter what you think is a people problem. You can easily discover what is bothering you, turn it into a clear work issue, and quickly move into action steps, just like you would do with any other business problem.

You may need to run your problem through the four-step process offered in Chapter 6 first, if you have started with labeling the employee. Once that is cleaned up, you can zero in on the facts of your people problem and decide what to do.

Here is a three-step process you can use:

1. State the issue
2. Define the problem and state the observable facts
3. Decide action steps

Typical Problems Managers Have with People

There are many communication problems that keep managers awake at night. This section will delve into several of the most common ones. You may not currently be experiencing these problems. However, they do crop up for many managers.

This chapter is intended as a reference chapter. You can scan the list below for a particular challenge you face and then go directly to that problem. Then later, you can return to the list as these familiar problems arise.

Problems that are unique to first-time managers are addressed in Appendix B.

A. Managing Friends
- When Your Friends Become Direct Reports
- You're Torn Between Being a Manager and Being a Friend

B. Managing Former Peers
- Preventing People Problems
- Handling People Problems

C. Dealing with Problems with Direct Reports

- ➤ She Wanted Your Job
- ➤ He Has More Experience
- ➤ She Went Around You to Your Boss
- ➤ He Is a Great Strategist but Can't Complete Tasks
- ➤ She Does Too Much Personal Stuff at Work
- ➤ Good Performer Starts to Come to Work Late

D. Clearing up Other Communication Problems

- ➤ Employees Work Virtually
- ➤ Leftover Problems with a New Group
- ➤ Getting Employees to Positively Accept Change

E. Helping Employees with Their Communication Problems

- ➤ Generational Differences
- ➤ Office Politics
- ➤ How to Get Work Done with Different "Personalities"
- ➤ When Two Employees Don't Get Along

F. Managing Up

- ➤ When the Relationship Is Going Well
- ➤ When the Relationship Is Not Going Well

G. Handling Organizational Concerns

- ➤ Handling Your Group When the Organization Has Problems

Examples Using the "Solving People Problems" Process

These examples are actual work problems managers mention and real-world solutions. Your problems may vary and you may choose to refer only to a few of these examples. Your problem definitions and action items might differ because your situation is unique. However, if you follow the three-step process for solving people problems, it will help you move to action, just like you do with other management challenges.

A. Managing Friends

When Your Friends Become Direct Reports

In your management career, no matter how high level the position to which you are promoted, at some point, you will probably be managing friends. I have both reported to and had direct reports who were friends.

What helped me work well with direct reports who were friends was hearing the late Peter Drucker give advice on the topic. Many thought leaders consider Drucker to be the inventor of management as we know it today and a great thinker on the topic. I was in an audience when he advised us managers to meet with all staff—including former peers and friends—whenever you are promoted. He said to ask them what helps them get their work done and what hinders them. I followed his advice each time and found it a great opener for collaborating on how my staff, including my friends, and I would work best together.

1. **Issue:** You are promoted to manage someone who is your friend.

2. **Problem definition/facts:** Other direct reports are watching to see if you will treat your friend with favoritism. They are uncomfortable. You and your friend have to set boundaries to clarify your new roles. If you, your friend, and the rest of your staff have no trouble with this new reporting relationship, keep on doing what is working for all of you (bravo). However, if there are any difficulties, you might want to choose some of the action steps listed below.

3. **Action Steps:**
   - Speak individually and immediately to each staff member about the new working relationship you will have and your intentions to treat each person fairly. Ask what helps and hinders them and what their suggestions are for working well together. Set clear

expectations. Listen to their concerns. Be empathetic. Follow through on items brought up during the meeting.

▸ Define each person's roles and responsibilities, including your own in your new management position.

▸ Be fair with everyone so there is no *perception* of favoritism. Other staff members' perceptions are their reality, even if the perception is not the same as your intention.

▸ Do not use the friendship as leverage to expect more or less than the job requirements of your friend.

▸ Speak immediately and individually to each friend about the new boundaries you both need to set so you can work well together in the new relationship. This may include not talking about work when socializing and not talking about socializing at work. Ask their opinions on how to make the new reporting relationship work. Approach your friends as team members, emphasizing their expertise (just like you do the rest of the staff). Mention that you will be relying on them to meet goals.

▸ Expect a transition phase to establish credibility in your new role and for direct reports to develop trust in your capabilities at the next level of management.

▸ Separate business from personal interactions and feelings.

▸ Consider how you would feel if the roles were reversed. How would you like your friend to treat you?

When You're Torn Between Being a Manager and Being a Friend

Even if you follow all the action steps in the previous example, you might still run into snags as you and your friend adjust to the new role of you as the manager. One conversation may not be enough to reinforce the boundaries and new roles. Be alert for signs that you are being distracted by your friendship. It is a normal transition that you both need time to adapt to. However, as the manager, it is up to you to take the initiative to quickly address any lack of performance. You owe it to the whole team.

1. **Issue:** The manager is uncomfortable executing management responsibilities with a direct report who is also a friend.

2. **Problem definition/facts:** A friend tries to bend the rules, overstep the work boundaries, and take advantage of the friendship instead of performing as expected.

3. **Action Steps:**

➤ Hold a one-on-one meeting with your friend to rediscuss work expectations and new roles. Emphasize that expectations and goals must be met and rules must be adhered to regardless of the friendship. Tell specifically what you observed in your direct report's work behavior and how it impacts you as the manager and the team. Explain what must now happen and consequences if your direct report does not comply.

➤ Discuss boundaries you previously agreed to. Now that you have worked together in the new roles for a while, you both may have a better idea of what will and won't work for you. Redefine boundaries, ask what their boundaries are, and make sure there is an understanding of what is acceptable to both.

➤ Separate work from friendship, and clarify what can be discussed during work and nonwork hours.

➤ Tone down the friendship aspect at work.

➤ Treat the friend with the same work expectations as the rest of the team. Review the expectations, reasons, and consequences.

➤ Don't shut down the friendship unless one of you is unable to separate the roles. It is okay to socialize, but best not to discuss it at work and best not to discuss work during socializing.

➤ Allow transition time as your friend gets used to the new boundaries.

➤ If it doesn't work, accept it.

B. Managing Former Peers

Preventing People Problems When Managing Former Peers

No matter how long you have been managing, every time you manage a new group or are promoted from within, there is the potential issue of how to manage former peers. Embracing your latest promotion and getting your feet on the ground as quickly as possible is certainly going to make you and your staff free from anxiety. However, your efforts to make them comfortable so they can stay productive outweigh your own comfort level. When staff have a new boss, no matter how well they knew you in your previous role, there is uncertainty for them about how to proceed in the future. The sooner you take the opportunity to handle the ambiguity they face, the better. Clear expectations and role definitions will help point them in a decisive direction. Listening to their feelings and dealing with them before they become stumbling blocks benefits everyone.

1. **Issue:** You begin your newest management role (any level of management) and there is uncertainty about what you will expect and how you will manage.

2. **Problem definition/facts:** You want to take action to prevent problems before any occur.

3. **Action Steps:**

➤ Don't make dramatic changes during initial stages. State what will and will not change initially. Be clear and decisive. Explain the changing dynamics and your new role. Validate/value what you bring to the new position. Put your conversations in language that benefits company goals. Encourage participation and feedback from former peers.

➤ Write job descriptions for your management position and for staff member positions (or review if already in place). Have an open dialogue about the differences in roles and responsibilities. Empower self and former peers to perform separate roles.

➤ Get feedback from ex-peers about their feelings. Listen. Using their own descriptions, acknowledge that you understand how they could feel that way. Don't take it personally. Be respectful and sensitive to their feelings, but do not shirk your responsibilities in order to be liked. Ask how you can best work together in the new situation.

➤ Define employee roles and responsibilities and levels of authority for tasks.

➤ Explain clear expectations and hold employees accountable to meet them. Ask about their expectations of you.

> Develop direct, regular, open communication with boss and staff.

> Be direct when assigning work, not as if you are asking a favor.

> Dress and deport yourself appropriately to your level of management.

> Don't play any favorites and discuss any perceived favoritism openly. Declare your intention not to play favorites. Ask exactly what employees saw or heard that led them to think there was favoritism.

Handling People Problems When Managing Former Peers

You have made your best effort to be understanding and inclusive while being clear about your expectations. Despite your efforts to initiate communication and prevent problems with former peers, inevitably there will be some problems at some time during your career. First, check your own comfort level when giving directions. Even if you are uneasy, you must assign work clearly with all direct reports. Next, are you managing the relationship with your boss? If your boss is ill at ease delegating authority to you because you are new in the position, your staff may pick up on that lack of trust. Work that out with your manager quickly.

1. **Issue:** The manager needs to cope with a myriad of problems that can occur with former peers.

2. **Problem definition/facts:** The former peer may exhibit jealousy and resentment, may resist your authority, and may not defer to your guidance. Former peers may think there is favoritism. They may not follow work procedures, they may resist the shuffling of the workload, or they may resent taking work assignments from a former peer.

3. **Action Steps:**

> Expect difficulties. Give it time. Embrace the experience and enjoy the new learning. Management skills grow by successfully working through these difficulties.

> Deal with problems at the time they occur. Do not procrastinate.

> Keep following the action steps outlined in the previous Prevent-

ing People Problems section. Focus on being objective and fair. Revisit the definition of roles/responsibilities and the levels of authority for your position and for your employees' positions.

➤ Solicit opinions and feedback to make former peers feel their opinions are valued.

➤ Recognize experienced team members by utilizing them as mentors or coaches within the team.

➤ Make all feel valued by giving regular positive feedback and mentioning their strengths and accomplishments.

➤ Work through difficulties with a positive and professional demeanor and as much confidence as possible. If needed, speak one-on-one to clear the air.

➤ Get management training on communication ASAP.

➤ When you need to reshuffle the workload of former peers, acknowledge the reality and need for rearranging the work. Explain the whys. Distribute work equally and according to skill level. Emphasize opportunities for growth and development on new tasks or projects.

➤ When assigning work to former peers, do the same thing you would do with all direct reports. Define goals, parameters, and requirements. Know the capabilities of each staff member and match them to the tasks. Find out which tasks they prefer and see if projects can be assigned to match preferences, especially if the work relates to development goals. Provide the resources to do the job successfully. Be clear about deadlines and follow up to ensure they are met. Hold weekly meetings to check on progress.

C. Dealing with Problems with Direct Reports

When She Wanted Your Job

When someone else wanted your new job and was not selected, open communication with your new direct report is essential. The first time I was promoted to manage managers, one of the contenders for the position had more management experience than I did and was certainly qualified for the job. She was also a peer with whom I had enjoyed a friendly relationship. Although we had managed groups in separate departments, we had supported each other with information and cooperation. Now that I was going to be her manager, we openly discussed the situation right away. I empathized with her sadness. I said I believed she could handle the job as well as I could, based on her background and specific strengths. I wanted the new working relationship to work for both of us. I asked how we could be a team and make our new unit be successful. We needed collaboration to pull the merging groups together into one new unit. She and I strategized a way to work together and created one of the most cohesive, productive teams I ever experienced.

1. **Issue:** Working through problems with people who wanted your job.

2. **Problem definition/facts:** They may say they deserved the job and you didn't. They may try to sabotage your success by making derogatory comments about you to coworkers and people outside the department. Or they may just be disappointed, but willing to work well with you.

3. **Action steps:**
   ▶ Have a one-on-one meeting immediately and discuss the situation openly. Allow the person to express opinions and vent. Listen to feelings with empathy. Discuss her strengths and achievements. Tell her you value her on the team and specifically why her contribution is important. Praise her accomplishments and skills. Ask how you can work together to make the new roles work well. Can you delegate special advanced tasks to her? Can she train and mentor others?
   ▶ Define separate roles, responsibilities, and levels of authority. Keep the chain of command clear and make sure your authority is not undermined. Build a united team with your boss to gain support for your level of authority and decision making. Respect yourself and be confident about the reasons for your selection.
   ▶ Keep open communication. Have weekly progress meetings with each staff member, including this person.
   ▶ Help this coworker with a skill development path (without making any promises of promotion).

> Periodically, discuss with this person how she feels about the relationship going forward.

When He Has More Experience

Many managers will hire or acquire direct reports who have more experience than they do. Some managers report discomfort in managing older or more experienced direct reports. I faced this challenge as a twenty-five-year-old first-time manager. Friday I went home as a senior analyst and Monday I suddenly managed my former peers, almost all of whom were more experienced than I was. Some had decades of experience in the company. This is tricky because you cannot change the experience level you each have. What you have to manage is all the feelings around that—yours and theirs. Your confidence in the knowledge and skills that led to your selection as manager is of utmost importance as you execute your management duties. What were your management strengths that got you promoted? Honest and open dialogue will also help clear the air and advance your working relationship.

1. **Issue:** Managing direct reports who have more experience than the manager.

2. **Problem definition/facts:** He has more technical, industry, and management experience. Since he has been with the company longer, he has more institutional knowledge. He resents reporting to a person with less job experience.

3. **Action steps:**
   > Meet with your boss to get clear expectations and levels of authority on responsibilities. Gain your manager's support and advice.
   > Let go of any fear of being upstaged. Gain trust by demonstrating your leadership and job expertise. Lead by example.
   > Meet one-on-one with the more experienced individual. Clearly define the meeting agenda and keep on track. Recognize his experience and past contributions. Discuss how he thinks his knowl-

edge can best be utilized going forward. Ask what new projects or career challenges might use his expertise. Ask what works best for him regarding types of tasks and how they are assigned and monitored.

➤ Collaborate on a way to proceed with his interests aligned with team interests. If he is qualified, invite him to lead others or designate him as your back up. Ask him to mentor or teach less experienced or newer staff. Set those opportunities in motion.

➤ Provide opportunity to showcase his talent and knowledge. Reinforce the high level of experience by giving high visibility projects. Embrace his knowledge and let the team know you appreciate it.

➤ Clear the air with regular, open one-on-one discussions. Tell him how his contribution impacts the organization/team and why.

➤ Consider his views on how to collaborate on projects, problem analysis, decisions, and planning. Ask his opinions on goals and strategies best for the team. Listen/be receptive to learning from him. Defer or delegate appropriate decisions to give him ownership. Keep him in the loop about goals, plans, and changes. Solicit his support. Use him as a resource. Ask for his opinions and reinforce his value to the project.

➤ Flex and adapt your communication style to best work with his style. (There are a number of style assessments available. Check with your Human Resources department, read up, or take a management class that includes styles.)

➤ Identify and support any skill gaps he has and give him chances to work in areas that would develop those skills. Keep challenging him for continued growth. Ask him what he wants to learn and what his career goals are. Support his career path development.

➤ Keep him busy and give regular feedback.

➤ Be flexible, firm, and fair, just like you are with all employees.

When She Went Around You to Your Boss

At some point in your career, you may have a direct report who goes directly to your boss to get what she wants instead of going through you. She knows you will find out and that will cause more communication problems with you, so that employee is communicating something indirectly to you. It happened to me when I was on a lengthy business trip in the United Kingdom. I came back to find out a manager who reported to me had gone to my boss and requested that he become the project manager on a worldwide project we were about to begin. Ironically, it was a good idea. It just was not done properly. He should have contacted me when I was in Europe, but chose to go to my boss instead. I realized that I did not have direct, open communication with this employee and that was the problem underlying the fact that he went to my boss. When your direct report goes around you, it is up to you to get communication back on track.

1. **Issue:** How to handle the situation when a direct report goes to your boss, and how to prevent it from recurring.

2. **Problem definition/facts:** Your employee did not discuss her request, suggestion, or complaint with you. Instead, she went directly to your boss. She did not communicate directly with you, but indirectly. Does she not trust you? Does she not think you are capable in your position? Is she afraid it will cause a confrontation if she speaks to you directly? Might you not give her what she wants? You probably do not know why she chose to not communicate with you until you ask her.

3. **Action steps:**
   - ▶ Discuss the situation with your boss and get agreement about how your boss will handle it next time by referring the person back to you. Get support that your boss will back you up in the meeting you are about to have with your direct report. Work back and forth with your manager until you are in complete agreement about the communication you are about to have with your direct report.
   - ▶ Make sure you have your emotions under control and you can conduct a neutral, fact-based conversation with your employee.
   - ▶ Hold a one-on-one meeting with the direct report (face-to-face if possible, and at least voice-to-voice if it can't be in person).
     - • Acknowledge what happened. Give direct eye contact. Ask why she went directly to your boss and listen carefully to her answers. Ask more open questions in a neutral tone until you cut

through all the excuses and find out the real reason. Explore the situation, "Can you help me understand why you went directly to my boss?"

- State why it was inappropriate. Discuss reasons for not going directly to your manager. Tell her that you and your boss are in agreement about this and what will happen if she goes to your boss again.
- Tell her you want to work well together and that communication needs to improve between you so that the work can get done appropriately. Communication is part of her job (if that is stated on her job description, show it to her). Get her agreement to improve communication. Put the onus on the employee. Ask "How do you think we should handle this?" Clarify her expectations of what she thinks you can do differently. If appropriate, agree to what you can change in the interest of the job. Ask what she will do differently. Clarify.
- Have your own idea of what needs to happen and discuss. State "This is what I expect . . ." and ask "Is there something I can do to help you be more comfortable with this situation?"
- Have employee restate the expectation and what she will do to meet it.

When He Is a Great Strategist but Can't Complete Tasks

When a person is an innovator and a great strategist, he has a conceptual, big-picture way of looking at the work. These abilities are essential for certain work, for example, starting a new department or creating new products and services or other projects that have not been done before. These skills are not needed for jobs that require following policy and procedure or doing things that are routine and must be done a certain way. The first question to ask when the strategist cannot complete tasks is, "Are his qualifications well matched with job requirements?" He may be in the wrong job. If he is matched appropriately to the work, a performance problem may be emerging.

1. **Issue:** How to deal with a manager (direct report) who has great ideas and is a good strategist but who can't focus on getting tasks completed.

2. **Problem definition/facts:** Direct report (who also is a manager) missed the last two deadlines. He did not prioritize his team's projects or the tasks within those projects last month. He surfs the Internet, engages in water cooler talk, and spends an hour a day on personal phone calls. He does not delegate to staff members. He creates effective strategies and contributes innovative ideas and approaches that save the company time and money. The manager of this direct report must separate the two issues of his strategic contribution and the management duties he is currently not accomplishing. The focus here needs to be on what changed in the last month and how to get him back on target.

3. **Action steps:**

> ► Ask questions to determine how well the employee thinks he is matched to the job, what has changed in the last month that he didn't prioritize projects and began missing deadlines, and what he can do to handle the situation.

> ► Have the employee clarify the expectations for schedules and responsibility to prioritize. Keep him focused on task at hand rather than big picture if that is the job requirement. Define milestones and checkpoints in the projects. Follow up weekly or twice a week for a while—monthly is too long between your progress check-ins. Find out what is helpful to the employee in completing tasks. Explain resources and tools available.

> ► Refer to company policy on Internet and personal phone time and discuss impact on the work. Define your expectations and get his agreement to comply with them.

> ► Discuss strategies for delegating, and have him review his priorities. Provide training for time management and delegation if needed.

> ► Ask how the employee's creative ideas can be addressed and perhaps used to better the workflow, processes, or organizational interests. Assign challenging projects that require innovative ideas.

When She Does Too Much Personal Stuff at Work

What if your direct report spends a lot of time doing personal things at work? There are many considerations before you tackle this one. Is the person working a lot of uncompensated extra hours (like working with people overseas at night) and needs to catch up on personal stuff during daytime hours? Is it really a problem for the work and the team? Is the individual's performance affected? If you conclude that your direct report or team's performance is affected, or the direct report could be more productive and take on more tasks, then you might want to choose some of the action items delineated by a manager who had this problem.

1. **Issue:** How to ask people to spend far less time doing personal stuff instead of working.

2. **Problem definition/facts:** The manager observed the employee doing social networking on the phone and on nonwork Internet sites over the last month. He does not know how much time the employee is spending doing personal activities, but he doesn't think she should do it at all. The manager made a joke about it once but the behavior didn't change.

3. **Action steps:**
   - ▶ Determine exactly how much personal time is being spent on the job. Is it worth discussing?
   - ▶ Discuss what's going on that is causing the personal time. Listen and empathize. State the company policy on computer and phone use. Get agreement on compliance to policy.
   - ▶ Outline important tasks in priority order. Discuss actual performance compared to what is expected. If the employee is not meeting job requirements, discuss what is needed to perform satisfactorily. If the employee is meeting expectations and has extra time, can she take on additional or more challenging assignments? Check the appropriate workload.
   - ▶ Ensure deadlines are set and clearly understood. Temporarily implement shorter-term checkpoints. Agree what the employee needs to accomplish so you can stretch out the time between checkpoints.
   - ▶ Calculate the hourly compensation and multiply it by the number of hours per day, week, or month spent on personal issues. This

is the cost to the company, and probably the person has not thought of it in those terms.

➤ If appropriate, educate the person on the ethics of exchanging work for compensation.

➤ Discuss distractions to other teammates and the necessity to role model good work habits.

When a Good Performer Starts to Come to Work Late

When performance suddenly changes, it is important to address it right away and see what caused the shift. If this is a new occurrence, it is best to approach the situation gently and get the facts of what has changed for the employee. At one client company I consulted with, a valued employee began coming to work ten minutes late every morning. His wise manager took a gentle approach and discovered that the employee had no car and the bus schedule had changed. The earliest the employee could get to work was on that bus. The company flexed his schedule for him even though it was a manufacturing job that had strict hours. The company kept an outstanding employee by finding out the cause and providing a workable solution. You might not be able to flex hours or see the need to do that.

1. **Issue:** What to do when a good performer starts coming to work late.

2. **Problem definition/facts:** Work hours are important to the nature of this job. The employee is needed at the workstation on time and has begun to be late. The cause is unknown.

3. **Action steps:**
   ➤ Follow the feedback process described in Chapter 8 of this book.
   ➤ The first time you notice lateness, immediately discuss it with employee. This teaches the employee that the behavior was noticed and that the policy is important. It also teaches the rest of the staff that you intend to enforce the policy.

> ➤ Ask what's going on in a neutral, friendly tone of voice. Listen and discuss.

> ➤ Explain the expectations and company policy. Let the employee know she is valued as a part of the team and why it is important to be on time. Explain the impact on the team and other implications of coming late.

> ➤ Ask what the employee can do to ensure she is on time. Get her solutions before you offer yours. Does she need your help?

> ➤ Hold the employee accountable for the tasks given her.

> ➤ If the lateness persists, there is a performance problem. Move into counseling, which is not covered in this book. Contact your manager and the Human Resources department to ensure you follow company policy on counseling.

D. Clearing Up Other Communication Problems

Employees Who Work Virtually

It is becoming more common, since the advent of the global economy, for managers to be responsible for goals that span the world. Their direct reports might reside in any continent of the world and not necessarily the same one as the manager. When direct reports work in a different facility, they are working remotely. Another common kind of remote work is telecommuting from home. Remote workers are connected via the Internet, which is referred to as working virtually. This arrangement might be full time or part time. Not having daily face time with employees is a challenge. It requires managing a long-distance relationship powered by trust. Expectations and process must be crystal clear, and opportunities for miscommunication are great.

1. **Issue:** How to clear up communication problems with employees who work virtually.

2. **Problem definition/facts:** There are time zone differences, which make it difficult to schedule Web meetings and phone conversations. There may be cultural differences. Lack of face-to-face communication

makes it difficult to interpret each other's verbal messages, because there is no body language to read. It is more difficult to give clear direction and follow up on progress. Some employees feel isolated because they are not at headquarters. Meetings are not consistent.

3. **Action steps:**

➤ Be clear about job guidelines and performance standards. Set expectations right from the beginning (working virtually is a privilege if it means working from home part time). If working with remote sites—including overseas—with time zone considerations, what routine processes and check-in meetings will you set up? What are your expectations regarding hours and days of work?

➤ Review goals and measure progress regularly. Give routine feedback.

➤ Address problems immediately.

➤ Return phone calls and e-mails promptly. Recheck the wording and tone of your e-mails before sending to prevent communication problems.

➤ Schedule regular phone calls ahead of time (try twice a week). Keep scheduled communications solid. Be there and expect direct reports to schedule around those events also—compromise on time difference (switch up on who is inconvenienced the most). Record notes from calls and send them out to confirm understanding.

➤ Schedule regular face-to-face meetings either in person or via available technology such as video conferencing or video chat, so you can see each other. Send out meeting minutes ASAP.

➤ Change location of in-person meetings based upon teammates' other needs to conduct business at various sites.

➤ Manager should fly to employees' locations on routine basis if budgets permit.

➤ Team-building meetings are effective. Conduct them at one work location where people can see how things work at that locale.

➤ Make time for visiting employees on a priority basis.

➤ At home office, post photos of remote employees.

Leftover Problems with a New Group

When you manage a new group, whether in the same company or elsewhere, there could be problems that were not taken care of by the previous management. These lingering problems need to be faced and discussed by whoever is the new manager so they do not fester or explode. Underlying issues can affect the work and the newly appointed manager's relationships with the team.

1. **Issue:** When starting a new management assignment, what is the best way to handle problems that were leftover from the previous manager?

2. **Problem definition/facts:** A number of problems might exist. Coworkers might not get along together. Some individuals might be underperforming and have not been given feedback to that effect. The new manager might hear complaints from team members. Technical, process, or workflow problems might be hampering productivity.

3. **Action steps:**
   - ➤ Identify the problem.
     - Why is it important?
     - What is the root cause?
     - Why does it still exist?
     - What personnel are involved?
   - ➤ Research the failed attempts to solve the problem.
   - ➤ Categorize severity of the problems and prioritize.
   - ➤ Work for a solution.
     - Read books and articles on the topic (don't reinvent the wheel).
     - Solicit input to solve the problem.
     - Interview the players involved to understand multiple perspectives.
     - Examine alternative approaches.
     - Establish acceptable behaviors and ground rules.
     - Set specific expectations.

- Formulate a plan to solve problems.
- Implement potential best solutions.
- Give positive reinforcement.
- Evaluate the outcome.

Getting Employees to Positively Accept Change

Since a manager is expected to continually introduce and implement change with his team, having a plan can help. Some people need more time to adapt to change than others. Some are early adopters and some like to hang back and avoid making mistakes. Also, people can take only so much change at one time. When they have a lot of change simultaneously—at work or in their personal lives—they may have more difficulty accepting the change in a positive way. The manager's reaction to the change serves as the role model of how the employees should react. Show that you as manager accept and embrace the change. Always be positive about and support the change since you are going to implement it anyway.

1. **Issue:** How to get direct reports to accept corporate changes with a positive reaction.

2. **Problem definition/facts:** The manager hears complaints when changes are communicated. Several of the employees don't change their behavior after the announcements. When discussing the change with the manager, these employees furrow their brows and use closed body language.

3. **Action steps:**
   - Introduce change with positive words, excited tone.
   - Announce change in a group meeting.
   - State the situation and expectations in an open and straightforward manner. Be clear (no gray areas) and concise about the change. Give clear "whys." Address rumors.
   - Tie the change to employees' personal wins. Emphasize the positive impact on their future.

- Allow enough time for people to air their concerns and ask questions.
- Listen to feedback and empathize. Respond to any uncertainty direct reports express.
- Emphasize the need to get on board and work together.
- Ask staff for suggestions on the best ways to incorporate the change.

➤ Provide necessary resources and remove obstacles that prevent staff members from making the change.

➤ Give employee feedback to your boss and strategize together.

➤ Find the informal "leader" of the employee team and try to get that person on board with the change.

➤ Reward employees who accept and demonstrate the change behaviors during the transition period.

➤ Get direct reports involved in the change, if possible.

➤ If individuals do not do what is expected to incorporate the change, handle this with one-on-one meetings to find out "What's going on." Restate expectations, find out what they will do to comply, and state consequences of noncompliance.

E. Helping Employees with Their Communication Problems

Generational Differences

There are four generations in the workforce right now. Typically they are called (from oldest to youngest): Traditionalists, Baby Boomers, Generation X, and Generation Y (or Millennials). There are many books and articles on the subject of their different perspectives, values, and beliefs about work. Each generation offers rich contributions due to the varied experiences they bring with them. When the manager is adept at identifying and facilitating conversations about differences, people problems can be prevented and/or solved.

1. **Issue:** How to help my team when generational differences cause them discomfort.

2. **Problem definition/facts:** People on my team are of all ages and thus representative of various generations. They sometimes get annoyed with each other when they have miscommunications. They tend to cluster with people of their own generation and complain about the other generations.

3. **Action steps:**

   - Openly discuss diversity of generation with the entire team. Ask for and give examples of benefits of having a diverse group.

   - Communicate with entire team about any disruptive behaviors observed and the impact on other team members.

   - Teach employees to adapt to each other's differences and grow together.

   - Showcase employees' unique offerings and how they think they can help teammates using their unique experiences.

   - Show that you value each person's offerings equally.

   - Ask how team members can learn from each other. What are their other ideas for profiting from this opportunity to work with differing generations?

   - Do team-building projects and/or training.

   - Mix and match team members. Some companies pair up people of different generations in a cubicle or on a project so they can share info and help each other. Some TV stations partner anchors of different generations; for example, CNBC pairs Erin Burnett, the youngest person to anchor a three-hour daily business news show, with broadcast veteran Mark Haines.

Office Politics

Different people define "office politics" differently, so it is important to define exactly what one means by office politics. This term usually means there is a communication problem, it is not being directly resolved, and there are bad feelings about whatever the real issue is. Once defined, a manager may or may not be able to fix the problem, depending on whether it is within his span of control. At the very least, the manager can listen and discuss the direct reports' concerns openly when they complain of office politics.

1. **Issue:** How to handle office politics that are distracting staff from their work.

2. **Problem definition/facts:** A direct report is advocating for his own personal agenda. This person is not operating in the company's greater interest, and his actions are causing a decrease in efficiency and motivation among teammates. The manager wants collaboration instead of blaming and manipulation.

3. **Action steps:**
   - ➤ Specify what management's agenda is. Identify and communicate corporate, group, and individual goals clearly.
     - Coach team toward goals.
     - Listen to feedback when team is not aligned.
     - Realign employee and the rest of the team toward goals.
     - Reward progress toward goals.
   - ➤ Determine what exactly the direct report is doing or saying that is referred to as a personal agenda. Meet with him to hear his perspective.
     - Identify what the direct report is doing to interfere with meeting goals. Determine how this impacts team members' ability to do their jobs.
     - Identify specific conflicts in the employee's agenda as it relates to management's agenda and goals.
     - Identify a strategy for the employee to make adjustments in an effort to resolve conflict.
     - Confirm agreement on future actions.
   - ➤ Create an open environment where opinions are honestly discussed and people listen to differing points of view.
     - Manage upwards, support upper management, and have regular communication with all disagreeing parties.
     - Expose issues and deal with them to avoid escalation.
     - Offer alternatives and be open to compromise.

Getting Work Done While Interacting with Different Personalities

Sometimes when people don't get along or when there is conflict, they use the phrases "personality conflict" or "personality differences." Phrasing the problem in "personality" terms makes it vague and difficult to resolve. A better idea is to get more specific about what you observe. Sometimes the problem is a just a difference in opinion or a disagreement about how to approach the work. Sometimes the problem occurs when behavioral styles clash. Behavioral style preferences are the way different people respond to situations, problems, timing, and other people. It's easier to get work done when people expect differences and do their best to state the facts.

1. **Issue:** How to help direct reports get their work done when they are having trouble interacting with different personalities.

2. **Problem definition/facts:** Some staff members are shutting out other personalities. People are afraid to express their opinions. There are miscommunications and misinterpretations of what coworkers mean. The manager wonders how to achieve goals with all these different points of view. These problems with coworkers have been stated by staff and are perceived as "personality" problems.

The first thing we needed to clarify was what this manager meant by personality problems. We worked together to turn the personality judgments into observable behaviors. In the following list, the first phrase is the original judgment and the actual observed behavior is shown in parentheses: no motivation (needs instructions), informational gap (needs better listening skills), too passive—asks no questions (needs direction and encouragement to ask questions), and easily distracted (changes focus and goes from task to task).

3. **Action steps:**
   ► Talk to Human Resources about doing a formal style assessment for your whole team to learn how each person works best and how to flex styles to improve relationships and get results. There

are several assessments available, but there may be concerns about how they are used in your organization.

- Help staff to be more open-minded by training them in style differences and how to work best with each style.
- Identify the different styles.
- Flex your own style to communicate in coworkers' styles.
- Find personal stimuli that help each person be productive.

► Don't judge people as "personality problems." Be specific about the behaviors that can be seen and heard and ensure that your staff do that also.

► Set clear expectations and goals about the work. Give clear deadlines and emphasize the importance of working together to meet goals and deadlines.

► Give regular feedback on progress.

► When there are differing perspectives, listen to all points of view. Prepare alternative solutions based on differing viewpoints.

► Provide excitement and enthusiasm about the work and its purpose. Establish trust and teamwork. Value contributions of all teammates.

► Teach staff listening skills through communication training.

When Two Employees Don't Get Along

Sometimes a manager ignores the situation when two employees don't get along. The manager might hope the two will sort out their problem by themselves or that the conflict is temporary and will go away. A better idea is to intervene early and facilitate a discussion with the two employees to identify the cause of the problem and talk about the impact on the work and the team. If left to fester, things generally get worse, as in the following example.

1. **Issue:** How to handle the situation when two employees do not get along.

2. **Problem definition/facts:** Coworkers say they are uncomfortable working nearby when two particular employees interact. Staff say these two create an uncomfortable work environment. These coworkers call each other names. Their behavior wastes their own time and that of co-workers and the manager. Emotional outbursts distract them from focusing on the work—occasionally one of them misses a deadline or goes home early. They do not share information with teammates when requested or when they should initiate it. They both refuse to communicate with other team members when approached for information.

3. **Action steps:** Immediately seek information from Human Resources (HR) about whether these two employees fit the description of creating a "hostile work environment." Follow all requirements and recommendations that HR makes. If it is not a hostile work environment, get HR's recommendations, which may include:

- Meet with both employees at the same time and discuss that job responsibilities require them to work together and with other team members.
- Discuss expectations and impact of deadlines being met.
- Discuss company policy regarding work hours.
- State the expectation that all employees must work together to help each other meet business goals and the corporate mission.
- Describe employees' observed behaviors in factual, neutral terms.
- Focus on the job-related impact of their behaviors.
- Set ground rules for how they must speak to people (no name calling and so on).
- Ask the coworkers to weigh in, one at a time, on how they each identify the problem.
- Ask them to offer solutions on how to resolve their differences.
- Offer both of them outside help if your company offers it (Employee Assistance Plan or HR).
- Discuss consequences of not changing behavior including the company procedure for counseling.
- Document the meeting according to HR's recommendations.

> Offer training in communication, conflict resolution, and team building.

> If behavior does not change, contact HR for next steps regarding counseling and documentation requirements.

F. Managing Up

When the Relationship Is Going Well

Your relationship with your boss can lead to your success or to problems. Many managers make the mistake of waiting for the boss to take the initiative. The care and feeding of a reporting relationship involves both of you. Maintaining a good working relationship does not happen by accident. You must demonstrate your strength and confidence in your abilities by managing the relationship with your manager—even when it is going well.

1. **Issue:** How to manage the relationship with your manager when the relationship is going well.

2. **Problem definition/facts:** You have no problems and want to keep it that way. The manager wants to prevent problems by managing up.

3. **Action steps:**
> Clarify your roles, responsibilities, and levels of authority (see Chapter 2). Know your manager's expectations and work within that realm.

> Establish a framework of goals/objectives and your method and frequency of communication. Can you meet weekly to discuss progress and plans? Keep your agreements on method and frequency of communication.

> Create a shared vision of what success looks like in detail. Go through potential examples. Walk through how the idea might get done.

> Assess where you are today vis-à-vis goals/objectives. Meet all goals or give early warning of why they won't be met with back-up plans of work-arounds.

- Present your plans and goals for your group earlier than your deadline. Be sure to indicate how they dovetail with your manager's goals and the overarching organizational goals.

- Send e-mail ahead of a one-on-one meeting with the agenda to give your manager time to think. Be prepared for routine progress meetings. Work from agendas/lists.

- Be considerate of your manager's time-management challenges. Be brief and brilliant. Give a high-level overview of the major points you would like to brief the manager on. Give only the details that the manager is interested in hearing at the time.

- Address the manager's needs. Remind your manager of what he committed to and offer to help deliver it.

- Be clear about what your manager has to communicate up and provide the necessary information or results on time.

- Be factual when presenting what your group needs. Back it up with evidence.

- Balance your manager's expectations with those of your direct reports. Support your group when you represent their accomplishments and needs to your manager. Get answers for them when needed.

- Discuss with your manager any variations in each other's styles and how you can best adapt to get the best communication results. Flex your communication style to best meet your boss's needs.

- Tailor what/how to communicate and how often so that communications meet the manager's needs.

- Discover what your manager's hottest topic is and be conversant on it.

- When you need approval or a decision, be thoroughly prepared with your recommendation, rationale, costs, benefits, opportunities, and potential problems. Think ahead about the questions your manager might ask and include the answers in your recommendation. Have a back-up alternative ready.

- If your manager is working remotely, the challenges are different. You need to take the initiative to speak more frequently despite time zone obstacles.

When the Relationship Is Not Going Well

Sometimes the relationship with your manager has not been developed, or it got off to a tough start. If so, it is up to you to decide on a plan to create a good working relationship with your manager. Don't wait for the manager to take the initiative. You cannot be successful without partnering with your manager.

This holds true even if your manager is ineffective or incompetent. I've witnessed situations where exceptionally competent people left organizations because they did not realize it was their responsibility to manage the unhappy relationship with incompetent or ineffective bosses. Since their boss's problems were well known throughout the organizations, they thought they would be covered. In fact, the people who did not manage up in adversity were perceived as having diminished organizational influence and power.

It's not only to your benefit to manage up in a difficult relationship, it is your responsibility to yourself, your staff, and your organization to initiate repair of the relationship and to manage the relationship with your boss.

1. **Issue:** How to manage the relationship with your manager when the relationship has problems or your manager is not effective.

2. **Problem definition/facts:** The boss makes unreasonable requests and gives unreasonable deadlines/goals. She requests something outside the scope of the job. Expectations and priorities are inconsistent and change from day to day. There are no written goals or deadlines. Staff feel intimidated because of her poor word choice and tone of voice. She tries to motivate people in a negative way instead of with positive recognition. She does not acknowledge job success. Her feedback does not match verbal goals. The impact of her behavior is loss of dollars due to people leaving, low morale, and low productivity.

3. **Action steps:**
   ► State your intention to work well together and to support her goals. Tell her of your need for clear expectations and directions. Relate this to how it impacts her goals.

- ► Ask for clarification on what needs to be accomplished. Ask for more structure, including written goals, so you can be sure to meet her expectations. Request prioritization of all projects and tasks. Clearly define responsibilities and priorities and give her a copy in writing. Clarify any misunderstandings right away and correct the written document.

- ► When she changes expectations, restate what was originally agreed upon—scope, goals, and deadlines. State what has changed and when it changed. Discuss inconsistent expectations. Ask for clarification and write up.

- ► Suggest that for "best results" more resources are needed (use statistics, failure data, historical data, person-hours needed to do tasks, and what other work is not getting done).

- ► Give your manager frequent status updates—overload with information until she tells you she wants less. This gives her the opportunity to give you frequent feedback so you will know where you stand.

- ► Suggest roundtable feedback with your manager and your team.

- ► Say how loss of teammates is impacting the work.

- ► Tell her what you are hearing from the team and express the desire to work together to improve the situation.

- ► Make specific suggestions and clarify your manager's needs. Ask specifically what you can do to help the situation.

- ► Meet with your boss's manager as a last resort if nothing works.

G. Handling Organizational Concerns

Handling Your Group When the Organization Has Problems

Organizational obstacles can hamper your team's progress and cause stress and frustration. You might want to look back at Chapter 3, "Communicating Your Expectations: What to Say and How to Say It," for more information on organizational obstacles. The "Six Communication Problems Arising from Unmet Expectations" section of Chapter 3 gives several specific concrete examples of what organizational obstacles are and how to handle them.

1. **Issue:** What to do when the organization has problems.

2. **Problem definition/facts:** Problems beyond the employees' control prohibit maximum productivity.

3. **Action steps:**
    - ➤ Identify the problem and discuss it with your boss first. How does the obstacle impact the work your group is trying to accomplish? How does it impede it?
    - ➤ Talk in the language of your team's action plans and goals.
    - ➤ Identify who can make decisions regarding possible solutions.
    - ➤ Work back and forth with your boss to provide possible solutions to the organization.
    - ➤ Be truthful with your group about the problem. Sometimes no organizational change is appropriate and the group needs to work around the obstacle.
    - ➤ Stick to facts and do not give opinions unless they are to advance a solution. Especially do not grouse or complain, as that invites morale problems.
    - ➤ Keep a positive approach and don't give up.
    - ➤ Keep trying to solve the problem and inform your employees of what you are doing.
    - ➤ Act as a role model and encourage patience and perseverance in spite of obstacles.

Summary

People problems are just business problems enveloped in concerns about interpersonal communication or about how to handle conflict among people. People problems can be cloaked in emotion and this makes them challenging. The simple process in this chapter helps managers dig down to the business facts and observed behaviors related to the work. This chapter relies on both the importance of relationship and an easy, three-step solution process.

In preventing and solving people problems, the manager's intention to preserve the working relationship is essential. So is the intention to discover the truth of both the work issue and the accompanying interpersonal issue. By describing the problem and facts, the manager can more easily solve the problem.

Next, Part III shows the importance of collaborative conversations in feedback, coaching, delegation, and listening. When you lead these management activities collaboratively, they *prevent* people problems. Each of these chapters pulls on the power of both relationship and having a repeatable process to follow and adds the dimension of collaboration.

PART

III

LEADING COLLABORATIVE CONVERSATIONS

P art III addresses feedback, coaching, delegating, and listening. These dialogues offer critical opportunities for the manager to energize direct reports about assignments. When you give feedback, you're collaborating. When you coach, you're collaborating. When you delegate, you're collaborating. When you listen, you're collaborating. Part III shows you how to do it.

How do Part I ("The Secrets to Creating and Sustaining Energized Relationships"), Part II ("How to Use Your Process Skills to Prevent and Solve Communication Problems"), and Part III ("Leading Collaborative Conversations") interconnect? When a manager has developed a close working relationship with an employee and a process is in place, he or she is positioned to lead a collaborative conversation.

The relationship is key to a successful collaborative conversation. The manager depends upon the relationship to set the environment for a frank, open talk about the work expectations and the observed progress toward those goals. When the relationship is in place, there is greater opportunity for honesty about what has occurred to date and how to continue or make midcourse changes so the employee can produce a successful outcome.

Both people listen with greater give-and-take when the relationship is solid. They have more desire to understand the issues as intended by the other person. New information can be learned, and each person can redirect his or her focus, if needed.

Process is equally valuable to the success of the collaborative conversation. When process is delineated, each person can lean on the structure to define terms and examine the alternatives for future action. This provides a common vocabulary and set of expectations, both of which facilitate collaborative conversation.

Partnership Behaviors

For feedback to be absorbed and applied, a collaborative discussion, in which the employee explores the issue and best alternatives, yields the most ownership of solutions going forward.

Collaborative conversations require the intention to develop partnerships. The manager leads this by demonstrating partnership behaviors. Working toward win-win outcomes, or mutual success, is critical. Try to answer why changing the way the employee does things will benefit him in the short and long term. How will such change help him achieve goals, and why should the employee care? On the other hand, does the employee have a better way of achieving the goal than the manager? Is there a third way to best benefit the needs of the organization that emerges through collaborative conversations?

Partners value the opinions of the other partner and appreciate their ideas on an equal basis. They recognize one another's talents, contributions, and knowledge. Associates are willing to learn from one another, listen to each other, and work as a team for mutual achievement. They share ownership of a goal.

An effective partnership builds on complementary knowledge, skills, and functional expertise. It creates common processes and vocabulary to enhance communication and goal accomplishment. Partnership is an opportunity to build and grow the working relationship for each other's benefit as well as the organization's.

Skilled managers develop partnerships with their direct reports. Partnerships lead to collaborative conversations.

Building and Maintaining Trust and Credibility

Collaborative conversations require trust. The manager needs to inspire trust before expecting to get it back. Sometime in your career you have probably heard someone say, "Trust me." What was your reaction? Words do not inspire trust. Management behaviors do. Being consistent and doing what you say you will do are trust-building behaviors.

Most of us look for patterns of behaviors before we trust someone, and that trust grows deeper as we see consistent actions. When people align their words with their actions, they signal trustworthiness. Being honest and able to admit mistakes conveys open communication, which makes most employees more comfortable at work. Employees also look for indications that the manager is approachable, encourages and accepts their feedback, and stands up for them. Caring for the employees' best interests, fostering mutual success, and getting to know employees grows trust.

The manager's competence and clear-cut goals trigger credibility. The ability to provide meaningful information, to follow through, and to hold people accountable generates credibility. The actual act of delegating extends trust to the employee and leads to faith in the manager's ability to assess the work and skills required to get it done. Removing obstacles to make the direct report's job easier demonstrates a willingness to work on a two-way street. Sharing experiences, showing commitment to the work and interest in employees, and adhering to high professional standards produce credibility.

Sometimes employees describe a manager who is credible as one who is willing to "roll up his sleeves and get dirty" to help employees in a crunch. When he does himself what he is asking employees to do, the manager engenders loyalty and collegiality. "We did it together" grows teamwork.

Involving others in decision making and asking for feedback and opinions demonstrates commitment to a "we" approach. This behavior corresponds with a manager's intention to work jointly. Behavior is what counts, not words or intentions. When a manager is always dependable, credibility and trust are built, and in turn grease the wheels of collaborative conversations and relationships.

CHAPTER 8

Giving Feedback— Sweet or Sour?

This chapter tackles the definition, types, and benefits of feedback. It calls attention to the importance of starting with the performance expectation and then stating the observed performance and its impact on the goal and/or team. It includes a real-world example of how to tie feedback to performance expectations.

Two types of feedback—positive reinforcement feedback and redirective feedback—are covered. Managers need to have a process for both types of feedback—one for supporting the current behavior of the employee and a separate process for redirecting the behavior. For redirective feedback, managers can plan what they will say before they discuss the situation with their direct report to feel more comfortable. This planning gives them fuller preparation and more confidence in the feedback conversation. Managers can assure themselves that there is no need for sweaty palms because they are prepared with facts and an intention to help the employee.

This chapter also addresses the value of managers inviting feedback from their direct reports and how that impacts business results.

What Is Feedback?

Feedback is telling people on a regular basis how they are doing in relation to the expectations and goals. This vital communication is honest and friendly and given with the intention of helping employees meet their objectives. It is an opportunity to keep the communication channels open. If delivered well, feedback contributes to relationship building. People want to know how they are doing in relation to the job at hand. They want to be affirmed when they are progressing. They want supportive help to redirect when they are off course, so they can achieve.

Feedback should be given immediately when behavior is observed, in person or at least voice-to-voice. When it is given on a regular basis, the employee can feel confident that he or she is on the right track. This reduces stress and uncertainty. When given frequently, feedback becomes part of collaborative, ongoing conversations rather than a big deal. It is a habit and therefore expected and nonthreatening.

When a manager chooses positive words, friendly (and nonjudgmental) tone of voice, and appropriate timing, feedback keeps people alert to what is important to the organization and how well they are fulfilling the expectations. This communication creates a comfortable, trustworthy environment because employees can trust that their performance will be observed and commented on with the intention of keeping them informed, developing their skills, and ensuring their optimum contribution to the team.

Chapter 2 ("Setting Expectations with Turbocharged Clarity") emphasized that feedback goes hand-in-hand with stating clear expectations. Expectations and feedback work in tandem. You cannot separate them, because feedback is geared toward communicating the extent to which expectations are met. Every time a manager gives feedback, he reinforces the importance of the expectation. When a manager does not give feedback, employees must guess if what they are doing is achieving the goals and meeting managerial expectations. Employees may operate out of fear of failure or may assume they are on the right course if the manager does not clarify expectations and does not deliver feedback. Trust, the relationship, and the work often suffer, as in the following example.

Unrealistic Expectations and Lack of Helpful Feedback

One Sunday I was riding the Hampton Jitney bus from Montauk, Long Island, to La Guardia Airport. When my seatmate learned I was writing this book, she told me a story about her daughter, Antoinette, who worked at an art gallery in Chelsea that had about ten employees. Antoinette was hired to sell art. When one of her coworkers, the bookkeeper, left on maternity leave, Antoinette's manager asked her to do the bookkeeping as well. Antoinette asked for more money to add those job duties. The manager said, "No. It will be good experience and will look good on your résumé."

According to Antoinette's mom, "The boss is cold and never compliments my daughter, who is doing two jobs. Antoinette has had no training in bookkeeping and sometimes makes mistakes. The boss reacts negatively instead of understanding that of course she will make mistakes—she is not a bookkeeper. The boss never thanks anyone. People who work there are afraid to admit errors. No one wants to take responsibility for anything that goes wrong."

Then she asked me if I thought all women managers think they have to act cold and curt and not be friendly to be effective as a boss. She had extrapolated from one unskilled manager (who did not set realistic expectations and who gave unhelpful, perhaps damaging, feedback) to all women managers. Just then, a man across the aisle handed me the *New York* magazine he had been reading. The blue cover sported titles like, "Do You Have to Be a Jerk to Succeed?" Apparently having an unknowledgeable, ineffective boss is a common theme. The issue seemed to be dedicated to articles about workplace problems.

Like Antoinette's boss, many untrained managers are unaware of the basics of building relationships, setting realistic expectations, providing resources including training, and giving job-related constructive feedback. Many managers have a difficult job handling these important communication activities, yet communication is the cornerstone for getting things done with and through others.

Why is workplace miscommunication such an area of interest for articles, research, surveys, television shows like *The Office*, and cartoons like *Dilbert?* There's a reason *The Office* is so well liked. The characters demonstrate relationship and communication problems that are played out every day in the workplace. Viewers laugh because the communication misfires are so familiar. At least the boss is likable and has all the best intentions for his staff. Still, his management skills are lackluster and affect results.

Example: Tying Expectations to Frequent Feedback

Fortunately, many managers are skilled at setting reasonable expectations and following up with friendly, job-related feedback that is constructive to the employees' success, to the relationships, and to the success of the business. An excellent model of a company that ties together expectations with feedback is the example we used in Chapter 2 on clarity of expectations: the Balboa Bay Club & Resort (BBC&R) of Newport Beach, California. The same example is used again here to complete the model of how to tie together setting expectations with giving feedback in a productive manner.

BBC&R provides an exemplary experience to their guests by both setting high expectations for all employees and making continual feedback about those expectations part of the daily work. Managers give feedback to employees. The quality manager, Cynthia Goins, gives feedback to managers and employees. Employees also give feedback to managers and Cynthia. The open-door policy flourishes because all are aware that they are striving for the same ultimate goals and everyone wants all employees to be happy. The leaders have built trust and relationships so all staff expect feedback on an ongoing basis.

Cynthia Goins works in Human Resources (HR), so most of the employees she gives feedback to are not her direct reports. However, she has the support of executives to go to housekeeping, the kitchen, and other departments to meet with department heads. She tells them, "I heard . . ." or "I saw . . .," and addresses what she heard or saw with the manager. This might be feedback from guests or employees. Cynthia says, "We treat employees as we would treat guests and members. We take time, listen to employees, and make them a priority. Once employees see it in a leader, they'll do it with guests."

Cynthia phones the hotel periodically to see how employees answer the phone. She gives feedback, so there is constant communication about the importance of how the phone is answered. Employees make every effort to go above and beyond expectations of the industry. Cynthia says, "The Balboa Bay Club & Resort is not in the business of selling service, but in the business of selling an *experience* for the guest— something unexpected. We accomplish this experience by really listening to and paying attention to guests, *engaging* them."

BBC&R has processes in place to ensure exceptional customer experience. It teaches techniques such as finding commonalities with guests, like noticing they have the same last name. BBC&R is continually looking for ways to enhance the experience for guests. The staff discuss, "What are we doing about this comment card?" They share best practices from other places they visit and never take for granted what they learn from other hotels.

Rather than sit at a desk, Cynthia walks around and asks employees about what happened yesterday. If there was a problem with package delivery, they talk about it. Standing outside in the porte cochere, if she sees a bellman taking guests to the front desk, she reinforces great behavior. While I interviewed her by phone, she asked me to wait a minute while she wrote down something she had just heard a room reservations agent say to a guest. As soon as we got off the phone, Cynthia intended to mention to the employee what he had said and why it was effective and important and to urge him to keep that up. "If we expect guests to be acknowledged, we have to do the same thing as managers and acknowledge both guests and employees," she said.

BBC&R encourages managers to write simple thank-you cards to employees when the manager observes outstanding behavior. Managers recognize that person in writing and give the card in public in front of peers. They also publicize it on the Daily Lineup Sheet because every employee sees that. Reinforcing good behavior is a regular part of feedback at the Balboa Bay Club & Resort. In addition to informal recognition, BBC&R also has formal recognition programs, such as employee of the quarter and of the year. The winners get a crystal award, a check, and their picture posted outside the galley—the employee dining area.

When managers give feedback, it is always about the standards. For example, if Cynthia forgets to wear her name tag, she expects other employees to give her immediate feedback so she can correct it:

> I would be disappointed if they didn't tell me, because we are supposed to be looking out for each other. We have open communication because we all understand what we are striving for and why we are doing it. We are not afraid to tell each other, "You're slouching" or "You've got a five o'clock shadow and you said you wouldn't come with one again." They're not offended, because of trust. Employees at BBC&R enjoy what they are doing and we enjoy working with our coworkers. It's all part of relationship and trust.

Two Types of Feedback

There are two important types of feedback: positive reinforcement and redirective. Both have a purpose and an appropriate use, depending upon whether or not the expectations are being met. Both are important communication tools.

Positive reinforcement feedback recognizes and reinforces specific desired behaviors. This feedback specifies positive behaviors that the manager wants to see repeated. Positive reinforcement feedback communicates that expectations are being met or exceeded and lets the employee know exactly what to keep doing.

Redirective feedback asks the employee to change, or redirect, her behavior to better align herself to meet goals and expectations. This feedback is sometimes called corrective because it helps the employee adjust her approach early on so she can meet expectations and be successful. This type of feedback assists the direct report in knowing exactly what to do differently so she can change her actions.

It is important to give both types of feedback on a regular basis so employees can count on knowing their performance status. When employees expect both types of feedback, they understand feedback in the greater context of helping them achieve the goals and expectations. This enables them to view both positive reinforcement and redirective feedback as collaborative conversations.

Guidelines for Both Types of Feedback

When delivering either type of feedback, there are some guidelines. These general tips contribute to making the conversations collaborative and most effective.

Feedback is an important communication tool, so give it in person or at least voice-to-voice (not by e-mail). E-mail is frequently misunderstood and can be blown out of proportion. Always link the feedback directly and explicitly to the expectation or goal and tell why that expectation is important. (Yes, even if you have said it many times before.)

Be sure to discuss only one specific situation at a time—not "you always, you never, you often, or you usually," even with positive reinforcement. It is also important to identify precise, observable behavior rather than making opinion or judging comments. A manager can also gather facts from project management milestones, plans, goals, required processes, procedures, and other stated expectations. Facts clarify the communication and allow both the manager and the direct report to remain objective and results oriented. Judgments or opinions can lead to conversational detours so the main point gets lost.

Be sure to give enough unambiguous and factual information to enable the employee to repeat the performance or make a requested change. While it's nice to hear, "Good job," it is insufficient information for a person to know exactly what that means. Similarly, comments such as, "Almost there" or "Not quite" do not identify what is expected and what the employee needs to change.

Feedback is never about the person. It is about the behavior—action or inaction related to the expectation. To keep the talk collaborative, be supportive in words and process. Keep building the relationship between you and the employee. Using a friendly, neutral tone of voice conveys your intention to help the employee succeed. Be sure to generate excitement for the person's potential to achieve the goal—frame the feedback in a positive context.

Positive Reinforcement Feedback—You Rock; Keep That Up!

Positive reinforcement feedback is recognizing desired behaviors and commenting on them when you see them. Some people call this supportive or positive feedback. The BBC&R example (immediately telling the room reservation agent specifically what he said that demonstrated he had anticipated a guest's need) is positive reinforcement. This type of feedback is essential if you want to see the behaviors repeated. This inexpensive form of recognition elevates the importance of the expectations and lets employees know right away that they are meeting those expectations.

Positive reinforcement feedback leads to *patterns* of positive behaviors. When this feedback is given frequently, it can be very motivating for people and help create forward-moving teamwork. The bottom line of this type of feedback is "you are succeeding at a specific job behavior—keep that up." Generally, this type of feedback is received well and enhances harmony individually and for the team atmosphere.

There are many opportunities to give positive reinforcement and employees never seem to get enough of it. Some managers might say, "That's their job. Why should I say anything at all? They should just do it." That is an impractical point of view. It is true that people are compensated to deliver certain results. However, a manager's job is to work *with* people—to collaborate, promote ownership, partner, and encourage participation. It is also a manager's responsibility to keep expectations visible and help people meet them.

Today's accomplished manager realizes that one of the most important communication skills to develop is influencing rather than telling employees to "just do it." Technology and the global economy have driven many of the communication changes, including the need to persuade rather than solely instruct. We are all more or less equal in our ability to gather information and thus are able to develop expert knowledge. This means people want to be treated collegially and be appreciated for their expertise. Most professionals do their best work when they are empowered to make decisions and use their ideas and work with other professionals. It is the manager's job to inject energy and enthusiasm into the workplace so people can enjoy working and concentrate on producing top results. Positive reinforcement infuses the environment with positive energy and recognition that an individual is progressing toward the goals.

Positive reinforcement also informs the employee what is important to you. Those are the behaviors you comment on because they impact the customer, the bottom line, the team, or the goal. You acknowledge and verbally reward the actions you want to recur. So positive reinforcement is one of a manager's most valuable tools.

Five-Step Process for Positive Reinforcement Feedback

Follow these steps when an employee meets or exceeds expectations and you want him to repeat the behaviors or actions.

1. State the goal, performance expectation, standard, or desired behavior. Be surgically precise. Eliminate any vagueness.
2. Describe the observed behavior or action in relation to the expectation.

3. Tell why the behavior the employee demonstrated is important and how it impacts the team or group goal.
4. Ask the employee to keep repeating that behavior.
5. Thank him for his contribution.

Here is a quick example that shows what a manager might say if he followed the above five steps:

1. "As you know, this job requires you to be at your desk at 8:00 a.m. every day."
2. "Since you are prompt, you were available to resolve that customer problem first thing this morning. That could have become a mini-crisis if you had not been here."
3. "I appreciate that you have developed a pattern of being on time every day because we can rely on you to handle customer issues during all of our service hours."
4. "Way to go—please keep that up!"
5. "Thank you for maintaining an outstanding attendance record. We appreciate that."

You might prefer combining steps 1 and 2 or reversing the order if it makes you and your direct report more comfortable. Collaborative conversations do not always follow a step-by-step process, since they involve back and forth. Regardless of how you decide to do it, the main point is to relate the observed behavior directly to the performance expectation.

If you want to see desired behaviors repeated, attach importance to them by showing you notice and appreciate them. Deliver positive, reinforcing feedback to elevate the significance of the performance and how it affects the team or organization. The following script shows an example of how to do that.

Script: Positive Reinforcement

Manager: "Tim, I noticed you stayed late last night to finish that report and I wanted to thank you."

Tim: "Well, thanks, but it's just my job."

Manager: "True enough, but it made a big difference that you put in the extra hours. Because that report was done on deadline, we were able to get it to Accounting in time for them to crunch the numbers today and make recommendations to our CEO at the 4:00 p.m. advisory meeting. She had some decisions to make that impact all of us and she really needed that information."

Tim: "I guess it was important then."

Manager: "It was vital. Thank you so much for the extra effort."

Tim: "You're welcome."

Tim is much more likely to repeat the behavior of staying late to meet a deadline because his manager noticed and acknowledged the effort. Also, because Tim was informed why it was important, he can put his task in context of a bigger picture. The feedback lends meaning to the task. It also might remind the manager to tell the importance of a particular deadline in advance next time. Consider what might have happened if the manager did not mention Tim's extra effort. Tim might feel overworked and undervalued. What happens to the relationship then? After a pattern of being ignored, Tim might opt out as a partner. Or the work might suffer if he gets tired of these late-night deadlines and loses commitment to the manager.

Redirective Feedback—Please Make a Change

The other type of feedback is redirective feedback. Some people call this corrective or constructive feedback. This type of feedback informs the employee that an expectation is not being met and asks for a change or improvement in what the employee is doing. The expectation can be wide-ranging. Some examples of expectations are: being on time, meeting a deadline, capturing a sale, serving a customer in a particular way, following a procedure, behaving professionally in a meeting or with co-workers, making quota, including certain information in a report, meeting safety requirements, or any number of job expectations. When any job expectation is not met, the manager needs to let the employee know as soon as feasible. The purpose of redirective feedback is to help the employee redirect her efforts and align them with goals and expectations. Giving redirective feedback assists the employee in knowing exactly what is off-track so she can correct actions. Oftentimes the employee has no idea that she is not meeting the expectation.

Many people view redirective feedback as "negative feedback" because it can be considered as delivering bad news. True, when a manager is not proficient in how to give redirective feedback, it may very well feel negative to both the manager and the direct report. It may feel like blaming or finding fault. If this type of feedback is not given well, it can come across as a "gotcha" ("I've been waiting for you to make a mistake and now I caught you"). Or it can feel punitive ("I'm disappointed with you personally"). In fact, sometimes ineffectively delivered feedback makes it seem as if the manager is angry with the employee. Poorly given feedback may even damage relationships. When a manager's feedback skills are underdeveloped, the feedback falls short of its purpose: to improve job performance.

But, properly delivered, redirective feedback is not negative. It is a positive communication tool to keep performance high and relationships growing. When managers give any feedback well, it displays their intention to support the employee. The purpose of feedback is to help the employee accomplish objectives and succeed. Done well, redirective feedback flows as a collaborative conversation and proves to be a benefit to the employee.

Redirective feedback is collegial and beneficial. It clears the air and creates certainty. It nudges people in a more productive direction while it preserves their dignity as people and as professionals. It leverages the thinking power of the person responsible for making the change and makes achievement possible. Now that is "sweet."

Five-Step Process for Redirective Feedback

Follow these steps when expectations are not met, so the employee has a chance to change his behavior or actions and achieve success. Notice Steps 1 and 2 are the same as in positive reinforcement feedback.

1. State the goal, performance expectation, standard, or desired behavior. Be surgically precise. Eliminate any vagueness.

2. Describe the observed behavior or action in relation to the expectation.

3. Tell why the behavior the employee demonstrated is not effective and how it impacts the team or group goal.

4. Ask the employee to tell you his views on the issue. He might have facts that you do not.

5. Ask the employee what actions he will take to meet the expectation. Move toward future performance.

As in positive reinforcement feedback, you might prefer combining steps or reversing the order to make the conversation collaborative. Regardless of how you decide to do it, the main point is to clearly relate the specific, observed behavior directly to the performance expectation.

Here is a quick example, based on a real situation, that shows what a manager might say if she followed the above five steps.

1. "As you know, this job requires you to be at your desk at 8:00 a.m. every day so you are available in the event of any network problems."

2. "When we had the network crash this morning at 8:15 a.m., you weren't here."

3. "So, your teammates were scrambling to solve the problem. That took them off their own deadlines for today. And it delayed getting the problem solved, since they had to wait until you got here anyway because no one knew how to handle 'X.'"

4. "Is there anything I should know about your being late?"

   Employee: "Not really. Nothing ever happens that early, and I noticed management is often not here until 8:30 a.m., so I began to think it wasn't important to be here."

5. "You bring up a good point. It might appear sometimes that managers are not working at 8:00 a.m. because they are working elsewhere. But your responsibilities require that you work right here every day. What do you think you can do about it?"

Employee: "Okay. I saw what a mess it was for everyone around here today and realize I'd better be at my desk on time. You can count on it."

Manager: "Thanks, and let's get Pranet and Joey cross-trained on the 'X' portion of the job so they can back you up in the event of an emergency. I'll talk to them later. Could you bring them up to speed by the end of next week?"

Employee: "Good idea. Yes, I'll talk to them after you do."

Script: Redirective Feedback Conversation

Here is an example of a feedback conversation. Although it is fictional, it is based on a real issue.

Manager: "Eduardo, I got a call from Hugh today saying you were fifteen minutes late on the weekly conference call you were supposed to host this morning. He said you were fifteen minutes late last week also."

Eduardo: "I was stuck in traffic."

Manager: "Eduardo, I can understand you might have difficulty talking on the phone when you are stuck in traffic. But we need you to host that call at exactly 9:00 a.m. every Wednesday wherever you are—whether you're in the office, in the field, or on the road. There are five other people who have scheduled that weekly time. They are waiting for you to host the meeting."

Eduardo: "I'll try."

Manager: "It is very costly to the company to have people's schedules disrupted. All those colleagues need to exchange information so they can meet their requirements. Plus we need their cooperation on many of our projects, so it's vital that they can trust our department to do what we say we will do. You are the key person on the call and it is necessary that you host it on time, every week. I need for you to more than *try*. I expect you to commit to meeting this critical job expectation."

Eduardo: "Or?"

Manager: "Eduardo, the job requires hosting that call at 9:00 a.m. every Wednesday. You have all the knowledge and expertise that is needed. Is there something going on that is preventing you from being on time for that call?"

Eduardo: "I didn't want to say anything, but due to a personal situation I now have to take my daughter to day care every morning for the next month. That means I can't be here by 9:00 a.m., and I hate talking in the car because I need to get online plus refer to some files for that meeting."

Manager: "I understand that must be tricky. What could you do to still host the call on time?"

Eduardo: "The day care is near home. I can double back there and host the call from home with no problem."

Manager: "Okay. Let's go with that plan for the next month. Let's touch base next Wednesday to confirm that you are back on track for placing the call."

Eduardo: "Okay then."

Use redirective feedback whenever expectations are not met so the employee has a chance to change his behavior or actions right away. When giving this feedback, use the process and always preserve the relationship. Season the feedback with your intuition about what to say and how to say it based on your intention to keep things positive and future-focused.

Phrases to Help You Be Direct and Clear

When giving redirective feedback, a manager *must* be crystal clear about the desired expectation, the actual performance, and the gap between them. If you are reluctant to state clearly what you mean in a feedback conversation, consider some of these phrases. Some of them are too strong for a first-time conversation, especially if it is with a direct report who is collaborating well on changing performance or behavior. But these phrases are helpful to have in your hip pocket in case the going gets tough:

"I heard you say . . ."

"I saw . . ."

"I understand your reservation to doing this differently, but the project calls for . . ."

"I expect . . . because . . ."

"This job requires . . ."

"The team needs you to . . . What will you do to make that happen?"

"The performance expectation is . . . What will you do to meet it?"

"The goal requires that you . . . because . . ."

"When you do "X," the impact of your behavior on the team is . . ."

Absence of Redirective Feedback Sours Performance

Managers are not doing their direct reports a favor by withholding comments when expectations are not met. No feedback at all is just as toxic as feedback given poorly. This lack of communication can have unfavorable consequences. The following example shows that when a manager ducks the responsibility to redirect behavior, the employee suffers.

One woman from the southern United States is a highly regarded sales account manager. She walked confidently into her annual performance appraisal meeting. She had always received an outstanding rating and her sales numbers were over quota. In the absence of feedback from her boss, she had every reason to believe she would receive the same rating she had received in the past. Instead, her boss blindsided her. He had lowered her rating. She was shocked and upset.

"Why?" she asked.

"Do you remember that report you did six months ago on _____?" he asked.

"Yes."

"Well I didn't like the way you did it," the manager said.

"Why didn't you tell me?" she queried. "I would have redone it the way you wanted."

"I didn't want to hurt your feelings."

"Well now you have *really* hurt my feelings," she said. "You have cost me my track record in this company as an outstanding performer. This has cost me financially in terms of a raise. You have really hurt my feelings now."

The manager had already submitted all his staff ratings to upper management and they had been approved. So, although he could change some of the wording, the rating stood. This is an example of poor management. Whose feelings was he really protecting? His own. He did not take responsibility for clarifying his expectations prior to the report getting done, or later, when his (private) expectations were not met. He did not exhibit strong management skills by holding a collaborative conversation about how he wanted the report handled. In fact, there was nothing collaborative about the performance management during the year. He surprised the employee during the performance appraisal. This should never happen. Employees should always know what to expect in the performance review.

Performance management is not about "gotcha." Effective managers work in partnership with employees. The conversations about expectations flow back and forth and get clarified for mutual understanding. Feedback is a tool that shows managers are trying to help employees do their best work. Failure to give feedback is abdication of managerial responsibility.

Noncollaborative Feedback Sours Relationships

One-way feedback, in which the employee has no say, is not likely to improve performance. In fact, it is probable that it will cause confusion, misunderstandings, and relationship damage. Lack of two-way communication can result in negative impacts, as this example of noncollaborative feedback shows.

One day when I entered the office of a small-business owner I know, he asked me how the front-desk employee treated me on my way into the office.

"Was she friendly to you?"

"Of course," I said. "She is a great ambassador for your business. She is always cheerful and helpful."

"She ignored me today," he said.

"Oh?"

"Yes," he continued. "I gave her some *feedback* two days ago. Then she missed work the next day. She always calls in sick the day after I give her feedback."

"How did you give her the feedback?" I asked.

"I sent her an e-mail."

"Have you considered just talking to her in person instead of sending feedback by e-mail?"

"No," he replied. "She always talks on and on and I don't have time for that."

He told me the scenario, which sounded like a misunderstanding about the expectation. It could easily have been handled in person in a positive, brief, and gentle way. This manager had no training in giving feedback, so he probably did not relate his comments in the e-mail to a previously expressed expectation. In fact, the expectation was probably not verbalized. Now feedback by e-mail was costing this small-business owner one day's salary for the absent employee, plus the cost of hiring a temp for the front desk. So it put a ding in the finances as well as the relationship. A collaborative conversation could have straightened out the misunderstanding and led to an instantaneous solution.

Benefits of Feedback

When properly delivered, feedback benefits the direct report in many ways. This communication aligns individual behavior and efforts with organizational interests and success, which is why people are at work in the first place. When an employee listens to feedback, she can develop skills and knowledge and achieve success that might not be accomplished without feedback. As the employee garners a sense of accomplishment, she is energized to persevere when times get tough.

Letting employees know where they stand, on a continual basis, reduces fear of the unknown. Knowledge, of how they are meeting or not meeting expectations, empowers employees to fine-tune their actions so they can achieve. This presents employees with a chance to improve performance and make midcourse corrections, which shows the manager has individuals' best interests at heart.

Feedback develops partnerships between employee and manager. It strengthens relationships as partners collaborate on reaching goals. Feedback invites participation and offers an opportunity for employees to voice their perspectives, concerns, and need for support. It offers the manager the opportunity to gather information from direct reports and collaborate on solutions. Collegial relationships eliminate blaming and finger-pointing and keep everyone focused on achieving the objectives.

Timely and regular feedback, of both types, lays the groundwork for a collaborative performance appraisal with honesty and continual learning as a focus. It leads to no surprises on the performance appraisal and better performance throughout the year.

Inviting and Receiving Feedback—How Are We Doing?

Communication is, of course, two way. Once trust and relationships have been established, asking for feedback is an important collegial conversation for the business. It can reap big benefits for the team, and you as a manager, and maybe for process improvements and innovation. Being able to not only deliver, but also hear challenging feedback is essential if a manager is to be influential and add value to the team and the organization as a whole.

Managers who want their direct reports to buy in and "own" not only their individual goals and results, but also those of the organization as a whole, must actively seek and invite feedback. A collaborative manager, with his eye on the strategic results of the business, asks for feedback from his team on a regular basis. It can be as simple as "How are we doing as a team?" or "How is my management style working or not working for you?" or "How can I better support you?" or "What could we do better?"

Listen carefully and restate what direct reports say in a nondefensive manner. "So it sounds like you are saying you would like me to delegate more authority to you?" "If I've got it right you think we should change this process to 'X' because. . . ." "Are you saying that there are organizational obstacles that prevent the team from . . . ?"

Take it to the next level. "You make a good case for changing. . . . What would you like me to do differently?" or "I'm glad you are assessing how our team is working. Let's get together with the whole group and you can facilitate a meeting on your ideas. Let's hear what they have to say and get their input too." or "So if the team has conflict about which way to proceed, that can be a good thing. Maybe we are on the brink of something new. Let's get the team together and examine the alternative next approaches."

Express appreciation. "Thank you for giving me feedback. I will think about it and get back to you." Or, "You're right. We will all benefit if I change. . . ."

Feedback to you as a manager is essential to your success and achieving desired results. It helps you know what is going on with your employees and vice versa. It emphasizes to employees that their ability to add value to the work is wanted, heard, and acted upon. When their feedback makes a difference, their level of commitment to you, your team, and the company increases.

Summary

Effective feedback relates to process (having structured work expectations) and relationship (candidness about performance develops trust). Winning feedback also requires collaborative conversations and intuition. You know *what* needs to be said—that's your intuition, based on your experience with this employee and with the type of work situation before you. You may need to focus on *how* best to say what needs to be said. That is where following a business-based process and recalling the importance of preserving the relationship connect. You're careful with your word choice and you keep the feedback job-related and specific.

Part I covered the importance of communicating clear expectations and how feedback describes the extent to which those expectations are met or not met. In Part II, Chapter 4 on workflow process and project management mentioned how having structured approaches creates a common language for communicating what is expected functionally on the job. This clarity helps managers and employees to discuss the expected steps and give objective, factual feedback on project progress. In addition to having facts about set expectations and observed behavior, a manager must be intuitive about what words and tone of voice to use so he will be heard and the employee will not become defensive. Successful feedback requires collaborative conversations. Two-way trust and collegiality grow through collaboration, and so do relationships and meaningful business results.

Feedback ties in directly with setting expectations, delegation, and coaching. In fact, feedback is an indispensable element of coaching, which Chapter 9 explains.

Compelling Coaching Techniques

This chapter addresses the definition, types, and timing of coaching. It points out how to use factual feedback within the coaching conversation. Emphasis is on revisiting performance expectations, providing help, and maintaining the relationship. Whether the employee believes that coaching is of benefit to her depends partially on how the manager positions the feedback and sets the tone for coaching. A manager must ask questions, listen, and convey friendliness to be an effective coach. The coaching session is an opportunity to help an employee self-discover ways to develop and enhance performance.

Definition and Purpose of Business Coaching

Business coaching is a collegial one-on-one process to help people excel in their job performance. Coaching is a series of meetings in which the manager and employee partner to define desired outcomes, plan how to achieve them, access resources, remove obstacles, and assess progress toward the desired outcomes.

Since you are responsible for the results of your entire team, it is essential that you give each teammate the resources to succeed. Coaching is a prime resource. Coaching is evolving as one of the top skills a manager must acquire because it strengthens individual, and thus team, performance.

Coaching starts with an evaluation of the needs and skills of your staff. The individual being coached may need your assistance so he can improve or enhance communication, leadership, teamwork, goal achievement, or technical aspects of his job. Coaching enables direct reports to meet goals, be productive, and learn new skills. As each individual enhances competencies, the entire team is strengthened.

Many managers do not understand the purpose of coaching direct reports. So let's look at a model that is familiar to almost everyone. Perhaps you have coached, or been coached, in sports, music, dance, acting, or another venue. Ideal coaches in these situations create and communicate long-range strategies as well as tactical maneuvers. These coaches have a process, plan, and schedule to train and practice. They constantly remind team members of the goals they are striving to achieve. They give immediate feedback—both positive reinforcement and redirective. Coaches motivate people to persevere under the toughest of conditions and challenges. They trust that the individuals being coached can accomplish the goals and continually say so. These coaches convey that they share the goals with the team members—everybody wins or nobody wins. No matter the degree of winning, development of knowledge and skills takes place during the process. The person being coached expects the coach to always be in the background for support, motivation, and tips on how to enhance performance.

Most people understand that the purpose of sports or arts coaching is to reach specific results for both individual and group success. The coach is a positive influence and a motivational force for teammates to persist and continually develop for some end goal—a performance, a game, or maybe even a Super Bowl.

Coaching has the same purpose in business. It is a partnership to help develop an individual's skills and knowledge so the team can prosper. It reduces employees' learning curve and thus increases their comfort and confidence. Yet some managers resist coaching. Some confuse coaching with discipline or counseling. It is neither. Counseling and discipline deal with performance problems that the employee did not correct after receiving feedback and coaching. These problems must be carefully documented and company policy followed because the problem is serious and may lead to the employee's termination. This book does not address discipline or counseling.

Although coaching is not counseling, coaching does involve tweaking performance, which is why some managers avoid it. But coaching is a gift that can be used to improve or prevent performance shortfalls, and to enhance already good performance. The manager assesses performance constantly throughout the year rather than only at annual or semiannual performance review time. By assessing performance regularly, the manager can help the employee boost it through positive reinforcement and redirective feedback and a coaching plan. Coaching divides up the time between formal appraisal meetings and helps ensure that the direct report owns the results of his or her work and is always supported to achieve them. In fact, many companies hire specialized coaches to work with their executives to support achievement or to prepare them for increased responsibilities.

One way to get clear on the positive purpose of coaching is to think of it as a communication "spa treatment." Coaching is an opportunity to relax as the manager and employee massage the muscles of getting the job done. The idea is to enhance learning, rid performance of pesky knots, and leave the employee glad he came in for the occasion. It is special one-on-one time dedicated to refreshing performance, communicating, and galvanizing the employee's energies toward the goals.

The coach is supportive and future oriented. She uses many communication skills: questioning techniques, listening, and keeping relationship central to addressing business challenges. The coach draws on both her content knowledge and ability to facilitate learning. Being a first-rate coach means the coach is highly evolved in the content and process of the work and highly confident in her ability to help others. It means she invests time in developing relationships, which facilitates coaching success.

Managing today includes influencing and invigorating people who are entrusted to your guidance. Inspirational guidance that managers provide through coaching fortifies the abilities of both the manager and the employee. It also fosters an energized, communicative environment in which everyone can work better together.

What Is the Relationship Between Feedback and Coaching?

The purpose of both coaching and feedback is to help employees achieve objectives and be self-sufficient in their work. Coaching is a long-term expression of a manager's intention to help the employee be all that he can be professionally and to meet performance goals. Feedback is the manager's input about a specific event or task. Coaching is a routine, scheduled boost to performance. Feedback can take place spontaneously when an employee needs it. Coaching needs to follow a process, because there is too much at stake to shoot from the hip.

Feedback is a miniprocess inside a bigger process. Coaching is a strategic process and part of performance management. Coaching links regular feedback with formal annual goal setting, professional development planning, the annual performance review, and back to setting the next year's performance goals. Feedback is tactical and takes place immediately upon observing behaviors. When managers want to reward performance behaviors and see them repeated, they describe the behavior and the impact it has. When managers wants to help employees tweak or improve performance behaviors, again, they describe the behavior just observed and the impact it has. They also ask the employees' ideas on how to redirect it. Feedback is to help an employee meet performance expectations, which are a subset of the annual performance goals.

Coaching Versus Feedback

A manager can coach *before* any work begins—for example, when delegating to clarify the assignment, when goal setting, when helping a person who is facing a new task or project, for career or professional development, during critical crossroads or milestones of a project, or when implementing a change initiative. You can't give feedback before you observe a behavior—feedback occurs *after* an observed action or inaction, if action was expected. Example: a person did not participate in a meeting at which his or her input was crucial. Or, an individual helped a coworker meet a deadline.

Coaching delivers performance information on a *routine* basis. It is planned, prepared for, scheduled, and expected. Feedback is not necessarily expected, since it is given *as an action occurs.*

Coaching implies an *ongoing relationship.* Feedback does not. For example, anyone can give feedback to anyone else with or without an ongoing relationship. The visiting VP of sales from headquarters might accompany a salesperson on calls once a year and give one-time feedback. But it is the sales manager who is the ongoing coach and maintains the daily relationship.

Coaching implies *agreement* that one person is the coach and one is the person who will get coached. It also implies that there is a *shared goal* both are aiming for. Both want to win the game, but the coach won't be out on the field actually playing. Feedback is not necessarily based on an agreement. Feedback is based on an observation in the moment, so anyone can give feedback to anyone: coworker to coworker, employee to manager, peer to peer, as well as manager to direct report. All coaching involves feedback. Not all feedback is part of coaching.

A coach wants to accomplish the most amount of change with the least amount of effort or force. The coach constantly makes decisions on how best to spend time. For example, how to word the feedback to effectively communicate the message, preserve the relationship, and affect results. Feedback, on the other hand, does not necessarily involve planning and preparation, since it must be given immediately in order for the employee's behavior to be recognized and rewarded or redirected. Since coaching is on a routine basis, a manager shares his technical expertise or ability to facilitate the employee to tap into his own expertise. Coaching involves pre-positioning. It requires setting up the rules of the game ahead of time and getting agreement on the terms, process, and end result.

Coaching implies a trusting relationship that the coach and team member are on the same team and both need the same outcome. A baseball player would not accept coaching from an opponent, or from the opponent team's coach. In business the analogy would be that your staff would not accept feedback from a manager from a competing company. The suspicion would be that the feedback is not in the team's best interest, so they would not trust it.

Example of Feedback Versus Coaching

Feedback gives people information about what others perceive and observe about a single issue and helps them figure out their own path of action based on that information or perception. It is tactical in nature because it is a one-time event. However, feedback can trigger the need for coaching. Coaching is a strategic plan that is implemented over time. It may be precipitated by one issue, but since the employee cannot solve it in one feedback session, it is integrated with big-picture goals and scheduled to take some time. The feedback in each coaching session will be new information.

The story below is an actual example of when poor feedback was given. Instead, it should have been put in the context of a long-term coaching strategy. This would have informed the direct report of why the behavior was important and would have provided all the resources necessary to make the change.

Marcella was a top-rated, experienced, first-line manager of professional groups. She was recently promoted to manage managers for the first time. She reports to Mark, the VP, and three group managers now report to her. Carol is one of the three group managers on Marcella's new staff. Carol is a newly promoted first-line manager with no previous management experience.

In this real-life example, Mark called Marcella into his office one day and told her that her staff call her "The Queen." This feedback shocked Marcella. Since the judging term, "Queen," was the nature of the feedback, Marcella did not know what it meant or what to do to fix it. Instead of using the hurtful label, Mark should have delineated specific communication behaviors that were causing tension between Marcella and Carol. Mark's words made it sound as if *all* of the staff had problems with Marcella, when it was specifically Carol that had the problem. Mark's tone of voice made it sound to Marcella as if he was rebuking her and siding with someone else.

In reality, the only person who had complained to Mark was Carol, who had not discussed any problems with Marcella. The communication misfire existed only among Marcella, Carol, and Carol's staff. The other two managers reporting to Marcella, and their staffs, had no issue with Marcella's management.

Mark should have asked questions of Carol to discover the real problem Carol and her staff were having with Marcella. If Mark had used the process in Chapter 6 and had untangled the judgment ("The Queen"), he could have discovered the facts and the observed behaviors that were not working.

Had Mark gathered facts, he could have given useful feedback (which would have been part of a general coaching conversation) to Marcella. Better feedback would have been:

> You have an outstanding track record as a first-level manager. I'd like to help you succeed in your new role of managing managers and want us to collaborate on how best to do that. You have a successful relationship with two of your direct report managers. Let's build on that for how you and Carol might work better together. You've been managing managers and setting up this new unit for only two months, so now is the ideal time to make a plan of where we go from here. I want to give you all the resources you need because I know you will be a terrific manager of managers with a little help.
>
> As you advance to higher-level management, the need for excellent communication skills is imperative. You will need to learn to work

well with larger groups and with direct report managers of differing styles. Let's make sure you get what you need to grow your skills as your job scope expands and your responsibilities for people increase. Let's work together to design a long-range coaching plan to help you develop the advanced communication skills you will need as a higher-level manager. I should have offered you management and communication training before you were promoted. I realize you have never had any of that training and yet you managed to be so successful. That's amazing. Managing and communicating at your new management level will be more complex, so we will include training as part of our plan. We will make sure part of that training is about learning about people's behavioral styles. You and I will meet regularly for coaching sessions so we can partner on your progress on our plan. With this coaching help, I know you will meet our mutual goal that you develop top-notch communication skills so you can continue your track record as a first-rate manager.

I want to tell you what Carol told me earlier today so we can figure out a plan of action to enhance your communication with Carol's team. Carol said that her team feels that you don't communicate well with them in terms of clarifying what you expect and then listening to their opinion of those expectations. They said you are not supportive in your ongoing assessment of their performance and you drive the project planning too hard. They are not used to formalized project planning and deadlines and may need some training. Let's hear what you have to say.

If Mark had given feedback like that, and positioned it as part of a collaborative coaching plan to develop Marcella's knowledge and skills, Marcella might not have run crying to the ladies' room and then left work as soon as she had composed herself. If Mark had given the ideal feedback, he could have asked Marcella questions to help her work out a plan to address her relationship with Carol and Carol's staff. Marcella would have been informed about specific observed behaviors, so she would know *what* to change, and given resources, so she could learn *how* to change. But this became a lost opportunity because Mark did not have the managerial and coaching skills himself. As it turned out, they never spoke of it again. The feedback evaporated into the air. But the problems and tension remained. Now, after several years of a good, collegial relationship with her boss, Marcella no longer trusted Mark. The relationship, unfortunately, was irreparably damaged. And Marcella struggled with communication issues, not knowing the root cause of the problems or how to fix them.

Feedback can be a one-time event. Coaching is an ongoing process. It incorporates feedback into a more *strategic and comprehensive* plan. It uses feedback as a foundation to fortify an ongoing partnership so that the employee can be successful. Using the previous "The Queen" example, the coaching would consist of identifying communication behaviors that prevented collaboration between Marcella and Carol and Carol's team. Mark and Marcella would explore what behaviors would be most effective and how Marcella thought she could best develop them.

Coaching and Generational Differences

Coaching is a one-on-one communication skill that is emerging as one of the key success factors for managers. The purpose of coaching is to aid direct reports so that they have the information, skills, and organizational support they need to be highly productive, achieve peak performance, and thus meet organizational goals. It is a very collegial process—a partnership. The intention is to use communication skills and a good relationship to raise the level of performance.

This partnership is increasingly important to members of Generation Y, who are known to be more collegial in approach. In general, this generation enjoys working with people rather than in isolation. Office furniture has even been designed to accommodate these workers, who want to be next to, not in cubicles away from, their coworkers. They need a manager who can lead casual, collaborative conversations with them to help them grow their portfolio of skills. They understand they will be changing jobs in their lifetime and will need to collect a wide range of abilities to make them marketable. They expect coaching.

Coaching is important to other generations in the workforce also. Most workers, regardless of generation, want acknowledgment that their contribution is important and is noticed. More-experienced employees reporting to less-experienced (code for younger) managers have different coaching needs. A manager may or may not think the more-experienced worker has skill-development needs. But in all likelihood, the older worker has had it reinforced for years that his skills and contributions are acceptable, or perhaps even exceed expectations. A savvy younger manager understands this and uses it as the beginning conversation when setting up a coaching plan.

If the relationship is to be truly collegial, the experienced employee must be acknowledged for his contribution and invited to share ideas on the inevitable changes in the working relationship with his manager. One of the questions to be answered is how to best use the expertise of the more-experienced employee. Many companies are pairing baby boomers with other generations and letting both parties contribute and enjoy the best each generation has to offer. It goes back to relationship, which knows no generational boundaries. Relationships can be nourished as long as there is mutual respect and intention to work amicably together. So, in coaching, if the intent is to grow the relationship as well as the performance, the focus is people, not generations.

Benefits of Coaching

Coaching benefits everyone—the manager, the organization as a whole, and the direct report who is the recipient of coaching.

Benefits to the Leader

One of the most rewarding activities a manager can perform is to help a direct report expand skills, develop potential, and achieve success. Promoting the advancement of others increases one's own skill sets and widens one's sphere of influence. This depth and breadth of competence and confidence in the people side of the business inspires respect and trust from both direct reports and upper management. It prepares a manager for even greater responsibilities.

Coaching is a gift you give to others who want to achieve greatness. You share your aptitude, talent, knowledge, and skill to help others develop their own. As employees move in the direction of accomplishment, the manager generates a comfortable, low-stress environment. Strong relationships and commitment to organizational processes are possible to attain as members of the team buy in to mutual success. This team commitment attracts better recruits from within and outside the organization as it grows. It also prevents people problems and thus decreases turnover—an expensive, time-consuming, and team-disrupting occurrence. In an economic downturn, coaching is just as important to help employees minimize stress and maximize productivity. Downsizing is distracting and emotional, as employees survive the parting of friends and coworkers, and the workload increases. Taking time to coach people in any type of economy saves the manager time and is more efficient over the long haul.

Benefits to the Organization

The entire organization benefits when its managers coach employees. Coaching is one of the best practices a manager can provide to the company. It creates an interactive environment that encourages positive and effective work behavior. This management practice leads to long-term success through constant team improvement and thus a stronger, more cohesive, better functioning team. Team success instills a sense of security for the team.

When coaching is a management habit, it fosters respect, loyalty, and commitment to the team and the whole organization. It shapes trusting relationships in which honest, open communication reduces stress for everyone.

Coaching helps people learn about their own ideas and develop competence, which leads to personal job satisfaction and empowerment. Developing others helps the manager succeed in a manager's main job: to get results through others. The partnership that coaching creates offers the opportunity to listen to feedback from employees and to work collaboratively. Ultimately, good relationships contribute to quality results, which translate to profitability and shareholder value. This spills over to the organization's reputation in the industry, to customers, and to job seekers.

When a continual learning environment is established, it sets people up for success. To achieve goals and higher performance from individuals, the manager acts as a sports coach would: training and providing immediate feedback as well as engaging in long-term supportive interactions. Coaching increases safety on the job, prevents disciplinary issues, and ups team morale. Most of all, coaching creates working partnerships that convey the manager's intention to help each employee develop competence and happiness in the organization so all employees can do their personal best.

Benefits to the Person Receiving Coaching

Coaching clarifies and communicates expectations over the long term. It reaffirms organizational goals and why they are important. People need to be reminded that what they are doing is important and how it fits into the big picture of the organization. This increases motivation and enhances relationships and team dynamics. When people are informed about how they are doing in relation to the goal, it keeps them on track. This constant communication about performance reduces stress and fear of the unknown. A more relaxed environment improves morale and enables people to focus on the work.

The personal attention of the coach is tailor-made for the individual's goals, talent development, and triumphs. Coaching makes it possible for employees to receive positive performance appraisals—which can lead to increases in compensation. It makes the learning and the job easier and more meaningful. Being an active member of a partnership for ideal performance encourages buy-in, ownership, commitment, and full participation. If your direct reports are managers or potential managers, they learn effective coaching skills by being coached well.

As coaching adds to employee professional growth and development, it builds self-assurance to accept greater responsibility. This promotes long-term success and career opportunities, and helps with succession planning.

Coaching Behaviors

It's important to neither overcoach nor undercoach, but to give the employee whatever information and support she needs to succeed. This implies the manager has developed a relationship with the employee and understands his or her talents. Assumptions that a person does or does not have certain knowledge or skills can derail coaching. The manager must continue the partnership throughout the coaching meetings.

The point of coaching is to enhance individual performance, which brims over into the well-being of the entire team. The purpose is not to point out shortcomings and hang people out to dry, call them out, or make them feel demoralized. If the gears of the relationship have been kept oiled, the coaching session will be a collaborative discussion. The manager is less likely to be defensive or fearful when she has built a relationship and established that her aim is always to support the employee's best interests and align them with the organizational interests. Coaching should demonstrate that the employee is a valued member of the team and that you want to help the person thrive on the job.

Positive coaching behaviors on the part of the manager will reinforce the message the coaching is meant to convey. Perhaps the most important action will be listening with a neutral, nonemotional reaction. True listening means not interrupting, not advising, but showing interest with open body language, eye contact, and enough silence to let the person explain the meaning of her comments. Listening is an action because it requires intention and attention. The intention is the desire to maintain the relationship and help the employee achieve greatness. The attention is taking the time to prepare for coaching sessions and then participating in partnering dialogues with as much time as is necessary. We talk more about listening in Chapter 11.

One of the overriding coaching behaviors is not judging, but defining facts and observable behaviors. Preparing for coaching incorporates the concepts discussed in Chapter 6 on breaking judging habits.

The preparation also includes a factual assessment of the direct report's skills and building the confidence to state them honestly and directly yet listen to the employee's viewpoint to gather more facts. Working out key take-away action items is an appropriate coaching behavior. Coaches need to present the information in a positive context of continual learning that directly benefits the employee. A coach who is excited about the possibilities of growth and development, she generates enthusiasm and forward movement with the direct report.

Preparing questions and also asking spontaneous questions to facilitate the employee's thinking so she can create her own plan of action contributes to buy-in and increased potential for changed behaviors. Empower the employee by agreeing to her plan (if workable), even if it is different from yours. Encourage and praise the person for current accomplishments. Consider role-playing, if it will help the employee. Share personal anecdotes of times when you were improving the same skills or how coaching has helped you progress. Provide the tools and resources the employee needs. Set a time for the next follow-up coaching session because it sets expectations that there should be progress on a timeline. Be accessible in between coaching meetings. Keep the follow-up coaching meeting that you committed to. It shows that skill development is important to you and increases your credibility.

Two Types of Coaching

There are two basic types of coaching: telling and asking. Both have a purpose and an appropriate use depending on the work that needs to get done and the skill level of the employee.

Telling coaching is sometimes called directive, or pushing, coaching, because you push information and directions on the person you are coaching. The coach does not ask the direct report's opinion because there is only one way to do it, there is a crucial deadline, and/or the person is new to this particular work.

Asking coaching is sometimes called discovery, exploring, or pulling coaching, because, by asking questions, the coach pulls information from the direct report, who discovers his own answers, solves his own problems, and makes his own decisions. This creates sought-after buy-in and ownership because the solutions belong to the employee. This kind of coaching is collegial in nature and requires partnership behaviors.

Telling Coaching

Telling coaching is appropriate in some situations. When telling, the role of the manager is to reinforce previous training, guide, and advise. The manager does not make *suggestions* because this gives a direct report an option to accept or reject the information. Telling is not suggesting. It is *expecting* the task to be done in one particular way. Asking a person's opinion when there is no option to include it will only make her angry, distrustful, and unwilling to contribute ideas when they are needed.

Managers often misuse telling coaching because it is most expedient. Sometimes an employee asks for help and the manager replies by telling him what to do. "Just do it this way" is faster than talking, asking questions, and listening. Sometimes managers improperly tell, instead of ask, when they want employees to do the job the way the manager used to do it. Other ways might work, but it is safer and faster to tell about a proven way to do it instead of exploring the employee's ideas. However, in the long run it takes longer for an employee to become fully competent and trust her own judgment if the manager keeps giving instructions instead of teaching the employee how to be responsible for her own work and be self-sufficient.

There seems to be a link between managers who are reluctant to delegate and those who slip into telling coaching. Some managers fear that employees will not get the work done as well as it would be done if the managers do it themselves. Some at least want the work done the way they always did it. It has worked well in the past to do the tasks that way. In fact, their methods of getting results may have been what earned them the promotion to manager. However, to fulfill their objectives of getting results through and with others, managers must move on and lead others to successfully do the work. Oftentimes, the employee has a different, new, or even better way of getting things done.

Asking Coaching

Asking coaching takes more time in the short run because the manager has to think of nonleading questions that will help the employee think about how to solve his own problem or make his own decision. Then the manager has to listen to the answers and, without casting judgments, ask more questions until the employee feels comfortable that he has a course of his own that will indeed work.

Many managers fall into the trap of solving employees' problems because "they asked." If an employee goes to the manager for direction, she may need it. However, often employees go because they don't trust themselves, a previous manager always told them to do it one way that was the manager's way, they fear repercussions, or they are trying to reduce the potential of rework.

Just because a direct report asks a manager to solve a problem for her does not mean it is the smartest course of action a manager can take. A manager's overarching job is to get quality work done through others. This means the manager must help each direct report develop to be the most knowledgeable and skilled worker she can be. A person whose manager is the source of all knowledge does not fully develop in the job she is paid to do.

An intelligent manager looks down the road at the cost of not doing asking coaching. If employees do not learn to take full control of their jobs, the manager's time will be sucked away. The manager will have little time to do strategic thinking and the level of work appropriate to his or her position and grade. So although asking coaching takes more time initially, in the long run it saves time. Eventually, employees learn to ask themselves the questions necessary to come up with effective answers.

When to Use Telling Coaching

Telling coaching communicates both *what* is expected and *how* to get a task done. It is a supportive tool to use because employees can feel confident that they are doing something the correct way when there is only one way to do something.

Suitable times to tell a direct report how to do the task are:

- ➤ For routine, repetitive tasks: for example, order fulfillment and purchase order follow-up
- ➤ For standard reports: for example, expense reports
- ➤ When procedures and policies are already defined
- ➤ For new task assignments
- ➤ When deadlines are looming
- ➤ When setting goals/corporate goals from upper management
- ➤ When following instruction manuals for machines
- ➤ For Standard Operating Procedures (SOPs)
- ➤ When introducing new policy
- ➤ During emergency, crisis situations when there is no time for asking coaching
- ➤ For simple tasks with no room for interpretation
- ➤ For impromptu projects with no lead time
- ➤ For anything with legal or compliance ramifications (when it must be done a certain way)
- ➤ For health and safety issues
- ➤ For disaster planning

➤ When directed by a boss to do it a certain way and passing it on to your direct report

➤ When telling "guidelines" for company objectives

➤ When setting expectations

➤ When choosing the direction/telling after ideas are generated

➤ For performance improvement plans

➤ For new hires

➤ During some training: for example, using software, operating machines

➤ When asking coaching fails and the employee is demonstrating a performance problem

➤ When dealing with a timid employee or one who does not want responsibility

When to Use Asking Coaching

Asking coaching communicates *what* needs to get done but helps the direct report figure out *how* to get a task done and to take ownership of the solution. This tool empowers and energizes the employee because the coach's questions allow a person to discover and explore his own solutions. This both demonstrates the manager's confidence in the employee and reinforces the employee's trust in himself. When the employee bears responsibility for deciding and taking action to achieve the outcome, the employee tends to own the outcome and the process to get there. The coach acts more as a catalyst to prompt the employee's own thinking.

Applicable times to use asking coaching are:

➤ Whenever a manager can delegate the "how"

➤ For research

➤ For professional development/personal growth

➤ When the project/process calls for an experienced person or one with specific education/certification to do the work (for example, an engineer, a librarian, etc.)

➤ When the employee has more domain-specific knowledge

- For more technical tasks
- During process improvements
- For individual challenges
- During problem solving, decision making, and planning
- For career progression and determining career path
- When the employee has done a similar task or project in the past
- When determining how an employee will reach a goal
- During participative training, where participants are highly involved
- When identifying roles, responsibilities, and level of authority
- During conflict resolution
- When building accountability/"ownership"
- When learning about an employee's process skills—how he approaches a project
- For discovering the depth of a direct report's knowledge
- When a competent employee asks for help or is not sure of an answer
- When a direct report asks for more responsibility and you need to create a plan
- During weekly progress meetings
- During annual performance review meetings
- When getting ideas on restructuring, creating new positions, introducing new products or projects
- For developing more advanced skills

Process for Asking Coaching

Relationships will always rule. Make all efforts to preserve the relationship while speaking in a neutral, nonjudgmental, but direct and honest way. Be supportive. Follow all the steps shown for "before" and "during" coaching for the best outcome in terms of both relationship and business results.

Before Coaching

> **Prepare ahead of time.** It is important to revisit job expectations when preparing for coaching. Then gather facts about performance as

they relate to expectations. Is performance at its peak, and you want to help keep it there? Is performance right on track, and you'd like to help the employee escalate it to excellence? Is performance off course, and you want to steer it back on target?

➤ **Decide if your coaching is telling or asking or a combination of both.** List questions you will ask the employee to stimulate her thinking about current performance, skills, organizational supports and obstacles, problem analysis, and decision making.

➤ **Set up the coaching meeting and give the employee time to prepare.** This can be part of your routine progress meeting or scheduled separately.

During the Coaching Meeting

➤ **Open the conversation.** Tell employee the purpose of coaching. Say you want to work together to set up a plan to help him develop a particular skill or meet a particular goal. Set your comments in positive terms and within the context of continual learning. (Remember the previous "Marcella/Queen" example on enhancing communication skills for higher-level management positions?)

➤ **Get agreement on the expectation or goal and how it benefits the employee.** Always ensure that the employee understands the benefit to him.

➤ **Find out the employee's assessment of his performance as it relates to the goal.** Ask open-ended questions and listen to the answers. Paraphrase the answers and clarify as you go. Facilitate a discussion in which the direct report does most of the talking and most of the thinking through of the issues.

➤ **Give feedback.** Keep it in the context of the big picture of the ongoing coaching plan. Offer specific, factual observations on progress as it directly relates to expectations. If the employee disagrees, ask questions, revisit facts, and keep conversing until you agree on the facts.

➤ **If there is resistance to the feedback, refocus the conversation.** Ask the employee's perspective through a neutral statement, such as, "Tell me more about that." Paraphrase the employee's point of view to show you understand what he is saying. (This does not mean you necessarily agree with the view, but it does mean you understand what he is trying to say.) If you don't understand the employee's viewpoint, ask questions to clarify meaning. Then ask open-ended questions to discover his rationale. There may be facts you don't know that change the direction to take next. But, if the employee is just offering excuses, refocus on observed behaviors and facts.

➤ **Work out the next steps together.** Learn about the employee's ideas of what he can do to move performance toward the goal. What would his next steps look like? What resources does he need? What obstacles do you need to remove so he can succeed? What are your own ideas for next steps? Decide mutually on what is best.

➤ **Energize the employee.** Infuse the conversation with enthusiasm and excitement about the employee's plan of action. Discuss the logic and benefits of the employee's approach.

➤ **Sum up and clarify.** Ask the employee to sum up the discussion of the expected performance goals, current performance, and the action steps and timeline to get there.

➤ **Set up the next collaborative coaching conversation.**

Is It the *Manager* Who Needs Coaching?

Sometimes an indication that the manager needs training or coaching is when she catches herself blaming or judging an employee. Mary, a manager participating in a management class, complained about a direct report.

"She is Mt. Vesuvius!" she exclaimed.

"What does Mt. Vesuvius mean?" I asked.

"She's like a volcano that erupts every day."

Mary was a newly promoted first-time supervisor who was Generation Y. Ginny was her direct report. Ginny, a baby boomer, had been doing the job for fifteen years. Mary was upset about having to work with Ginny because she felt Ginny was "Mt. Vesuvius."

As mentioned in Chapter 6 on unraveling judgments, managers sometimes judge and blame the employee when there is a problem. Mary first defined her problem by blaming Ginny and calling her "Mt. Vesuvius." Imagine the scenario from Ginny's vantage point. She comes in to work every day and her boss sees her as a giant volcano about to spill over with hot lava, instead of seeing her as a person. Ginny cannot meet her boss's expectations because she does not know what they are.

As Mary and I used the unraveling judgments process explained in Chapter 6, Mary tried to redefine the problem in factual, behavioral terms. This was difficult. At first Mary redefined the problem as, "Ginny does not respect me because I am younger than she is." I kept asking open-ended questions to help Mary peel back one layer at a time. Finally, Mary got to the actual behavior she had observed.

The observed behavior was that Ginny was following the same procedures she had always followed. She did the job exactly the same way she had done it for years. All those years she was rewarded for her performance and got high performance appraisal ratings. Now Ginny had a new manager but the new manager had not stated any change in what Ginny was to do.

As we worked at solving the problem, Mary recognized she had not made her expectations clear. She also realized that the procedures were probably out of date. In this case, the employee was getting blamed daily because of organizational obstacles: out-of-date procedures, lack of clear managerial direction, and no notification that a change in the way to do the work had taken place.

Although Mary had bruised the relationship, it could be healed. Mary, the manager, made a plan for what to do when she got back to work. She intended to tell Ginny that she wanted to make a fresh beginning of working well together. Then she would discuss the misunderstanding. Her next step would be to seek Ginny's input on why she was doing the work the way she was doing it. Mary would read the procedures and discuss whether they were useful or should be changed with Ginny. Mary planned to ask questions to seek Ginny's expertise and experience and show she valued both.

Mary would then decide if there was discretion for Ginny to determine the *how* or if the work demanded strictly following procedure. Mary would also determine if she was insisting on work being done her own way when Ginny's way might work just as well. If the work needed to be done only one way, she would lead a conversation about the new expectations and the logic behind why the changes had been made. She would discuss why it was important to do the work the new way.

Perhaps most important, Mary would acknowledge that Ginny was previously reinforced to do the job a different way by previous managers. Mary would clarify that her expectations represented a *change.*

During the discussions with Ginny, Mary said she planned to ask open-ended questions to help Ginny express her feelings about the changed expectations. Questions would also help Ginny figure out how to work the new way so she could meet the new expectations.

Mary was excited about how much she learned in the management training. She had a roadmap of what to do to solve people problems and prevent them in the future. She realized that she needed to create a plan for growing her management knowledge and expertise. She decided to ask her manager for ongoing coaching so she could learn more about how to effectively delegate, give feedback, and coach.

Summary

Coaching, including giving targeted feedback, offers a collaborative approach to helping direct reports do their best work and succeed. Isn't that one of a manager's primary goals—to help others achieve success? Using a logical coaching process helps the manager stay on track to give the employee what he needs based on the goals or project. When coaching is done well, it strengthens the working relationships between managers and their employees.

Coaching assumes that setting clear expectations and delegating have been done well in the first place. We look more closely at delegating in the next chapter, Chapter 10.

CHAPTER

10

DREAM Delegating Ensures Clarity and Collaboration

This chapter helps managers define the task or project to be done and determine who should be doing it. This chapter draws on the content of many of the previous chapters. Proficient delegation requires clarifying and communicating expectations, using process and project management skills to identify tasks and timelines, asking questions, not judging people, but seeking facts, and leaning on collaborative relationships.

Delegation starts with the performance expectation and not with assumptions that direct reports may interpret. This chapter reinforces the importance of the ideas in Chapter 2 on turbocharged clarity and in Chapter 3 on communicating your expectations.

What Is Delegation?

Delegation is assigning a task or project for which you are accountable but do not necessarily have to do yourself. It is trusting someone else to accomplish work and obtain a specified outcome, with certain performance standards. Level of authority varies for each responsibility and must be clearly identified before the employee starts work on the assignment.

Delegating work with low opportunity and high boredom will not build camaraderie. There should be positive reasons for delegating—

getting more work done, seeking more viewpoints and employee development, or making time for managerial tasks. Another measure to consider is what salary level is appropriate to the task. (How much would a completed task cost based on the number of hours times the "hourly" rate of pay for the manager versus that of the direct report?) A manager must also decide how to distribute the work to the team so each person can balance his or her workload.

Criteria for choosing the person to whom to delegate varies and must be clearly delineated. What is the nature of the task? What knowledge and skills are required to successfully complete it? How much time is available? Can I train someone? Can this be a development opportunity for a particular employee? Do we need someone who already has the experience on this or similar tasks because of criticality of the project, visibility, or time constraints?

Determining required skills and experience for a task or project is essential. The manager can identify who has the necessary capability to minimize the manager's involvement in the tasks. Or, the manager can delegate the task to someone who needs to develop those skills. This will necessitate proper training and more coaching but bring a return on that investment over time.

When to Delegate and How to Trust

Managers are often concerned about how to balance their time and responsibilities and those of their direct reports. Sometimes they wonder what to delegate and when. You cannot delegate if you do not have the authority over the task or project. This leads us back to Chapter 2 on turbocharged clarity. Remember Figure 2-1: "Clarifying Expectations Worksheet"? Once you understand areas where you have full authority, you can decide how much of that authority you are willing or able to delegate.

After you decide how much of the task and what level of authority you will delegate, decide how much to delegate to each individual.

Chunk it down into pieces if you are not comfortable delegating the whole task or project. You can keep parts and parcel out parts to one or more people.

Then, pick the correct people and trust them to drive it to completion. But, one of the ways to increase trust is to set checkpoints and monitor progress along the way. So trust your intuition. What does your intuition tell you about this particular task or project delegated to this particular person? What information will you need and when will you need it to feel comfortable that the job is getting done according to specification, within budget, and on time? Schedule progress check-ins accordingly. Maybe your weekly progress meeting is sufficient and maybe not. A manager does not need to apologize for needing to know status. As time goes on, you might decide to stretch the checkpoints further apart. Trust grows, dependent on consistent delivery, not on how much we like people.

How to Increase Collaboration When Delegating

Some managers worry about the way they delegate. They think they are too authoritarian in their approach and get resistance from their employees because of it. They have asked, "How can I be more diplomatic in the way I request that something get done?"

One thing to remember is that delegation is not really a request—it is an assignment. A confident manager might word it as a request knowing that will increase collegiality and the employee's ownership of the task. That approach can work quite well to maintain good working relationships. But it takes a self-assured manager who has established a collaborative relationship to make it work.

Similarly, managers are not asking for a favor when they delegate work. It is the manager's job to decide who is best suited to do what by when. Sometimes managers who have well-built two-way relationships with employees will delegate by saying, "Can you do me a favor?" because they know the person will say yes and it is the nature of their relationship. It keeps things feeling more reciprocal. In fact, their employee might say the same to them, "Can you do me a favor?" when they need resources or help to get a project done. It all depends upon the relationship.

These phrases are ways to hold collaborative conversations in which both people view themselves as colleagues trying to meet the shared goals. They do not look at the organizational hierarchy when they work together. The energy flows. Managers who have not yet developed strong relationships might find themselves in the situation of one manager who intended to "request" something but actually displayed an authoritarian demeanor.

To increase collaboration, try these tips:

- Be confident that delegating is part of your job.
- Use a neutral, friendly tone of voice.
- Tell how the tasks fit company goals and why they are important.
- Tell why the delegatee was specifically selected.
- Invite questions.
- Listen.
- Understand the employee's style and adapt yours.
- Be respectful in language, tone and volume of voice, and body language.

Benefits of Delegation

Managers report numerous benefits of delegation to both themselves and to the delegatee. Here are some reasons to delegate for the greater use of each person's talents and abilities.

Benefits to the Manager

The more a manager delegates, the better he develops that skill. This prepares him for a broader scope of responsibilities. Not only does the manager enhance delegation skills, he builds other managerial skills by focusing on higher-level tasks. The manager can focus on long-term strategies and planning, for example. This creates a more efficient use of time for the whole team.

Because delegation frees up time, the manager can attend to more advanced work that demands and improves managerial skills. Having these skills leads to success as a leader. Part of leading is having time to enhance training and mentoring of staff, so the effect is cyclical.

Frequent delegating helps managers build trust in people because direct reports have the opportunity to demonstrate that they can and will deliver results. A pattern of accomplishment emerges and shows that delegating pays off. And the manager gets a chance to learn about the skills and abilities of his employees. This can lead to delegating more complex work.

The more the direct reports have an opportunity to showcase their knowledge and expertise, the more strengthened and motivated the team. Teamwork is built when many hands are working collaboratively toward shared goals. The more team members that a manager delegates to, the greater the diversity of ideas and new perspectives. Inviting fresh perspectives leads to innovation and process streamlining. Eliciting full team involvement increases commitment and enjoyment for everyone.

Delegating leverages the technical skills of individual contributors, who are often better matched to the technical demands of the project than the manager. In addition, delegation offers cross-training, which is in the best interest of the business. It also ensures productivity when the manager is away and increases the readiness of employees to step up to new accountabilities and to be potentially promoted from within.

Delegating provides variety for both managers and employees when they take on different tasks. It also offers efficient use of skills and talent appropriate to the task. This should have the effect of productivity and higher output for the team, perhaps leading to increased revenue.

When a manager confidently delegates, it demonstrates achievement of the overall management responsibility to develop others and get ideal results with and through direct reports. It improves the organization by creating a well-knit, smooth running, collaborative team. Delegation trains future leaders, which strengthens the fabric of the organization. And managers find they can discover "diamonds in the rough" when they give direct reports opportunities to excel.

Benefits to the Direct Report

When the manager trusts an employee with new, perhaps higher-level work, it also engenders the employee's trust in the manager. Trust flows reciprocally. Trust and increased levels of responsibility empower direct reports and offer them more visibility in the team and organization.

Trust builds rapport and a feeling of working "with," not "for." This collegiality often makes direct reports feel valued and useful. It can motivate and engage employees. It can also secure buy-in, project ownership, and accountability.

Sometimes these delegated tasks offer networking opportunities, which benefit the individual as well as the whole team. Advanced-level tasks provide the opportunity to do something new, develop new skill sets, prove knowledge in another area, and get recognition. The tasks or projects may present the opportunity for the employee to make recommendations, do things in his own way, or demonstrate his unique expertise. This proven success enhances employees' qualifications for broader responsibilities and promotion. The direct report might develop the reputation as a "go-to" resident expert or subject matter expert (SME). He may also earn the skills necessary to fill in or be the backup replacement for the manager.

As people learn new tasks and progress in abilities, they gain a sense of accomplishment and job satisfaction. They may experience a heightened confidence level in their knowledge and value to the organization. Staff morale is enhanced with an increased sense of competencies.

Why Are Managers Reluctant to Delegate?

Managers recognize the many benefits of delegation; why, then, is it so difficult to delegate? Managers can come up with many barriers to delegating. They say they are reluctant to delegate for personal reasons of their own and for reactions they suspect their employees *might* have.

Managers' Personal Reasons

One reason some managers do not delegate is because they fear they will lose their technical skills. They want to keep them honed, especially to be prepared when there is an economic downturn. Also they may feel that they are better at the old job than they are at the new one if they are a new manager. Since they were probably promoted because of outstanding technical skills, they may feel, correctly, that no one on the team measures up to the expertise they achieved. This means it is easier for the manager to do it herself because she can do it faster or better than any of her direct reports. Some managers fear that time will be wasted on rework. This may be the case until direct reports come up to speed on the new responsibilities. But the manager will end up doing the task forever if she does not delegate, and this will take a lot more time than developing an employee.

In the short term, delegating may take more time for the manager than doing it himself. The manager may think it will be more stress to delegate because he will have to set and clarify goals, decide and communicate timelines, train, follow up, and give feedback. There may be communication difficulties, and he may think there is no time for questions or instruction. If the manager has time-management issues, the manager may think he has no time to spend with direct reports. We are all limited by the time available, but a big part of the manager's job is to spend time with staff and help them grow and produce work.

Some managers doubt their own abilities. They may feel a sense of insecurity. Some say they have weak training skills and it is time-consuming to train direct reports. Others say they are unskilled in how to prioritize and properly decide what to delegate and to whom. These skills can be developed in training classes or by coaching from the manager's boss. Reaching out to managers who are more experienced in delegating easily solves lack of current ability.

Fear prevents some managers from delegating. They may fear loss of control, that quality and standards might dive, that employees do not have the competency, or that they cannot trust others to do the work. Still others are afraid that a strong-minded employee will intimidate them. Experience will nurture confidence to overcome these fears. It is a bit like swimming. You cannot learn to swim until you get into the pool.

When managers lack authority or are unsure of their level of authority, they rightfully avoid delegating. Following the recommended steps in Chapter 2 on getting turbocharged clarity from your boss can prevent this. If you lack upper management support and guidance this must also be discussed immediately with your manager. Managers cannot successfully delegate without having authority in the first place and knowing that management will back them up.

Reluctance to delegate can be caused by a lack of resources and qualified, competent employees. Sometimes a manager is concerned about adding stress to employees and does not want to overload or overwhelm them. Some managers feel guilty, or do not want to be perceived as lazy or taking the easy way out.

If a manager got burned in the past when an employee did not come through with a completed assignment, she may not want to delegate. Or, the manager may find it difficult to balance check-ins and oversight with leaving direct reports alone to work independently.

Virtual and remote delegation requires more complex communication. The work may be 24/7, 365 days a year. Lack of face-to-face contact is challenging when the manager needs to discuss and clarify delegation issues. In addition, there are time barriers when managing people remotely around the world. Language and cultural barriers also play a part in reluctance to delegate when managing remotely or virtually. Sometimes e-mail delegation is the only option, and e-mail can easily be misunderstood or ignored.

A manager who worries about not getting personal kudos after delegating tasks need not be troubled. If a manager is a skilled delegator, his staff will accomplish the goals and meet all the specifications. This is the manager's true responsibility, so the manager should receive recognition for succeeding in managerial work.

Concerns About Employee Opinion

Some managers are disinclined to delegate because they imagine the employees might view the delegation negatively. These managers think employees may not be committed enough to the manager or the organization. Or they think direct reports might resist accepting more work; another assignment could be perceived as punishment. Employees might say, "It is not my job." Employees could think that there are unequal workloads among team members.

Assigning certain plum tasks could generate comments about favoritism and cause dissension among team members. On the other side of the coin, unimportant, tedious tasks could demotivate employees, and they could think the boring task assignment is not fair. Managers say that employees fear getting an increased workload on a continual basis if they agree to take on one new task—especially if they do it well.

Delegatees may think they do not have the skill or experience to do a certain task and fear making mistakes or even failure. They may worry about lack of support or have an opinion that the manager is pushing work down on them. Direct reports might have concerns that the priorities will change midstream and the work will be for naught.

All of these delegatee concerns can be controlled by a skillful delegator who follows a process and keeps communication channels open. If direct reports think they will do all the work and someone else will get all the credit, assure them you will provide them with plenty of positive recognition when the task is completed as required.

Challenges When Delegating

Managers mention many challenges when delegating. These include:

- ➤ Virtual or remote delegation (staff work on other continents, countries, cities, sites, or at home, rather than physically where the manager works)

- Language barriers
- All communication being via e-mail and phone because of location
- Time needed to provide support when delegating
- Delegating to a "green" staff (little experience)
- Knowing how to delegate to different skill levels (adjusting to each delegatee's experience)
- Work that changes and grows daily
- Allowing others to do it their way, which may be different than the manager's way
- Knowledge transfer challenges (for example, details on software)
- Employees who are more experienced than the delegator

When an Employee Refuses an Assignment

One manager, Rosa, asked me, "What can I do when an employee I am delegating to is constantly negative?" I probed to find out what she meant by "negative"—what were the observable behaviors that the manager could see and hear.

When the manager attempted to delegate, the employee, Brenda, had a plethora of replies. I've included all of them in the dialogue of the role-play that follows. Brenda consistently refuses the assignment. Brenda makes firm, rigid comments such as, "This is not going to work."

If this ever happens to you, here are a few suggestions. First, don't get rattled—stay calm and neutral. If you cannot stay composed, set a time to resume the conversation and go do some deep breathing and deep thinking. Next, when you are ready to continue the conversation, start asking open-ended questions to gain information. Stay with the facts and do not deviate into judgments or emotions.

I suggested to Rosa that we role-play to show how to deal with an employee who refuses an assignment. Here is a reconstruction of the role-play using Brenda's actual comments and reactions.

Role Play: How to Handle an Employee Who Refuses an Assignment
Employee: "This is not going to work."
Manager: "Well Brenda, what exactly is not going to work?"

Employee: "This extra assignment! What do you think I'm talking about?"

Manager: "What is happening with your responsibilities that makes you say it won't work?"

Employee: "I'm not going to do it. I have other things to do."

Manager: "Let's review your workload and see what we can rearrange. What do you see as your current priorities?"

Employee: "We're wasting valuable time here just talking when I could be working."

Manager: "Well, discussing workloads and priorities is a responsibility we both share as part of our jobs. Let's talk about what is on your plate and I will take a few notes. What is your most important project (task)?"

Employee: "Look. I've got witnesses, examples, and supportive evidence that I am overworked." (Goes into detail on each of the three.)

Manager: "This is very interesting. How long did it take you to compile all this?"

Employee: "I've been tracking it for a while."

Manager: "I wish you had come to discuss your feelings with me, but let's think about this. Do you know what your salary equates to on an hourly basis?"

Employee: "No."

Manager: "About $30 an hour, so think about how much it cost the company to pay you to compile this."

Employee: "I did it at home."

Manager: "Okay, fair enough. But you could have saved a lot of time by talking to me. I want us to have a good working relationship. If you feel overworked, we need to talk specifically about what your tasks and priorities are.

Employee: "Sigh." (Rolls eyes.)

Manager: "You know, Brenda, I have valued your expertise in. . . . We need that expertise now on this new task/project."

Employee: "Flattery will get you nowhere. I'm not going to do it."

Manager: "Brenda, I'm sorry you feel that way. I was hoping we could work collaboratively toward our goals. It does not seem like you want to work this out with me."

Employee: "You got that right."

Manager: "Brenda, your job requires you to take on assignments that need to be done and to work with me on status. I am going to give you tonight to think over how we still might work together on defining a balanced workload and priorities. Tomorrow I want to meet with you at 10:00 a.m. in my office. If you have decided to work with me we will talk about your priorities and this new one in particular. We will discuss all your job requirements and how you plan to meet them looking forward. If you need help from me, we will plan that in. However, if you decide not to accept assignments and not to discuss your workload and status with me, I'm going to begin the counseling process, which will include documenting our discussions and getting Human Resources involved. It's your choice, but I do value your contribution and hope you decide to work with me as a team. I'll see you at 10:00 a.m. tomorrow."

After such a discussion with an employee, stand up with neutral, friendly body language and end the meeting. Go directly to your boss and, in a competent, businesslike way, discuss the situation and how you are handling it before your direct report goes to your boss or begins rumors. Write up your notes as an incident report to be kept for future reference if you need to start the counseling process. Contact Human Resources for advice if you think it would prepare you for the 10:00 a.m. meeting.

Process or Hallway Delegation?

More formal delegation, using a process, will assure the most success for the majority of assignments, especially for long-term project work. This is because of the time the delegator takes to clarify exactly what is and what is not desired. Using a process provides the logical steps that remind a manager to consider all the parameters, such as the interdependencies of tasks and projects with other coworkers or departments. What happens to the big-picture goal if this delegation is made? Chapter 4 on process and project management covers these critical issues. Using a process also gives the manager and employee time to clarify specifics and ramifications, clear the air on any concerns or workload issues that require reprioritizing, and prevent people problems through making it a collaborative conversation. If a manager is going to entrust someone else to achieve results for which she is accountable, the manager can get the best results by following a rational process rather than spontaneously assigning accountability in passing.

Corporate culture must also be taken into consideration in terms of how work is usually delegated. But, sometimes corporate culture must be challenged. Just because it is the usual way of doing things does not mean it provides the best communication, the most cost-effective method, the least-confusing way, or the best way to ensure all projects coordinate with each other. "We have always done it this way," does not guarantee the best outcome or the most effective way to reach a goal. For example, one senior management high-tech group I conducted training with rebuffed the concept of setting clear expectations and using a process when delegating.

"We do 'hallway delegation' here," one of them said emphatically.

"Maybe that is why we have so many problems," the CEO commented. He continued that they needed to explore the idea of adding structure to their delegations since they were a growing company and might have outgrown hallway delegations.

Hallway delegation might work fine for some tactical delegations or for one-off tasks. For example:

"Will you go to the meeting for me tomorrow? You will need to prepare a, b, and c to present to the committee."

"Can you prepare a summary report on X by Thursday at 5:00 p.m.?"

"Would someone on your staff be able to edit this proposal for me by the end of the week?"

For more strategic work, hallway delegation may prevent success or cause communication and people problems. Lack of clarity when delegating can cost time, cause rework, and inadvertently pit groups against each other. Information might be incorrect or inconsistent with previous delegations. When the person accepting the responsibility is not clear enough on what to do, he or she may not meet the manager's expectations. The employee may stray from the desired direction.

At times, every manager must squeeze out as much quality work with as few staff members as possible. It is essential that delegation starts with communicating clear expectations so both manager and report have the same understanding of the expectation the first time. Everyone needs to save time.

A manager must be sure of the interdependencies of how this delegation relates to other teammates, projects, tasks, teams, and departments. This requires using a systematic process and not assigning work without considering the possible effects.

The DREAM process described in this chapter helps increase clarity and minimize stress for both the delegator and the employee accepting the assignment. It is imperative that managers do all they can to preserve employee commitment in times when every person is asked to do more.

DREAM Delegating Process

This DREAM process can help you gather your thoughts and prepare to delegate in a systematic way. It may take a little time to learn the process in the beginning, but it will save you time in the long run because it is a repeatable process that ensures as much clarity and collaboration as possible.

1. **Decide What and Who**
   - ➤ What task/project or portion of a project are you delegating?
   - ➤ To whom are you selecting to delegate and why?
   - ➤ What will you tell the delegatee about her skills and experience as they relate to the delegated work?

2. **Resources**
   - ➤ What help will you provide the delegatee to do the assignment?
   - ➤ What access to subject-matter experts, budget, equipment, staff or temporary staff, and materials will be available?
   - ➤ What will you do to ensure employee gets those resources?
   - ➤ How and when will you give feedback on progress?

➤ What kind of coaching and support will you provide the delegatee?

3. Expectations

➤ What is the goal of the work?

➤ What exactly does a successful outcome look like?

➤ What will a high-quality job look like in terms of quality, quantity, timeliness, and behaviors that contribute to teamwork?

➤ Are there other desired results, such as innovation and creativity?

➤ What will the evaluation criteria for success be?

➤ What is the budget and specified criteria?

➤ What is the deadline?

➤ What are the potential problems and opportunities? If problems occur, what support will be available? Who is the proper person to contact?

➤ What happens if critical performance standards are not met on time, within budget, and according to specified criteria?

4. Authority Level

➤ What level of authority does the delegatee have on this task or project? This can range from complete autonomy (she makes all the decisions and tells you what she has done) to low authority (she does it your way) or anything in between (such as making a recommendation and asking you before acting). Be very specific.

➤ How much discretion does the delegatee have about how to do the task or project? Be specific to prevent people and project problems.

5. Monitor with Milestone Reporting

➤ What are the milestones or check-in points along the way?

➤ At what events or dates will the check-ins be?

➤ Is there a computer system the employee must update?

➤ What feedback do you want to receive in between check-ins? How do you want to receive it—verbally or in writing?

To Delegate or Not to Delegate—That Is the Question

What to delegate depends on a number of variables. Every manager must decide continually what is appropriate to delegate depending on the task, workload, deadlines, priorities, and availability of people with the needed skills.

Sometimes managers can create innovative projects that did not exist before and delegate them. For example, in my first management job in systems and procedures, I decided our group would systematize and document our workflow just like we did for all the other areas of the company. The senior procedures analysts divided up all the work we did into areas that interested them. They streamlined any processes and documented them. I modified or approved the procedures. We now had a reference manual as well as a training tool. Each of the senior analysts became the go-to expert or SME for a phase of our work. They trained the new hires. And the manual made it possible for other analysts to hone skills and develop the capability to train people in all areas. The project developed great teamwork among existing staff, who showcased their expert knowledge. And the new people immediately had the opportunity to get to know an informal mentor who could help them as they developed skills.

What to Delegate

What could you delegate to your team right now? A list of possibilities follows. Other managers have said they could delegate these responsibilities, and maybe this list will trigger ideas for your situation:

- Data entry and data recording on reports
- Running some meetings
- Attending some meetings for the manager
- Routine reports
- Technical troubleshooting
- Safety meeting presentation
- Discovering or researching solutions to problems
- Scheduling
- Certain client interactions

- Orientation and training for new employees
- Preparing and delivering presentations
- Case reports for legal arbitration
- Inventory planning
- Engineering drawing requests
- Weekly report on invoice data
- Coordinating with purchasing department
- Workflow and process improvement

What Not to Delegate

Your situation may vary, but here are general guidelines for what not to delegate:

- Any assignments you don't have full authority on
- Work with legal consequences for the organization
- Confidential activities (giving feedback, coaching, counseling, final hiring decisions, terminations, performance reviews, salary decisions, payroll information, and any performance documentation to Human Resources)
- Monitoring and evaluating staff's work
- Final budgeting decisions—although you might ask for input
- Running staff meetings
- Final decisions on strategic planning, goal setting, developing a vision (although a collaborative manager will include employees in formulating these)
- Audits

When Your Boss Overdelegates to You

Have you ever had a manager give you more work and say, "Just figure out a way to get it all done"? If you think your boss has overdelegated to you and your staff, be sure to do your homework before discussing it with him. First, think about what you *can* do to adjust and possibly do what your boss has asked.

Probably you won't want to compromise the quality. It's usually a given that quality should not be sacrificed. However, sometimes *perception* of quality might need adjusting with direct reports. For example, in my first management job as the corporate procedures officer, my responsibility was to publish and maintain all the corporate operations manuals. Sometimes because of deadlines, the procedures analysts would approach me about whether I was looking for quality or quantity. They wanted me to pick one, as if they were mutually exclusive. All of us wanted top quality. But a challenge for many analysts and writers (my direct reports were both) is knowing when it is time to stop. To the analyst and writer mind there is always infinite room for new ideas and enhancement. Since we all wanted the best, we had to discuss how to deliver quality *and* quantity within the company's established deadlines of implementing new hardware, software, and major new methodologies. People's jobs were going to be transformed in major ways. The train was going to move ahead with or without us. Were we going to provide assistance on how to do their changing jobs throughout the corporation? Or were we going to hold off until we had perfected every word?

When more work than can be done descends on your desk, examine the quality versus quantity issue. Next, if you are savvy on project management, you know approximately what each task in your area of responsibility takes in terms of person-hours to accomplish. If you do not know, estimate and calculate it. This knowledge increases your confidence when delegating, monitoring, giving feedback on progress, and discussing resource needs with your manager. Analyze all the possibilities that might assist you in meeting your boss's expectations. Where might there be wiggle room: the budget, number of people, materials, machines, or supplies? Figure out the deadlines of each project or task within your purview and where the conflicts are. Is there any give in the budget to hire temporary staff? Can you borrow staff from other departments? Can some deadlines be stretched out?

When it is impossible to do everything that is asked, a top-drawer manager will do the homework on how long things should take, how much time is actually available, and what it would cost to align the deadline with the current available person-hours.

After analyzing the facts and preparing for a discussion with your boss, realize that there are times when it will be physically impossible to get it all done—you just cannot will it to happen, as much as you want to. One of a manager's goals is to retain superstar employees. In a good economy, burnout can lead to employees searching for outside employment. In an economic downturn, when your superstars have little choice but to stay, they may become disgruntled and worn out. They may become less productive and less committed at a time when everyone's passion to reach the goals and give extra effort may be necessary for organizational survival.

If your boss is overdelegating, communication is essential. Don't withdraw. Initiate a conversation. Collaborate with your boss on how to handle the workload. Ask for reprioritization.

If you cannot deliver, find a way to say no without saying, "No." During downsizing, when everyone is clinging to their jobs and willing to do more, it still may not be possible to do the new task no matter how many extra hours the team works. Here is where your project management skills can help. Prepare for a logical, process-oriented discussion with your manager. Tell him how much you *want* to deliver all that is expected but that you need his help to figure out how to accomplish everything. Revisit organizational goals and needs. Perhaps something like this would work:

> I appreciate the opportunity to manage this project and your faith in our team to meet the goals. However, with the current deadline set and the amount of work left to complete, we will have some challenges. Let's discuss the priorities, timelines, and available resources. Based on my analysis, this new project will take X person-hours. Our current workload takes Y hours. So, we are faced with some decisions. I've got some questions before we look at potential alternatives. How firm is the deadline of the new project? Is other staff available to

assist us? Can we authorize overtime? Let's review the scope of the project and the other projects my team is working on.

Summary

How does delegating relate to feedback and coaching? Once managers have delegated an assignment, they must monitor progress and give regular feedback on how the employee is doing. Coaching sessions may be planned before the work begins if it will help the employee achieve success. Or, if at any time during the project the employee needs a boost, coaching sessions can be set up at that time to help.

Whether delegating, coaching, giving feedback, or performing any other communication activity, one of the most important skills a manager needs to master is the art of listening. Listening is the subject of the next chapter, Chapter 11.

CHAPTER

11

Don't Have Time to Listen?
Try These Tips

Listening is perhaps the greatest skill an expert communicator can develop. This capability can make the difference between communication
and miscommunication, and between enhancing relationships and
harming them. How well do you really listen? Have you ever said you are
"multitasking" while attempting to listen? In this age of working flat out,
to what extent do you make yourself available to listen? What are the
benefits of listening to achieving top individual and corporate performance?

Managers are responsible for the success of the communication. Listening intently—to be sure you understand what the speaker means—is
a part of all communication. It takes a few minutes of concentrated attention, but it can save an immense amount of time. If you and your
team are under pressure because of leaner staffing, listening heightens
your chances of success. It is critical to understand the messages the first
time to save time.

Why Listen?

In one seminar I teach we do a three-minute listening exercise. People
are amazed how much they can learn from the other person in only
three minutes. And the speakers report how good it feels to be truly lis-

tened to—a luxury most do not enjoy very often. Once, a participant said, "This is fine for a role-play, but in real life I do not have three minutes to listen to my employees." I was astounded. Three minutes? I gently took listening to the next step by showing how it weaves through every single management function.

Listening is an integral part of developing relationships. A manager cannot show she cares about people and earn their trust if she does not fully listen to them. In previous chapters this book has established the importance of relationships to getting work done and preventing and solving communication problems with people. Real listening builds credibility and trust, which are necessary for influence and persuasion.

Listening is crucial when delegating and clarifying expectations. Managers must communicate back and forth with direct reports to ensure that both manager and employee have the same understanding of the goals or informal expectations.

How could managers give feedback without listening to the employee's perspective? Expert coaches have highly developed listening skills since coaching is a collaborative conversation. In fact, any collaborative conversation implies that both parties are listening to one another.

Tips for Collaborative Listening

The listener's body language lets the speaker know that he has the listener's attention. Eye contact—not eyes glazing over, but genuine, attentive eye contact—is the first indication of listening. Open body language, where the manager faces the direct report with arms open—not crossed, not working on a handheld or a computer, and not fussing with papers— shows it is the employee's turn to talk and that what the employee has to say is valued. Other listening body language consists of facial expressions and head movement. The listener might use such facial expressions as a slight frown or a general confused look in the eyes if she does not understand. Or the listener might nod her head slightly to show that she does understand.

Comments such as "Uh-huh," "Hmmm," "Yes," "I see," and "Oh?" said in a neutral, friendly tone of voice are nonjudgmental and noncommittal and encourage the speaker to continue talking. They are indicators that the listener is interested in hearing more detail about this topic.

Employee: "So accounting has not gotten back to me on that report . . ."
Manager: "Oh?"
Employee: "No. I guess I had better call them right now to follow up."

Clarifying What We Think We Heard

Another valuable act of listening is clarifying what we *think* we heard. This is done by restating comments the direct report makes, asking clarification questions, and paraphrasing what we thought we heard. This way we can be sure we understand the real meaning of what the person meant to say. It does not necessarily mean we *agree* with what the person said. It does mean we respect her enough to let her know her message has been received the way she wanted it to be heard. This is easy to do if we take the time to clarify, rather than tuning out what has been said or accepting it at face value.

1. **Restate comments.** When you use the speaker's own words, you prove that you are still listening and want a more in-depth explanation. These comments reflect what the direct report says or implies. These comments can be used to draw out more information and to establish empathy. Here is an example:

Employee: "I'm not sure I can make that deadline for project X. I've got so many other projects right now."

Manager: "So you might not be able to meet the deadline because of your other projects?"

2. **Ask clarification questions.** When you want to probe deeper to clarify your understanding of what the direct report really means, request clarification. For example:

Employee: "I need more employees if we are going to meet the target date."

Manager: "Tell me a little more about why you think you need more staff."

Or

Employee: "That sales department is such a loser. They promise the moon to our customers and we can't even get the products developed by then."

Manager: "What exactly did the sales department promise and to which customer? When do you think your team will finish the product development?"

3. **Paraphrase.** Paraphrasing is similar to restating, except that in paraphrasing you use your own words instead of the speaker's. Also, listeners often paraphrase using a question instead of a statement. The purpose of paraphrasing is to be sure you understand what the direct report meant—by saying it a different way. Especially when used in question form, paraphrasing is collaborative because it invites the speaker to continue.

Employee: "Heather, we've got a problem. Those guys from manufacturing are messing up our schedule with the customers. We, the sales department, promised our top customer that we would deliver the new product to them by next Wednesday. We based this promise on what Ron, the head of manufacturing, told us. Now they are blaming us and we won't have the product by Wednesday. This is going to dent our relationship with our highest-revenue customer. This could mean the company misses our quarterly revenue target."

Manager: "Let me see if I've got this straight, Eliot. There are a lot of issues you are raising. Are you saying that we are not going to make corporate revenue projections this quarter?"

Employee: "Well, no. I'm just saying we might not."

Manager: "So just to be sure I understand your other concerns, is it definite that we will not deliver the product by Wednesday?"

Notice that, with the three techniques of restating the employee's comment, asking clarifying questions, and paraphrasing, the only purpose is to understand the speaker's meaning. The manager does not give advice and jump in with a solution. A solution might not be appropriate, because the manager might not grasp what the employee actually meant or have enough facts yet. Notice also that the manager does not change the attention from the direct report to himself by saying, "Me too. I had that same problem." The manager does not agree or disagree with the employee's statements—he or she merely tries to accurately comprehend them. This requires neutrality and withholding judgment.

Listening Is the Key to Delivering Desired Results

Scott Torok, co-owner of Descend Salon in San Francisco, prides himself on purposeful consideration for creating beauty and style—for the well-being of his clients. To achieve this high standard, he has acquired expert communication skills. "A communication breakdown equals a bad haircut," Scott says. He continues, "You have to *really* listen. Not just half listen and think, 'I'll just do haircut #2.'"

Scott always paraphrases what the client *says* to be sure he understands what it is the client really *means*. He cites two examples of potential miscommunication. The client says, "I want my hair over my ears." Does that mean covering the ears, or the ability to tuck it behind the ears, or cut above the ears? So he moves the hair one position at a time and says, "Do you mean you want it this way, or this way?" Another common issue is the client with hair layers who says, "I want my hair all one length." Scott takes a section of hair from the top and shows her that to have her hair all one length, he would need to cut the bottom of the hair off to meet the end of the top layer. This would result in a short haircut that was unwanted. Sometimes the client really wants layers on top.

"That's why a lot of hairstylists fail to give clients what they want," Scott says. "They don't listen carefully enough to understand what the client *means*. Listening and paraphrasing can take a little time up front, but it sure improves the outcome and it builds trust and relationships.

This can result in repeat business with long-term customers and can generate goodwill for the next interaction."

Scott's example can be applied to any situation at work. If we don't listen and clarify, we are likely to misunderstand the facts, which could have results ranging from minor to disastrous for a project or client. In order to work collaboratively, managers must listen. It is impossible to be collegial and not listen to and understand the other person's point of view.

Not listening can isolate employees and limit organizations from reaching their goals. Near Boston, Massachusetts, Jared, an engineer in his mid-twenties was recently disenchanted with his start-up company because he and his peers were not listened to. Jared got frustrated and began to pull back his commitment because the engineering recommendations were being disregarded.

Jared said, "Senior management has risen so far above that they don't take the advice of the people in the trenches—the technical experts. Upper management doesn't know what they are doing. This can impact our company's success." It was like learning that there is no Santa Claus. Jared, an MIT graduate with international exposure on a team project, was hired because of his knowledge and invention capabilities. Suddenly his bubble of security was burst. He was on the first rung of realizing the world is not necessarily logical. The senior managers don't always listen to the people who can help propel the product suite forward.

Listening Can Change Relationships

Allison, a single mom of a teenaged boy, came to me privately at the end of the first day of a three-day seminar. She and her fifteen-year-old son were having difficulty communicating. Although she attended the class to enhance management skills, a greater, more basic need emerged—her desire to parent well. She wanted to improve her relationship with her son and *then* transfer the new skills to work. She needed to do this because her home relationship was distracting her from her work.

Allison said that her son would storm out of the room when she tried to talk with him. She resorted to shouting. She was astounded by how the class discussion that day, and the listening process in particular, had stimulated changes in other participants. Christopher, another participant, had a parallel situation to Allison's. One of his direct reports displayed the same behavior on the job as Allison's son did at home. Christopher's previous reaction to the employee was also to shout.

Throughout the seminars, I encourage people to make commitments to change back on the job by stating specific action items. Christopher said he was never going to shout on the job again. Allison was inspired that Christopher could make such a strong statement of his intention. She said she was going to do the same thing at home—not ever shout again. She went home to try it out.

The next morning, Allison came in quite early to talk to me. She dabbed off the tears rolling down her cheeks. She said she had practiced the listening process with her son and it had worked. In fact, he was so surprised that she was listening to what he said that he asked her, "What's wrong?"

"Nothing's wrong," she replied to him. "I'm starting to listen. I am never going to shout at you again. I'm listening to what you have to say from now on." He stayed seated in the room and talked with her. A week later, Allison e-mailed me that she was not only successfully listening at home, but also to her direct reports at work. She noted favorable changes in relationships and impact on getting things done.

A Simple Listening Process

Listening is easy if a manager makes a commitment to listen. Sometimes you will be too busy to listen. You might be solving a crisis, be on a deadline, or have an appointment. If you do not have time to listen, say so. Tell your reports that what they have to say is important to you and you want to give it the attention it deserves. Invite employees to come back at a specific time when you will be able to concentrate fully on their message. When you are ready, here are four tips:

1. Clear all other thoughts and focus only on the person.
2. Eliminate thoughts of yourself—no advice, no "me too."
3. Use open, listening body language as described earlier in this chapter.
4. Clarify what you think you heard by restating, asking clarifying questions, and paraphrasing.

That is it. When managers use this easy process instead of assuming they know what the speaker means, amazing relationships and understanding about the work emerge. When managers do not interrupt, multitask, or act hurried, but actually listen, rework is reduced and better products are produced.

Listening with Your Heart—Speak Their Language

Jane Rundle, from Vancouver, British Columbia (BC), Canada, has an interesting story to tell. Jane said that, throughout her life, she attempted to get collaborative results with whomever she was working. Jane said, "The common thread from being an art educator in New York City to being an art administrator in the Okanagan, BC, to being co-editor of the North Shore Stroke Recovery Centre newsletter in Vancouver was speaking their language.

"When I say speak their language," Jane continues, "I mean finding what works for them so we could reach the goals." In order to do this, Jane had to pay close attention to whomever she was working with and listen with her heart. She set the intention to both develop the relationships and achieve the objectives.

"In New York City, I taught art in a public high school. We had a common goal that the students would be able to create art. However, I realized that my students were not comprehending the design concepts that I was trying to teach them. I also noticed that they danced as they made their hand-built pottery. So I utilized their passion for dance and made arrangements to do dance movement in various galleries of the Metropolitan Museum. As they moved from Greek sculpture to African sculpture, I realized that they were slowly internalizing design concepts of line. By the time we got to the modern art gallery, they were shouting, 'I'll be the blue line and you be the red line.' Their subsequent work at school just blossomed. Our goal of learning concepts of design so they might enjoy creating art was achieved.

"In Penticton, I was director curator of the city's art gallery. I was sensitive to what the community would enjoy seeing so as to get them to come to the gallery. Again, I spoke their language. Without judgment, I observed, intuited, and assessed where the community was and met them where they were. Community involvement was low prior to my being hired. A goal was to attract the community. Coming from Manhattan, I was familiar with art exhibits. This was not Manhattan. It was a small, rural community in an isolated area of BC. I needed to meet *their* needs, not mine. By exhibiting many shows that I might not have considered high art, I established a trust with them so that when I did bring in 'higher-risk' exhibits, a trust relationship had been established. They were more receptive to the exhibitions. I also wrote a weekly column in the local newspaper. This gave them a hook or springboard from which to start to view the abstract art. Speaking their language worked."

Jane says her approach continues to work.

"Now with editing the newsletter for a readership of stroke survivors, caregivers, and medical professionals, I again speak their language. Being a stroke survivor myself, I am aware that what I write needs to include their accommodations. The articles need to be short for attention spans. If I write a recipe, I also include how this can be done with one hand or with limited muscle strength.

"I also speak their language when we are together in person. For those friends with left-sided deficit (they cannot see midline to the left of their bodies), I stand to their right side so they can see me. I do not finish sentences with aphasic friends. I use humor and suggest we play charades when they have trouble speaking. I'll laugh and say 'Three words? First word, two syllables?' I smile and sincerely appreciate people for who they are—just as they are. Without judgment, I build on their strengths, not mine. I care about them as if they are my family."

When a person listens with her heart to what others need, it is genuine communication. You get the other person on board and work together side by side. Also, he will listen better to you when you respect, appreciate, and listen to him.

Listening with your heart so you can speak another's language and meet common goals is an extraordinary skill managers can develop. It is a fundamental part of collaboration to understand the needs and approaches of others and work toward meeting them.

Summary

Listening, including asking appropriate questions, is the fulcrum to the lever that coaching offers. Listening multiplies the effect that coaching can have on the desired behavioral change. Listening combines relationship—intention to understand the other person's point of view—with process—a step-by-step approach.

Strong listening validates the other person's thoughts. Listening carefully shows that you heard what the speaker meant to convey, not just his words. It demonstrates patience and desire to enhance the working relationship because the person and his ideas are worth the time to be aired and assimilated. Listening is an important part of persuasion, which is at the top of the skills list for most of today's professionals.

CONCLUSION

Be a Gold Medal Communicator!

This last chapter provides nine more communication tips for busy managers. To be a first-rate manager and communicator, you need to believe communication is the most important skill you can develop and you must practice it every day. Great managers engage their staff, help them have good days, and treat them nicely. Managers who make the effort to stay positive attract people like magnets and get things done. Exceptional managers remove communication barriers, support their employees, and trust their intuition. World-class managers lead change with extraordinary communication skills. They have highly honed influence and persuasion skills. These tips will point you to becoming a gold medal communicator and a top-notch manager.

Tip #1. Continually Practice Good Communication

Communication is the underpinning of everything you do. Your overarching responsibility as a manager is to get quality work delivered on time with and through your direct reports. The greater the demands on you to achieve these results with and through your team, the greater your need for superior communication skills. As a manager, your staff expects you to prevent and diminish friction in the way people talk to each other so the team can concentrate on the work and not be distracted. Through *relationship, process,* and *collaboration* you can reduce discomfort about sticky conversations at work. You can expand your competence and confidence to handle the tough stuff. You lessen your stress when you are confident that you have data, not opinion. Each time you clearly set expectations, you increase productivity in the team, because clarity minimizes rework. Clarity also reduces time wasted due to misunderstandings and perks up your ability to form relationships.

Creating an energized, positive work environment during any economy reduces your colleagues' stress and slashes sick and other lost time. Simple kindness and engendering good days for your team can move them to push on and thrive. One manager from Alaska said of his boss, "I *want* to work for him. We can have a pleasant conversation about mistakes, but it doesn't hurt. He gives specific feedback and invites me into the conversation. He asks me questions and lets me decide how to proceed." Communicating, as a knowledgeable partner, can earn any manager these accolades.

The better a communicator you are, the more valuable you are to any organization in any economy. Communication is a transportable skill to any job, working with any group, anywhere. The more adept you are at building rapport and leading collaborative conversations, the more you advance your opportunities.

Tip #2. Engage Your Staff in Their Roles and Be a "Keeper"

An epidemic of workplace dissatisfaction is infecting the United States. In 2007, "the *Gallup Management Journal* (*GMJ*) surveyed U.S. employees to discover if employees would fire their boss—and what effect workplace engagement might have on their willingness to give their boss the boot," says Eric Nielsen, Gallup's senior director of Media Relations. Survey respondents fell into one of three types of employees: engaged, not engaged, or actively disengaged. Engaged employees made up only 26 percent of respondents. Those who were not engaged made up 56 percent, and the actively disengaged made up 18 percent of the respondents. On September 13, 2007, *GMJ* reported in the article "Would You

Fire Your Boss?" by Bryant Ott and Emily Kilham that "Nearly one quarter of U.S. employees—and 51% of actively disengaged workers—would sack their managers if given the chance. . . . Engaged employees, however, are far more charitable to their supervisors."

Make sure upper management sees that you are a manager supported by your staff—staff that are engaged in their jobs. When your employees are allied to you, it reinforces your stature as a leader. It also impacts how well you can assist employees in aligning their personal professional goals with organizational objectives. Position work assignments in terms of importance and benefit to employee skill development to acquire their committed involvement.

Employees also want to work in an environment that is congenial and cooperative. It is the manager's job to lead by example and facilitate communication in a way that creates a harmonious atmosphere free of unnecessary stress. This means taking the time to build and maintain friendly relationships that encourage people to do their very best work.

Tip #3. Help Staff Have a Good Day—Every Day

The environment you shape for your team makes the difference in how they feel about their work, the organization, you, and their coworkers. When you lower the stress and create a comfortable workplace, you make it easy for employees to focus on their jobs so they can be highly productive. You can achieve this through communicating, motivating, and inspiring every day.

Bernie Haas, a former meeting coordinator at the San Francisco Center of the American Management Association (AMA), and I recently lunched to celebrate his retirement. In discussing his more than twenty years with AMA, I was stunned when Bernie told me, "I have never had a bad day at AMA. A major factor has been the attitude of the managers and the working atmosphere they created."

No one had ever said that to me before. The more I thought about it, the more I thought it would really help managers to hear his comment. After all, this is the reason I began writing this book in the first place—to help managers create a work environment where everyone has good days. When I went back to the afternoon part of the seminar I was leading that day, I told the class what Bernie had said. They were taken aback when I told them Bernie said he had never had a bad day at AMA and that he attributed it to the management. Jaws dropped. Eyes popped. People sat back speechless in their chairs. Then we began a discussion on how the participants could use what they were learning in the class to provide that kind of environment for their own staffs.

The next week, when I e-mailed Bernie to see if I could quote him in this book, he wrote: "My days with AMA were all good ones, no question about it. At my retirement lunch, I thanked my AMA manager, Gordon Silvera, for 'creating an atmosphere in which I could work.' I think that if more people found something that they really like to do in an atmosphere in which they really like to work, there would be fewer folks trying to retire at forty-five. Finding such a situation is easier said than done. I think it's a matter of knowing oneself and finding a place where one can use one's talents and work comfortably. A good thing for managers to remember is not to make mountains out of molehills. When managers don't make mountains out of molehills, employees have a better day and do better work."

People need work they like and that makes them feel successful. But the atmosphere the manager creates may be even more significant. The manager makes the environment conducive to productivity through a blend of clear expectations, process, and relationship.

Tip #4. Be Nice

The secret to being viewed as a collaborative professional is a simple one: be nice. Persuasion and kindness are more effective than confrontation. When others feel they are well treated, they are more willing to grease the wheels and get things done. Observe what happens when people feel they are being condescended to or are expected to jump through hoops. They sometimes find ways to take control of the situation by not delivering. It can become an unnecessary power struggle that is so easily prevented when managers are just plain nice.

Why did the Chamber of Commerce of the resort town of Montauk, Long Island, recognize Marilyn Bogdan, owner of the clothing store Summer Stock? Marilyn started this retail business thirty-two years ago, and through tough and good economic times, her business has succeeded. She attributes the success to being nice. And recognition from the Chamber proves that being nice works.

When I asked Marilyn how she motivates her staff, she said, "It works best when they can feel you really care about them. They want to please you and work hard for you. When they see you working hard, they put in extra effort." Some of Marilyn's employees have been with her for twenty-five years. They stay because they know Marilyn appreciates them and cares about them.

"We do get involved with their families," Marilyn says. "If there is an emergency, we are there for them. If they are ill, we make life as easy as possible. And financially we take good care of them. I constantly tell them about the great job they do. I give them little handwritten notes that say, 'I couldn't have done (specific situation) without you.' I consistently let them know how valuable they are."

Marilyn continues, "I try to be nice. I care and they know it. The retail business is all about people. The customers come in because we are all nice to them. So the employees have to feel cared for so they can treat the customers nicely. It has to start at the top. When they see us act that way to them, the employees act that way to the customers."

Summer Stock does not pay commissions, because that makes employees compete against each other and the customers can tell. The employees get bonuses at the end of the year, so they feel free to step in and help coworkers. The customers benefit from this cooperation and teamwork.

"If you were to teach someone how to be nice," I said, "what would they be doing?"

"We always tell them to act as if it's not a store," Marilyn said. "We say to act as if it's your home and people choose to come visit you. Greet them with a big smile. Show you are glad to see them with a little opening conversation. Let the customers know if they need anything, you are available. But don't follow them around and hound them."

Sometimes the employees sit and talk with the husbands of the women who shop there. Some people have had bad experiences at other stores. Marilyn feels a responsibility to make visiting her store a good experience so it affects customers' opinion of all of Montauk in a positive way.

Marilyn always focuses on the positive and demonstrates an attitude of gratitude. "You feel fortunate that you've been able to stay in business so long," she said. "You don't take things for granted. Being nice always comes back to you."

"Sometimes managers are afraid if they are nice they will be taken advantage of," I said.

"I've found it just the opposite," Marilyn said. "The employees don't want to disappoint you. Being nice also works best when dealing with suppliers. If you need something quickly, and you've been nice to them over the years, they take care of you. It works in your favor."

It also is effective to be nice to customers. "Customers have a choice of what stores to go to," Marilyn said. "We look at baby pictures and wedding pictures. We remember their names and give little gifts. Some people come in just to talk. So we hire people who can easily work like that and have feeling for people. That's why we've stayed in business thirty-two years. Being nice works."

Tip #5. Stay Positive

Charismatic leaders consistently emphasize the good and demonstrate a constructive disposition toward the future. Earning a reputation for being positive helps attract people to you, your goals, and your organization. Staying positive under pressure displays your consummate leadership agility.

William (Bill) C. Torchiana, is president of Torchiana, Mastrov & Sapiro (TMS) and a founding member of Career Partners International, the global leader in talent management consulting services. Bill exemplifies charismatic, positive leadership. He draws people in by his inclusive, uplifting, and optimistic manner. TMS is the San Francisco Bay Area's leading independent career management and leadership development consulting firm. The service it offers requires that every team member act and speak positively, because the mission is to share hope and energy with people who need that in their career transition or leadership growth.

Bill says, "Being positive is an option to choose even if it takes some effort on your part to do that. All successful leaders that I know are positive by nature or by choice. One of the best ways that managers energize an organization is to craft an authentic and positive vision of the future, clearly convey it, and create excitement about it. They tell the story to attract followers who will join them and pursue the aspirations and the cause. I don't think there is any other good alternative to that approach. It is a strong belief that I hold."

He continues, "I've met a few leaders in my lifetime who are at *all* times positive and nice about *everything* they say about people and things. That shows up to me as world class. I think most of us can be uncomplimentary at some time or slip up once in a while. But the exceptional people never deviate from being positive.

"Some people pride themselves on being honest, and in doing so, might not be so nice. Some people have trouble being too blunt. Follow the Golden Rule—treat others as you'd like to be treated."

Bill also notes, "In the work I've done I have seen some naysayers, doomsayers, and energy suckers. Some people unintentionally try to break us down and would not be good people to have in the lifeboat in that they might cry, 'We've got a leak. Oh, no. We've got another leak.'"

People act like naysayers, according to Bill, because there are people who are discouraged or in pain, even leaders in pain. And in tough economic times, some people become pessimistic. "The question is how to help them develop a more optimistic view; optimism and the entrepreneurial spirit have worked well in the past and will prevail in the future," Bill adds.

"What I do is not magical," Bill says. "It's a belief system I choose to live by. There are several findings that suggest many of us will live to be 100 years old. So what do I choose for the years between now and then? I expect those years to be positive and hopefully healthy. They will not be lived day-by-day, but rather with a positive view of the things to come."

What is Bill's advice for managers who have people on their team who are not being positive? "When managers are evaluating a skill set necessary to hold the business together, you have to pick people who are positive about the future," Bill says. " It gets us through the difficulties of the present. I will not let anyone pull us down on our team, because at our work we live in hope. We need lifeboat people. A positive view of the future is essential for our work. TMS provides our view of the future to our clients. And being positive is a vital quality of a winning leader," Bill concludes.

Tip # 6. Remove Communication Barriers and Support Employees

Irene Goldberg, the library director of the Monroe Township Public Library in New Jersey, faces unique challenges in public service. Irene says, "In a busy public library, service is our product; books and materials are borrowed, not bought. For the most part, money does not change hands significantly. So, why would working at a public service desk in a library bring with it conflict and stress for the employee? In many cases, the fact that a desk—be it a cashier desk in a commercial establishment, or a service desk in a public library—separates the two parties creates an expectation in the mind of the customer that the service person may not have her best interests at heart. Often I've heard contentious words spoken as the patron steps up to the desk that the employee behind the desk has done nothing to provoke. Does a piece of furniture have such power?"

Irene continues, "There is a movement in library service to get staff out from behind the desks as much as possible. The intent is to remove barriers to service, but the side benefit is that it seems to remove some of that stress. The person on the inside of the desk no longer appears to be the 'enemy' when met beyond the desk."

As in any job, collaboration and collegiality offer entrée to communication opportunities. As organizations have flattened and become less hierarchical, so coworkers and customers have emerged as side-by-side colleagues. The prevailing Internet use has also equalized people and reduced a sense of looking to authorities for the answers. In the Monroe Township Public Library, removing desk barriers is one way to achieve this type of communication and ease employee stress.

"We provide walk-around opportunities for staff willing to do so," says Irene. "Some cannot leave the protection of the anchor (desk). Those who do walk around find it gives them an opportunity to smile and exchange pleasantries as they get a book down off a high shelf, recommend a great read, or just explain policies or procedures. They walk a figure-eight path, being sure to be welcoming and accessible."

As welcoming as staff are, they still have to deal with some cranky customers. This demands that managers be alert to how their staff are handling these situations and how the employees are impacted. It presents challenges for how managers can be supportive and help employees navigate their way through this aspect of their jobs.

At the library, Irene energizes the managers and staff with periodic staff gatherings: "We discuss certain tenets of our service model, as a gentle reminder. In Monroe there are seven planned retirement communities. For many people living alone, we are the first human beings they speak to that day. And for some, complaining is a communication style, unpleasant as it is to the listener. In some cases, retired people, used to being the boss in their previous work life, are a little too emphatic when they speak. Some people use a condescending tone of voice or sound like they are ordering the staff to do something instead of asking. Regular staff meetings allow the staff members to talk about these concerns and problem solve among themselves with positive ways they've defused a situation."

Such meetings motivate employees and grow their skills. Meetings also reinforce expectations that serving the public means being adept at conversing with all types of communicators—even if they complain.

No one expects employees to be mistreated by the public, and co-workers and managers team up to lend a hand to each other. Irene says, "Staff members always know that their supervisor, up to the library director level, will always intervene if needed (or wanted) and always watch their backs. Staff watch out for each other, and a beleaguered first person can look to his or her side and communicate a silent message that they need to cycle away from the situation. No one wants a situation to spiral out of control."

A vital way to show your direct reports how important they are—both to you and to the organization—is to go the extra mile in supporting them. Actions speak louder than words.

Tip #7. Use Your Intuition

One way a confident communicator supports staff is to ensure that you energize your staff with enthusiasm and positive energy. Since managers are role models for how to communicate, you teach your team how to integrate relationships, process, and collaboration by how you do it yourself. Use the concepts in this book and use your intuition. Trust your insight.

Sharon Lawrence of Walnut Creek, California, is a chemist by training who has worked in both research and start-up organizations. She has also taught yoga and meditation for ten years and uses healing touch and sound therapy with her clients and students to help them relax and connect with their intuition. Sharon says, "True relationship comes from intuition—from our inner knowing. Intuition drives the decision of when to stay with the process and when to let it go in order to connect and create a true relationship. When we trust our intuition and are authentic in how we communicate with people, relationships not only grow, but relaxed positive energy flows.''

Using intuition makes it more comfortable to be natural at work. Many people feel compelled to play a role at work instead of just being themselves. Some managers think everything has to be "by the book" and authoritative. But when people are at ease, quality work gets done because people can focus on the task without the underlying tension that swells when good relationships are not in place.

Tip #8. Lead Change with Extraordinary Communication

Some management tasks remain constant. A manager will always need to plan, organize, monitor progress, control resources, and lead. Setting team goals according to corporate goals, implementing the corporate core values, resolving conflict, providing a motivational atmosphere, helping employees grow and develop, determining and monitoring budget and schedules, operating from ethical values, and getting the job done are basic requirements. Organizations will always need goal-oriented managers who are clear on the mission. But the manager with extraordinary communication skills who can lead people through the uncertainties of change boosts his value to the organization.

With all the changes occurring in workplaces today, including economic changes, managers must stand out as proponents of change. Communication is the most important skill a manager can develop to introduce and implement change initiatives. Communication suggests a commitment to change, lifelong learning, and flexibility. These attributes are needed to negotiate the major changes that managers must deal with, including endless technology improvements, increasing diversity and language differences in the workforce, employees who are more empowered and have higher expectations than in the past, and volatility in the global market affecting the business models.

There are constant explosions in technology and processes. These alterations require continual learning and training for the manager and staff. A manager must embrace and implement the new technology and perhaps research new applications. Recruiting new talent may require updating hiring processes and team adaptation to different skills of teammates. Leaders must be amenable to fast-changing budgetary issues for leasing and purchasing equipment and software.

Greater workforce diversity demands awareness and education, leading the charge in breaking down any barriers, and inclusion of all employees. Diversity necessitates an open-minded frame of reference and modeling that framework for employees. Communication may require greater effort and time. A manager may need to work harder at clarifying expectations and meeting them.

With the need to empower employees today, there is a shift in accountability directly to the employee. This demands greater clarity when the manager sets the bar and communicates the vision. A manager must encourage trust and walk the talk. More accountability also rests with the manager to manage risk—business and personnel—and protect the company and the manager from lawsuits.

Employee expectations exact management behaviors such as identifying and meeting the needs of followers. Managers must look for opportunities to chunk down the work in acceptable bites and look for occasions to reward and praise. Direct reports expect the manager to initiate open and frequent communications. They anticipate support and encouragement in both their work and their professional development.

Globalization has modified business models and people management. In any seminar I give, usually several managers attending have the responsibility to manage folks at remote locations, ranging from people working at home to people on the other side of the globe in completely different time zones. This calls for enormous flexibility and communication skills. Often voice-to-voice communication is difficult to achieve, much less interpersonal contact. Unprecedented knowledge of cultures and how people do business is needed. Managing virtually compels the manager to exert extraordinary efforts to clarify expectations and follow up on progress in a collegial, collaborative way.

There have always been regulatory changes, and a manager can expect them to differ from year to year based on new federal and state laws. Managers need to be knowledgeable of current regulations and any impact on their goals and their teams.

Other changes, such as those to ergonomics, safety and security, ethics, and a loss of productivity due to learning curves, all require that managers have the ability to describe expectations and action items clearly, listen, deal with resistance, keep morale high, and collaborate. Communication methods such as e-mail, handheld devices, and cell phones require continual adaptation. Many feel that managers are now held to higher standards. They must justify their existence with tighter financial and other metrics than ever before. Many managers must manage risk in the business.

Tip #9. Influence and Persuade

Today there is a much greater emphasis on a manager's ability to persuade and influence others at all levels of the organization, including direct reports. Being directive is important at certain times and is addressed in Chapter 9 on coaching. However, being directive is no longer the only skill a manager must have to be successful. Nor is it the most advanced or complex. Communicating with people now requires influence and persuasion skills.

The higher level the manager, the greater the wings of influence need to spread. To persuade, a manager hones his skills in educating others on the benefits and logic of a project or an approach. To be convinced, people are interested in learning the reasoning and value of what the persuader has to say before they make up their own minds. This puts the onus of being very clear about the whys and wherefores directly on the shoulders of the manager. It also requires relationship building and knowing how to partner with people. This in-depth knowledge and ability to communicate is a far cry from telling employees to "just get it done."

Partnering with direct reports requires a high degree of persuasion skills to include the other person, instead of just ordering him about. By being included, the employee's commitment to his manager, the organization, and the work itself expands. This leads to ownership, which induces employees to produce optimal results.

Influence and persuasion skills are significant communication skills that proficient managers use to collaborate in delegating, monitoring progress, giving feedback, and coaching.

Summary

I know that you will want to refer to this book again and again as you master one of the communication tips and want to learn another. When you prepare to hold a feedback, coaching, or delegating conversation you can freshen up your approach with ideas from this book. When you face new people problems or you want to strategize to prevent them, return to a chapter. When you manage a new group or get promoted and face different communication challenges, revisit the pages and the processes. Have fun in your communication journey. As a continual communication learner, you will open many professional and personal doors of opportunity.

This book provides all the tips and techniques you need to ramp up your interpersonal communication to "gold medal status." Happy managing, and cheerful communicating!

Basic Job Expectations

Goals, Job Descriptions, and Performance Standards

This appendix defines three formal tools that are used to communicate basic job expectations: goals, job descriptions, and performance standards. Two examples show how these three communication tools are linked together.

Goals

Most employees need to understand not only what to do but also how each responsibility fits with the larger view of the group, department, division, and the company. This moves us to goals.

Goals are formal, measurable, written expectations. They are planned end results or outcomes that guide individuals and groups in their responsibility to achieve their part of the corporate direction. Goals transform hope and wishes into strategic direction.

Peter Drucker, renowned management consultant, introduced Management by Objectives (MBO) in 1954 in his classic book, *The Practice of Management*. MBO has morphed into other ways to set goals. But the concept of goals has withstood the test of time. They are still necessary. Currently, many organizations use SMART goals. This acronym helps people remember the key components of an effective goal. The written goal must be:

Specific (has a desired outcome)

Measurable (through evaluation criteria—often expressed by percent, number, or dollar amount)

Attainable (achievable, reachable even if it is a stretch goal)

Relevant (aligns with corporate objectives)

Time bound (has a target completion date)

Examples of SMART goals are:

1. Distribute news releases to three new TV news stations and three new Internet sites by 9/30/20XX.

> S–Distribute news releases (desired outcome)
>
> M–Three new TV news stations and three new Internet sites (both the number *three* and the adjective *new* are measurements)
>
> A–(manager and employee agree that they are attainable given the employee's entire workload and the marketplace realities)
>
> R–(assume it aligns with a corporate objective to increase news coverage)
>
> T–9/30/20XX (target date)

2. Improve customer satisfaction during sales/service handoffs and installations by 5 percent as measured by the customer survey on 12/31/20XX.

> S–Improve customer satisfaction
>
> M–by 5 percent
>
> A–(assume it is a realistic increase given the time available)
>
> R–(assume it is aligned with corporate customer service objectives)
>
> T–12/31/20XX

Job Descriptions

Job descriptions tell people *what* their duties are. These job descriptions list the responsibilities for a particular position, not for a particular person. Each accountability listed includes an action verb to depict the activities this job requires.

Applicants usually see the job description during the prehire interviewing process to help both the interviewer and the candidate assess whether the job and the person's qualifications are a match. Newly hired employees then use this list of job duties as reference tools when they begin the job. Oftentimes managers revisit the job descriptions at performance appraisal time when evaluating performance against the job duties.

Job descriptions are useful to draw the framework of activities an employee is to accomplish. But they are general in nature and frequently used for similar positions in many areas of the organization. They are an excellent guideline but by no means the only way expectations are set for most professional and managerial work.

Examples of job responsibilities on job descriptions as they relate to the two SMART goal examples:

For goal 1, a job responsibility could be: Writes news releases and distributes them to media on subjects that may be complex; makes decisions about the news releases regarding the format of information and which media to contact.

For goal 2, a job responsibility could be: Ensures that all customer service standards are met during sales/service handoffs and installations.

Job descriptions are essential communication tools before and after hiring. A manager explores a candidate's ability to execute the responsibilities during the interview. A manager then trains or orients the new employee to the job, referring to the job description. When job descriptions are revised, this calls for another clarification meeting. Discussing the job descriptions—new or revised—is important managerial communication. The conversation about new or revised job responsibilities is a dialogue until the manager is satisfied that the employee has the same understanding as the manager about what the words on the job description mean for this specific job. Then the manager reinforces the responsibilities in the weekly one-on-one or group staff meetings when reviewing progress until they become second nature to the employee.

Performance Standards

Performance standards are the parameters that employees will be evaluated on in the performance appraisal. They are introduced with the job description or whenever work is assigned. They specify what a high-quality job will look like in terms of conditions, quality, quantity, budget, timeliness, safety, and behaviors that contribute to teamwork and other desired results. Depending upon the type of project or task and the level of employee expertise, performance standards may be imposed or may be mutually decided with the direct report.

Examples of performance standards for the two previous job responsibilities are:

For job responsibility 1: Writes news releases and distributes them to media on subjects that may be complex; makes decisions about the news releases regarding the format of information and which media to contact.

- ➤ Meets specified deadlines.
- ➤ Uses approved sources of information.
- ➤ Gets written approval for quotes in advance of distribution.
- ➤ Meets company guidelines for news releases.

For job responsibility 2: Ensures that all customer service standards are met during sales/service handoffs and installations.

- ➤ Follows company service standards and procedures completely.
- ➤ Completes service agreement forms and documents any promises to meet the individual needs of the customer.
- ➤ Ensures that solutions are mutually acceptable and signed off on by the customer, the sales manager, and the customer service manager.

- Completes and submits reports that track progress, including, but not limited to, daily, weekly, and monthly sales call plans, appointments, and orders obtained.
- Provides accurate and complete information.
- Uses company format.
- Meets deadlines for each report.

The more specific the performance standards are, the better the chance the employee has for success. When managers are not clear on the performance standards, the employee often cannot be given excellent ratings. This is because the manager can't define "fully satisfactory," much less "excellent." Frequently this lack of clarity leads to misunderstandings, lack of trust, and decrease in morale. Employees may feel that they cannot succeed because success cannot be defined; the performance rating might be designated based on gut feel, which is not predictable.

When managers determine performance appraisal ratings, they are using performance standards. The standards may be formal, written, and discussed. Or they may be personal to the manager, informal, unwritten, and not discussed. Managers must measure observable results against a yardstick of some sort. The more openly discussed and clarified, the easier it is for the employee to achieve and thus stay motivated. It also prevents surprises on performance reviews.

Oftentimes I have heard from managers that their bosses do not give excellent ratings. In one particular management class, a woman stated that her boss never gave anyone an excellent rating on a performance evaluation. He said no one is ever excellent. She said she'd gotten used to it and was now applying that dictate to her staff. She also said it upset her and her staff and had negative effects. Since employees were frustrated that they could not achieve greatness, they did not give extra effort to make results excellent. She felt the quality of the work was less than it could have been with no incentive to go above and beyond. Other class participants said they would leave a boss who refused on principle to give excellent ratings. They said it is demoralizing to know you can never earn a top rating.

The boss in question confuses "people" with "performance standards and results." It's true that humans are not perfect, but that is not what is at stake in setting performance expectations and evaluating against them. Job responsibilities and performance standards are specific to a job, not to a person. If the results exceed the basic requirements, then the performance can be rated excellent. The person may not be considered perfect, but it is the work that is being evaluated, not the person.

Communication Issues Unique to First-Time Managers

First-time managers experience special challenges, especially when it comes to communication. The two main problem areas are (1) handling the dual roles of being both a manager and an individual contributor simultaneously and (2) making the transition to being a manager. This appendix includes action steps to handle some typical issues that arise, including:

Dual Roles

- ➤ How to strike a balance between functioning as a manager and an individual contributor
- ➤ How to handle problem managing peer with greater seniority and experience
- ➤ Time management (balancing time for direct reports and managerial work)

Transition to Being a Manager

- ➤ Transitioning from an individual contributor to a manager role
- ➤ How to prove capable in new role
- ➤ How to get comfortable managing people

Dual Roles—Being Both a Manager and an Individual Contributor Simultaneously

A trend today is that many first-time managers are required to function in two roles. They are expected to continue in their technical individual contributor role working alongside their peers. They are also expected to assume the role of manager of these current peers. In addition to time-management challenges that arise, dual roles are difficult to handle for both the new manager and the direct reports because the roles are blurred. It is unclear when the manager wears the peer hat and when she wears the manager hat.

When you are given the new management duties, the first thing to do is to meet with your manager. Do you have a title and/or grade-level change? How and when will your manager announce your new role to the team? Get clarity on your manager's expectations and your level of authority for each of your responsibilities. What percent of your time is to be spent on these new managerial responsibilities? What are your manager's suggestions for making the new arrangement work well for the team? Who is responsible for evaluating performance of your team-mates—you or your manager? Set a plan with your new manager. Be sure you and your boss are clear on his expectations of you.

How to Strike a Balance Between Functioning as a Manager and as an Individual Contributor

1. **Issues:**
   - ➤ Time management.
   - ➤ Defining roles and expectations—confusion about separating roles.
   - ➤ Prioritization (individual versus team needs).
   - ➤ Friction with teammates and managing friends (see Chapter 7).
   - ➤ How to get teammates to do the work without micromanaging.
   - ➤ Defining boundaries of delegation.

2. **Action Steps:**
   - ➤ Clearly define goals and objectives and job responsibilities for self and for reports. Ask for clarification from your manager and communicate that to your entire team. Ask your boss to make the formal announcement of your new role.

- Identify all tasks for each role. Classify tasks based on individual, team, and organizational needs. Prioritize each task.
- Evaluate all the work processes. Streamline processes and work-flow with input from peers.
- Acknowledge the new role to the team and ask for their input on how to make the new relationships and work assignments work for everyone. Redefine roles if necessary.
- Adapt to the demands of each team members' needs.
- Schedule one-on-one meetings with peers to discuss how you will handle the dual role. Set expectations with your direct reports.
- Assign equal or greater priority to new management role while continuing in individual role. Allow time as necessary to be accessible to your team.
- Discuss the change with peers. Understand and address your peers' feelings. Accommodate their needs as much as possible.
- Lead from the front—pull the team, rather than push them. Contribute as part of the team in the new managerial role—not aloof and not apart.
- Assign work and follow up to ensure it gets done. If workload is unrealistic, clarify what your team *is* able to accomplish. You may need to reset your boss's expectations or request resources.
- Define the need to hire an individual contributor to fill your old position, if necessary. Present detailed workload information to your boss and prioritize.
- Clearly define your new role and transition your former roles over to someone else or distribute them among several others. Learn to delegate and trust (define authority level for tasks). Train team members to pick up some of your previous tasks. Don't take back the assignment once delegated.
- Know your direct reports' strengths and work preferences.
- Plan for the future.

How to Handle a Problem Managing a Peer with Greater Seniority and Experience

1. **Issues:**
   - Peer doesn't meet established deadlines.
   - Peer resets already established priorities.

➤ Peer's general performance level has decreased. The quality of her work is lower. For example, she deviated from the standard operating procedures and that led to poor software installation. The result was higher cost.

➤ Peer goes over the manager's head to higher-level management.

2. **Action Steps:**

➤ Gain your manager's support for the priorities and deadlines. Clarify that he agrees with your plan to meet with the nonperforming direct report.

➤ Hold face-to-face meeting. Clarify goals and rules. Emphasize the priorities and deadlines and why they are important. Compare expectations to observed performance to recue the gap issues.

➤ Discuss how to better capitalize on the peer's experience. Does she need more independence or more challenging tasks?

➤ Discuss what the peer will do from here on in to meet agreed expectations. What help does she need? State consequences of not meeting priorities and deadlines.

➤ Tell your manager your plan and ask him to send the peer back to you if she goes over your head again. Gain your manager's support for the priorities and deadlines.

Time Management (Balancing Time for Direct Reports and Managerial Work)

1. **Issue:** How to prevent people problems by organizing your time to do both jobs.

2. **Action Steps:**

➤ Organize time for managerial work.
- Plan and schedule your work.
- Review your progress daily and plan the next day.
- Close the door occasionally, or specify a "quiet hour."
- Set time in morning and afternoon for dialogue.
- Manage your boss's expectations.

➤ Organize time for direct reports.
- Have a weekly or biweekly pulse check one-on-one meeting

with direct reports. Each person saves up nonurgent items for the meetings.

- When delegating, communicate performance standards, objectives, timelines, and checkpoints.
- Ensure direct reports understand what to do.
- Assign nonurgent work direct reports can do when they have downtime.
- Expect that newer employees or lower-performing employees will require more feedback and coaching time.
- Understand each person's strengths, limitations, and talents.

Transition to Being a Manager

Transitioning to a management role is an exciting challenge. It offers opportunities for growth and development of communication skills. Your skills now need to be broader and deeper. There will be roles and tasks you will need to let go of. What a first-time manager lets go of when ceasing to be an individual contributor depends on the situation. Be sure to clarify your specific responsibilities and levels of authority (see Chapter 2, "Setting Expectations with Turbocharged Clarity"). It is important to know precisely what your boss expects. Most managers also do individual work, although at a higher level. If you are still expected to do some detailed technical work, you need to clarify to what extent. In general, here are some things to consider as you move forward.

Transitioning from an Individual Contributor to a Manager Role

1. **Issue:** Changing roles from doing the work to managing the individual contributors.

2. **Action Steps:**
   - ➤ Define new roles for yourself and your direct reports. Get buy-in from your manager. Find out your manager's expectations and set expectations for your staff. Adapt and adjust.
   - ➤ Clearly communicate your expectations to staff and ask them to clarify their understanding.

➤ Set up a transition plan for delegating work. Execute and monitor the plan.

➤ Communicate continually with your manager and direct reports. Be approachable so staff feel comfortable approaching you (what is important is that they *perceive* an open door, not just that you tell them you have an open door). Be inclusive and understanding so direct reports are able to ask questions. Demonstrate your intention to preserve relationships and help them succeed on the job.

➤ Behave as you would have other staff behave. The manager is a mirror, so the behaviors you demonstrate are the behaviors you are likely to see in your staff (honesty, consistency, meeting deadlines, keeping commitments, listening, not judging, not gossiping, and being positive).

➤ Act confident in your own abilities so the employees will be confident in your ability to steer the group.

➤ Know your information before you explain to staff. Be consistent in decisions.

➤ Continually develop expertise in your job. Grow skills and learn as much as you can.

➤ Possibly let go of some aspects of your individual contributor role that you enjoyed. This is your decision, based on the needs of your new management role. Some managers find they need to let go of their perception of self as a technical expert, certain friendships, detail work, projects and tasks, gossip, and avoiding people they didn't like to work with. These depend on the situation and people involved.

How to Prove Capable in a New Role

1. **Issue:** Want to be capable and viewed by others as a capable manager.

2. **Action Steps:**
   ➤ Continue learning the new job quickly.
   ➤ Attend management training programs as soon as possible.
   ➤ Read management books and articles ASAP.
   ➤ Find a mentor inside or outside the organization.

- Develop a plan with your boss to increase your skills. Ask for coaching.
- Make new peer relationships with other managers.
- Read everything you can find on the subject of your new job to be fully competent in the industry and functional areas.
- Demonstrate confidence and knowledge.
- Make decisions and trust yourself. If you make mistakes, acknowledge them and try a new tactic.
- Manage the relationships with your direct reports, your manager, and your new peers, and maintain previous relationships.
- Treat each person with respect, listen thoroughly, and communicate well.
- Resist the temptation to make changes right away.

How to Get Comfortable Managing People

1. **Issue:** New management role is uncomfortable because of the people aspects of the job.

2. **Action Steps:**
   - Talk to your manager and get a comprehensive understanding of job requirements and level of authority for each. Get advice. Role-play feedback and coaching situations with your manager.
   - Develop a thorough knowledge of direct reports' responsibilities and levels of authority. Be completely familiar with their job descriptions.
   - Get complete knowledge of all company policies, standard operating procedures, workflow and processes, legalities, safety procedures, and HR requirements.
   - Ask HR what support is available for new managers. Learn how delegation, feedback, coaching, performance evaluations, and counseling are done in your organization.
   - Go to management classes. Read communication and management books and periodicals.
   - Set and meet goals for your group. Assign tasks and follow-through decisively.

- ➤ Take communication training courses to develop knowledge of how to talk to direct reports, give feedback, and coach.

- ➤ Know your direct reports and their work backgrounds and full range of expertise.

- ➤ Develop direct reports' skills and knowledge through appropriate assignments. Give direct reports opportunities for visibility. Coach them to help them succeed.

- ➤ Give positive and redirective feedback regularly.

- ➤ Hold team meetings to cross-fertilize the ideas, goals, and accomplishments of the entire group. This also builds camaraderie and teamwork.

- ➤ Get a mentor and new peers who are managers.

- ➤ Keep a professional journal of what works and what you need to rethink and improve.

Index

NANNETTE RUNDLE CARROLL is a popular speaker, management trainer, and communications consultant. She is also a top-rated faculty member with the American Management Association. She lives in the San Francisco Bay Area.

Photo by Rachel Capil Photography, www.rachelcapil.com